BECOMING FULLY HUMAN

Becoming Fully Human

Patrick Whitworth

Terra Nova Publications

Published in Great Britain by
Terra Nova Publications Ltd
PO Box 2400, Bradford on Avon, Wiltshire BA15 2YN

Except where indicated,
Scripture quotations taken from the
Holy Bible, New International Version.
Copyright © 1973, 1978, 1984 by International Bible Society.
Used by permission of Hodder and Stoughton Ltd.
All rights reserved.

Scripture quotations marked NKJV are taken from the
New King James Version Copyright © 1982 by Thomas Nelson, Inc.
Used by permission. All rights reserved.

Cover design by Gazelle Creative Productions Ltd.
Cover illustration:
A fresco of the Resurrection,
in the St Saviour Church, Chora, Istanbul (Kariye Camii).
The frescoes were commissioned by Theodore Metochites.

ISBN 1 90194 923 0

Printed in Great Britain
by Bookmarque Ltd, Croydon.

Contents

Foreword

Lord Carey of Clifton

In modern societies that tend to promote cults of health and human well being the 'disease' at the heart of humanity is strangely neglected. Even the churches are generally silent about this issue and it is rare to hear effective and convincing preaching that shows that the preacher has really grasped the grandeur and sadness of the human condition. But this is the bread and butter of great literature. From Shakespeare's *Macbeth* to modern writers like Kafka, Camus, Bellow, Golding and Updike we are shown the power of evil, its tragic consequences and suffocating power. Quite recently I reread William Golding's *Darkness Visible* about an ordinary, basically decent man, Simon Goodchild. Through Golding's lucid description we are given a glimpse of a man labouring under a burden of guilt as he remembers a malicious trick he played on a colleague: 'You could not embark on the long voyage of reparation that could make all well.. could not do it because, to change the metaphor, this latest piece of wantonness was only a bit on the top of the pile. The pile was a vast heap of rubbish, of ordure, of filthy rags, was a mountain — it did not matter what one did, the pile was too big. Why pick the last bit of filth off the top?'[1]

In those few sentences Golding goes to the very heart of what we all long to be — free of guilt and free to be the kind of person we feel should be our destiny.

Patrick Whitworth's book *Becoming Fully Human* is a readable, enjoyable yet serious description of human beings before Almighty God because, let's be clear about it, if this life is all, then all is futile and nothing is of value —nothing whatsoever. Few people believe that or live like that. Deep in the hearts of most thinking people are moral persons struggling to get out. We know that God is and that he is to be reckoned with. It has often struck me that the description of people as 'human beings' is less than accurate. A 'being' suggests something that is formed and static and clearly unlike any of us. Perhaps we should start to talk of people as 'human becomings', because destiny tingles in the fingertips of every child of God as, in Michelangelo's great painting, we reach out to touch the outstretched hands of God and so become fully human.

Patrick's intelligent book emanates not only from much reading and deep thought about the subject but from years of ministry in which he has seen much suffering and too much human sinfulness. He has also witnessed time and again the overwhelming love and grace of God expressed in the majestic and attractive life of Jesus Christ. That person, Jesus Christ, is the model for human nature. It is my hope, and certainly that of the author, that this book will lead many to him.

George Carey
103rd Archbishop of Canterbury

[1] William Golding, *Darkness Visible* Faber & Faber Ltd. Used by permission. Also by kind permission of Farrar, Straus and Giroux (USA, 1979).

Prologue

In the film *The Shawshank Redemption* there is a wonderful moment when Andy Dufresne, the wrongly convicted city banker, has obtained books and records to start a prison library. One day he plays a piece of Mozart over the prison tannoy system whilst most of the inmates are exercising in the yard. It is a moment of great humanity in a brutal and brutalising prison system. Most of us can recall moments of humanity, and know what we mean by them even if they are not as stark as in that film. But this book looks at the deep underlying question of what it means to be fully human, and how we can break out of whatever brutalising systems confront us. Surely, one of the greatest questions we can ask today is: what does it mean to be human? —And *how* can I become fully human? It is a question that must be asked and answered by each person.

In his enthronement address as the new Archbishop of Canterbury, Dr. Rowan Williams put it like this: "We only become completely human when we allow God to remake us. Like the conservationist in the art gallery, God works patiently to remove the grime, the oil and dust of ages, and let us appear, as we say, in our true colours. Wonderful, yes;

but it means also God will lay bare all the ways we hide from him and each other, all the sad and compromised and cowardly things we do to stop ourselves being human."

So this book presents what I like to think is a classic Christian answer to this question —the answer which was lived out by Jesus and then cogently explained by Paul.

As with many such undertakings, it started out as a series of talks, in this case Lent talks on the Seven Deadly Sins, for St Peter and St Paul, Shepton Mallet at the invitation of John Woolmer, their Rector then, in 2001. Since then, the book has evolved. It was, in thought form, a travelling companion from Bath, where I live, to Amman in Jordan, a journey of some four thousand miles overland, which I made as part of my sabbatical last year. The very Pauline flavour of much of the text, together with references to the early years of Christianity in the days of Constantine, is partly due to the route we took through Istanbul (Constantinople), central Turkey (Galatia) and Damascus. Thanks must go to my intrepid companion on this expedition, Michael Fowler, for his interest in the project.

I would also like to thank Gay Carder for her helpful reading and suggestions, Lord Carey for his Foreword, my publishers for their editorial assistance, and my family: Olivia, Rachel, Louisa, Sophia, and David, amongst whom I am hopefully edging my way forward to greater humanity! Only they know the true story!

Needless to say, the shortcomings, of which there will be many in such an endeavour, are entirely mine, but I pray that it may bring a little illumination in our common quest of becoming fully human.

Finally, it is possible that this might become the first in a trilogy (trilogies seem to be fashionable these days, from *The Matrix* onwards) of *Becoming* books, but we must wait and see! Or, to make it more Christian, I must "pray and see"!

25th May, 20003, The Feast of the Venerable Bede (whose commemorative chapel in Durham Cathedral I much enjoyed when training for the ministry at St John's Durham).

Part One

DEAD SOULS

1

The Fractured Image

"So what's this book called?" one of our eldest daughter's university friends asked.

"Well it's called "Becoming Fully Human", I replied.

"But what's it about?" she further quizzed.

"At its simplest, I suppose it is saying that the closer we get to God, the more truly human we become. After all, God is good, generous, creative, loving and just, and the more we become like him then the more we become what we were created to be. I know that begs all kinds of questions, but if you read on you can see the answers that Christianity comes up with and see if you agree. Hopefully the book will answer some of the questions you have and which the title begs. Anyhow, one of the most important questions to decide is, 'What does it mean to be truly human?' —so let's begin there."

****

In the opening sentence of his systematic theology entitled *The Institutes*, the French reformer John Calvin wrote, "Our wisdom, in so far as it ought to be deemed true and solid wisdom, consists almost entirely of two parts: the knowledge of God and ourselves."[1] In our secular and self-absorbed world, that is an assumption or hypothesis which would be hotly contested, but it is the working premise of this book. Building on that premise, I would go on to say that we can only become fully human if we have a true knowledge of God and a proper understanding of ourselves.

When I was growing up my parents would often state their views on someone we had just met; their good points or bad points would be highlighted as either something to emulate or avoid; and occasionally the comment that he or she was "very human" would be given to a particular individual. It was undoubtedly a compliment and probably meant a cluster of things. It meant that he or she was approachable, humble, and possibly a little vulnerable, and especially that they combined a mixture of integrity and dignity. It is not now a compliment that I hear paid very often, and that may well be because it is a phrase which is passing with their generation, but it may also be that the concept of what it is to be truly human is passing, and I fear that this may be the case.

A BRIEF HISTORY OF "BEING HUMAN"

A study of history which, it has been said, is simply the study of human behaviour and thought spread over time, shows that our view of what it means to be human has varied greatly down the centuries and in different societies. In broad-brush terms we can see different views of what it is to be human rise and fall.

The classical Greek and Roman view was bound up with what we have come to call the humanities. They strove to develop the potential in each person, and in particular his skills as orator, philosopher, fighter, athlete, artist and mathematician. Plato, who developed the ideas of Socrates in Athens in the fourth century BC, thought systematically about morals and politics, science and mathematics and above all sought knowledge from the soul to discover the "highest good". He was interested in what could be said to be eternal and unchangeable in nature, especially in ethics and society. He concluded that there must be a realm of ideas behind the material world of our existence. For him, and for the Stoic philosophers later, this meant the submission of the body to the interests of the soul or the submission of the actual or material to the idea that they expressed.

For Plato the human body was made up of three parts: they are the head, the chest and abdomen. To each part of the body there is a corresponding faculty: to the head, reason; to the chest, will; and to the abdomen, appetite. Likewise, to each faculty there is linked an ideal. So wisdom is the ideal form of reason; courage the ideal exercise of the will, and temperance the ideal exercise of our instincts or appetites. Only when each of these parts is exercised in a harmonious and unified way is the person truly "virtuous". Aristotle developed these ideas further in Greek culture, systematising their effects, and Cicero, some three hundred years later, in Roman thought.

However, this philosophy—brilliant, influential and persisting as it may have been—was tethered to human perception alone. It was not until the apostle Paul came to the same Athens where Plato and Socrates had taught some four hundred years previously that another wisdom was revealed. Paul's speech to the Athenians in Acts 17 contained a piece of revelation which would challenge world views that see human reason as paramount. Luke tells us,

> Paul then stood up in the meeting of the Areopagus and said: "Men of Athens! I see that in every way you are very religious. For as I walked around and looked carefully at your objects of worship, I even found an altar with this inscription: TO AN UNKNOWN GOD. Now what you worship as something unknown I am going to proclaim to you."[2]

It was this proclamation concerning who God is, and the proclamation that he has revealed himself in Jesus Christ, which was, in time, to transform their society.

After an extraordinary period of 250 years of mission, proclamation and persecution, the Christian faith would take root in the Roman Empire with the conversion of Constantine though a vision which he related to Bishop Eusebius of Caesarea. From the time that the Emperor Constantine made Christianity the official religion of the Roman Empire in AD 312, the accepted view of what it meant to be human began to change. The life, ministry and death of Christ now informed it. Here was a new model of humanity, which replaced the purely classical view, and it eventually came to dominate European thought until the French Revolution and the Age of Enlightenment. This model of humanity has been most lucidly expressed in the prayer of St Francis of Assisi. Francis was a friar; one of those itinerant preachers who turned his back on the institutional church and its corrupt ways, and went around like his Master, "doing good". He was a preacher, teacher, and role model for the faith, as well as being in touch with both people and the environment. The prayer that bears his name became a template of Christian living. In the latter part of the prayer, Francis expresses the essence of Jesus' teaching, which is that in losing our life for the sake of the kingdom of God we find ourselves; Francis puts it as follows:

> Grant that we may not seek so much to be consoled, as to console; to be understood as to understand; to be loved as to love; for it is in giving we receive, in pardoning we are pardoned and dying that we are born to eternal life.

However, rulers and power structures, not least the church herself, would use this new model of humanity to their own political ends; so tarnishing the image of Christ, and in turn provoking movements of either Christian reform, like the Reformation, or secular revolutions like those in France and, later, Russia. The old story of the leaders of the church in St Petersburg debating the question of how many fingers should be raised in the Orthodox blessing, when a group of revolutionaries were next door, planning the most significant revolution in the twentieth century, serves only to show how far church hierarchies can be removed from the aspirations of human beings. It also shows that not only does power have the tendency to corrupt but also to isolate.

Secularism and humanism (themselves in part reactions to corrupted Christianity) had earlier propelled the French Revolution and helped to overthrow the old order. A hundred and thirty years later, similar forces were at work in Russia, provoked by the poverty of the masses. Once again they swept away the old order. This time the revolution was dressed up in Leninist Marxism which sought to replace another almost absolute monarchy and corrupt church with aggressive secularism.

But secularism and Marxism were optimistic about human nature. The former, secularism, held that if the human spirit could be freed from the dictatorship of church and state and then given proper conditions of equality, fraternity and liberty, then we human beings would truly become what we should be. Later Marxism, with its class structure dialectic, stated that if the working class or proletariat were freed from the conditions in which the ruling classes held them, then they would enjoy both freedom and prosperity. For this to happen, both the means of production and all raw materials should be owned and directed by the state.

Only comparatively recently in the West was Marxism and her children finally discredited when the jury of Eastern European populations rose up and gave their verdict on the communist or socialist experiment to which they had been subjected for fifty years and more —with the dismantling of the Berlin Wall, and the subsequent collapse of the Eastern bloc's political dictatorships. Marxism in the West was more or less consigned to the history books and seen as another political philosophy in which power hungry men could masquerade as guardians of freedom. To underline this, the commonest noise in the offices of the former leaders of these Eastern-bloc countries was the whirr of the shredder machines as evidence of their deeds was consigned to the bin before it could be brought against them.

As the truth dawned on the populations of the Eastern bloc, they realised that the Marxist experiment, far from bringing them freedom, had enslaved them to falsehoods served up as truth, and this was no more ironically demonstrated than in the main Soviet newspaper and organ of propaganda called *Pravda*, which of course means truth!

If, on the one hand, the end of the Marxist experiment in Europe occurred with the dismantling of the Berlin Wall in 1989, the break-up of that form of secularism, which stemmed from the Enlightenment, is now thought to have happened in the 1960s. Generally speaking, through the 19th century, humanism—the belief that man had his own destiny within his grasp—gradually strengthened. By the beginning of the 20th century there was a much greater optimism about man's ability to control his own future, but two world wars, and the holocaust, were soon to dismantle these expectant hopes. Although the 1950s saw a period of retrenchment and social stability (in the UK for instance, churchgoing became much stronger, and many men offered themselves for full time ministry in the mainline denominations) those years now look like an Indian summer before a new epoch was to begin.

This epoch is essentially a mixture of often-contradictory values and beliefs. It is non-ideological and at the same time intensely individualistic; it is romantic and yet thoroughly consumerist. Actions are determined not by any objective set of duties but by what feels good; and, understandably, alongside this there is a deep craving for intimacy and a search for what is common to us all. This characteristic of our age has been identified by many writers and commentators.

But ironically there is also an increasing inability to sustain intimate relationships, so that solitariness is more and more common and intimate relationships exist vicariously, especially through the ever-increasing number of soap operas. This means that characters in soap opera, media stars and celebrities fill a vacuum in people's lives created by the failure of relationships close to them. In part this explains the extraordinary outpouring of grief at the tragic death of Princess Diana.

Technology has on the one hand enhanced ease of communication, but on the other gives governments an ever-increasing control over their populations. People are prepared to offer more of their personal freedom to their employer, provided they are given prosperity as a quid pro quo. There is an intense search for what it means to be human and an increasing doubt as to what is masculine and what is feminine. There is a search for "the hero inside" which is quickly supplanted by the worship of a hero outside who is either a sporting or entertainments industry celebrity, often mutating as the media re-creates his or her image. We have now reached the stage where our humanity in the secular West is essentially an ever-changing construct in which we are capable of presenting an image, which is a kaleidoscope of other images, handed down by either advertising or the media in general. So we mostly experience a brew of fluctuating elements that has been given the title "post-modern", but poses the age-old question: "what does it mean to be truly human?"

This is a question of burning significance and lies at the heart of modern debate on various issues from embryo research to euthanasia. It is a question very many are asking and the answer we give literally dictates our role in relation to the world around us, our view of our own significance, and our hope for the future and the way we set about relating to each other.

The rise of voyeur television programmes such as *Big Brother* is a parable of our times. People are put together in virtual isolation from their normal lifestyle and friendships, but in fact are under the perpetual scrutiny of the viewing public. There they are given a series of monotonous tasks, which have little significance other than the opportunity of testing and sometimes degrading their relationships. The contestants are given the solitary power of ejecting a member from their community, sometimes through a conspiracy against a particular individual, and the motivation for it all is winning a large sum of money or temporary fame. So many of the modern Western "values" are on parade in these programmes: an excessive, almost voracious, interest by viewers in people whom they have never met, but whose secrets, personality and pain they expect to invade; the abdication of personal freedom and choice to *Big Brother*, who controls the contestants through their hope for the big prize. The only power that is given to the viewer is to eject from this "community" those who do not conform, or whom you find least attractive or convincing; and the motive force for the contestants taking part is usually "being on telly", having brief fame and money. I suppose the big underlying lie about it is that it appears to be about building a community, whereas in fact it is about the projection of one person who comes out winner —and it feeds our prurient interest in the intimacies of others' lives. It exemplifies the cocktail of neuroses that shape modern western life. "Only a game," I hear them cry; have a laugh —but humour is sometimes the betrayer of what so many really think, which is that humanity may be observed, invaded, bought, dispensed and finally discarded, except for the winner, who gets all! Is it the modern televisual equivalent of Golding's *Lord of the Flies*? Have our social groupings become parodies of the great *Big Brother* game, in which people can be slung out if they do not conform or are voted out by the majority, leaving a few beautiful people, who have what it takes, holding the prizes? Which humans do we want in and which out? We all cry that surely we have not reached such a pitch, but then what *is* the basis on which we now relate to each other?

So where do we start in our exploration of what it means to be human?

THE IMAGE OF GOD

G. K. Chesterton put it well when, to describe something of the character of man, he employed the simile of a tree —its roots in the earth, and its highest branches seeming to rise almost to the sky.

The early chapters of Genesis majestically describe the creation of the human race. There are two accounts of this creation in Genesis chapters one and two. In the former we are given a window into the divine mind before the act of creating the first human:

> Then God said, "Let us make man in our image, in our likeness, and let them rule over the fish of the sea and the birds of the air, over the livestock, over all the earth, and over all the creatures that move along the ground."[3]

This sentence appears as a pause in the rolling creation process described hitherto in the account, and then the divine creative action continues:

> So God created man in his own image,
> in the image of God he created him;
> male and female he created them.[4]

Having created male and female, he firstly blessed them, gave them the command to multiply and made them his stewards of all that he had made on the earth. In a few sentences, God lays down the purpose and privileges of humanity.

The origins of the human race continue to fascinate, tease and provoke furious discussion. Archaeological evidence suggests that there have been hominids on planet earth for some two million years. Earlier this year I visited Oldupai Gorge in Tanzania, where the Leakeys discovered in volcanic sediment the footprints of hominids that lived hundreds of thousands years ago. They may well have borne some kind of partial resemblance to us physiologically, as do other primates, but the essence of human-ness is not merely inherent in a degree of physiological similarity; it consists in being made in the image of God. This image was conferred on man in a divine creative action, which made *Homo sapiens* what he is. Evolutionists maintain that the human body has developed over millions of years. Biblical creationists resist that view (claiming that there is no evidence to suggest that one species has ever developed into another, but that the gaps in the putative evolutionary theory are too great) and maintain that the Genesis account of a special creation of man is the historic truth. Whoever is right in that debate, God granted the principal constituent part of our humanness—being made in the image of God—to Adam and Eve, who were both the prototype of our humanity—real historical people—and representatives of the human race. To put it simply: they were real; and they were, historically, a distinct, unique, new creation. To say these things is not a scientifically provable statement. It is a faith statement, drawn from the teaching of Scripture. Of course, it is possible to be a Christian without subscribing to this particular understanding of the origin of the human race. At the very least, a Christian believes that humans were God's specific creation, accountable to him and made in his image; the Bible encourages us to believe that Adam and Eve were the first humans, with a history which is significant for the whole race.

Sometimes the Church, in its ignorance of science, has been far too simplistic and over-confident in its approach to questions of science though, admittedly, it was only reflecting the thinking of its time. A most notable example of this came from the pen of Archbishop Ussher of Dublin who wrote with real confidence that Adam was created in 4004 BC. John Lightfoot, a seventeenth century scholar using Ussher's work, went further and declared that Adam had been born on the 23rd October of that year at 9 a.m.! In an amusing and ironic comment on this statement, E. T. Brewster wrote in a scientific review of Lightfoot's work: "The Vice-Chancellor of Cambridge University closer than this would not commit himself!" Or again, in the sixteenth century, it was Galileo's telescope, not his church, that conclusively refuted the previous interpretation of Psalm 96:10 which says,

> Say among the nations, "The LORD reigns."
> The world is firmly established, it cannot be moved:
> he will judge the peoples with equity.

The church had hitherto taken the view that the earth remained fixed, until Galileo discovered that it orbited the sun each year. But for a long time he was penalised for his discovery.

Equally science, in its secular form, can be far too simplistic in its presentation of evolution, drawing up classroom charts that simply assert that all life forms may be directly traced back to primitive species such as sponge-like substances that floated in the primeval soup. The theory, for that is what is, seems to suggest that it was simply the passage of time operating within the principles of evolution and survival of the fittest that drove these lower life forms to become higher ones, until almost inevitably we reach the existence of *Homo sapiens*. However, as the creationist position asserts, there is indeed remarkably little fossil evidence to substantiate the theory that one species developed into another in such a smooth process.

The biblical account of the creation of human beings revolves around a few simple principles. Firstly, it is clear that the idea of a human being was conceived in the mind of God, so that he said, "Let us make man" before they were created in reality. The second principle was that the essential and defining characteristic of this creative act by God was that this new creation "man" would be made in "the image of God." The third principle was that this image of God was expressed in male and female together, finding community and companionship in each other, and the final principle was that the essence of man's being is the unique combination of the dust of the earth and the breath of God whereby they became living souls.

Indeed, there has been some debate down the years amongst theologians as to whether man is essentially a dichotomy (being made up of two basic constituents) or a trichotomy (being made of three basic constituents). In the former view, man is taken as being essentially body and spirit or in the Genesis account a combination of dust, representing matter, and the breath of God, representing Spirit. The latter view holds that man is made of three parts, namely body, spirit and soul. Rather than force the issue between these two views, it is more important to hold to the **unity** of the person; for according to Scripture we are not a compound of constituent parts, which could be isolated from each other, but rather a psychosomatic unity. We are not two *separable* parts, spirit and body, which combine in the womb and separate at death, which was the classical Greek view of man, nor are we infused with an immortal soul which pre-existed our bodily life, as Origen appears to have taught and Wordsworth wrote of in his poem *Immortality of the Soul*, but rather we are a unity of different parts each of which can be developed by God's interaction with us. The terms the Bible uses, whether "soul", "spirit", "body", "heart" or "mind", are simply different ways of looking at the same person. The person is a unique combination of each of these parts, who is invested with the image of God.

If the defining characteristic of being human is being made in the image of God, it is also a guiding principle. So, in the final analysis, we are not defined as humans by the size of our cranium, the shape of our spine or the length of our limbs but by whether or not we are discernibly made in "the image of God". Archaeological finds can shed little light on this defining characteristic. Only other discoveries associated with a find of skeletal remains could begin to tell you that; whether, for instance, there are signs of worship, community or family life, which suggest something of "the image of God" in man.

In the Blombos Cave, 180 miles from Cape Town, small

pieces of engraved ochre were found, dated by laser as being around 70,000 years old. Professor Henshilwood of the Iziko South African Museum believes that these two small pieces of engraved ochre are the work of *Homo sapiens*. Until this discovery, the earliest signs of human art were to be found in the caves of France and Spain. In any event, traces of human activity on planet earth are comparatively recent when it is estimated that there were fish in the sea three million years ago. Human beings are latecomers to the stage of earth. But all this begs a question: what does it mean to be made in the image of God?

WHOSE IMAGE?

The word "image" in our modern world is deceptive. In fact, in the context of this secular and theological interface, it has a double meaning. Nowadays, "image" means, above all, what we want to project. It is an idea which is substantially driven by the media, advertising, fashion and clothes. Most products have brand images if they are to succeed in the market place; and the entire world is a market place as globalisation continues. But where there are no competing philosophies, except that of globalisation, humans become "products", too, with a need for our own brand image. So "image" is what we present, and that presentation is our identity, which can be changed as necessary, as we seek to re-position ourselves. Celebrities do this all the time to promote their careers; in fact the very media on which they rely demand this; so "image" can be a changing thing, which describes us at a given time.

Not so the image of God. God is not a construct but is unchanging; and therefore his image, which he has given to man, is in its essence unchanging, although it will be expressed in a myriad of cultures and human personality types. So we have two almost opposite meanings attached to the term "image". Our secular, Western image is forever changing, responding and re-defining our identity, whereas

God's image, which is constant, and is essentially his **likeness** in us, remains fundamentally the same. We must explore how this likeness was given and what it means.

Michelangelo, in his famous fresco on the roof of the Sistine Chapel in the Vatican, depicts the moment of the creation of Adam: the finger of God is extended and reaches out to the extended hand of Adam. There is a remarkable sense of energy in his painting, and the beauty and magnificence of Adam's body is startling, but the physical strength and beauty of Adam's body should not be the summation of his humanity. Humans are more than beautiful or not-so-beautiful bodies. Nor are we simply the sum of our genetic parts. Nor are we simply driven by instincts alone, as Lord Winston would have us believe. With the completion of the human genome project in the year 2000, which has mapped all the DNA bases present in the human body's 1,000 billion cells, we have unparalleled information about the genetic pattern of the human body, but still do not understand, to put it non-scientifically, how we tick! But scientific commentators have pointed out that this advance in knowledge does not mean that science understands how the genome actually does its work, which affects every cell in the body. There is no adequate theory to explain how it performs all its amazingly complex work. That kind of understanding remains as elusive as an unfamiliar language.

To be made in the image of God means a cluster of different things that have been boiled down to these essential characteristics: man's ability to reason or understand; his desire for social relationships in which he finds satisfaction; his ability to be creative, whether in art, construction or in support of his lifestyle; above all, his desire for a transcendent relationship with God, in which he finds true significance. As the writer of Ecclesiastes said, "He has also set eternity in the hearts of men...."[5] These characteristics reflect something of the nature of God himself, in whose image or likeness man was created. Throughout the Bible, God is understanding, wise, reasonable and full of knowledge; he is creative beyond our wildest imaginings, creating extraordinary life forms in prodigious numbers; he is intensely intimate, and there is relationship of the deepest kind both within the godhead and with his creation; and he is eternal, giving to us that longing for eternal significance. So man was created in the image of God. And yet, as the Jewish philosopher Martin Buber said, "There is a tragedy at the heart of things." I first started writing this book a week after 9/11 and the attack on the World Trade Centre in New York, where around three thousand died on a day of dazzling beauty when, out of the clear blue skies of early autumn, death rained on countless unsuspecting people, and with that event the perceptions of a generation were suddenly and violently changed.

The tragedy is, of course, that having been made in God's image, his creature went tragically and terribly wrong, so that the image of God in man was fractured and the likeness of his Creator could no longer be so discernible. The tell-tale signs of God's handiwork in our human existence have been obscured by the effects of our choice to pursue our own self-interest, to our own and others' great cost. The result of this, which we shall consider more fully in our next chapter, is that we are left with a shattered image, like a broken mirror in which it is harder to discern the image of the one we are supposed to project. In fact, human beings are walking paradoxes, displaying, on the one hand, wonderful courage, skill, love and intelligence, while at the same time showing unbelievable cruelty, self-centredness and brutality.

THE PARADOX OF MAN

The evidence for this paradox is not hard to find. It lies over the pages of human history; yet in the last hundred years the horror that stems from our fallenness appears to have reached a new peak.

After the fall of the Berlin Wall in 1989, which incidentally I had known as a child, growing up in Berlin in the early sixties soon after it had been put up by the East Germans, I went with a small group from our South London church to visit Poland. We went at the invitation of some young Christian students, to help open a Christian bookshop in Katowice in Southern Poland. It was a mind-opening and unforgettable visit and we felt the excitement of these students on the edge of a new future without the shackles of communism and Soviet domination.

Whilst we were staying for a few days in Katowice, our hosts insisted on taking us to Auschwitz. Most of us are familiar with the sinister front of the extermination camp with the high arch at its centre, through which the trains brought Jews and other people from across the Nazi Reich. But nothing can prepare you for the piles of shoes of all sizes, and human hair, taken from the victims in the systematic stripping of human beings before their extinction in "the shower room", and now displayed so sparsely in glass cases. The utter bleakness and clinging cold assaults you. Our hosts told us that every schoolchild in the area is taken there, so that we, collectively, should not forget.

In 1980, some eleven years before we visited, Primo Levi, a survivor of the camp, was asked by the Polish government to write an inscription at the entrance to the Italian section; of the eight paragraphs he submitted, only one survives today:

> Visitor, observe the remains of the camp and consider; whatever country you come from, you are not a stranger. Act so that your journey is not useless, and our deaths not useless. For you and your sons, the ashes of Auschwitz hold a message. Act so that the fruit of hatred, whose traces you have seen, bears no more seed, either tomorrow or for ever.[6]

On April 11, 1987, Primo Levi took his own life, plunging to his death down a stairwell at his home in Torino, Italy. In a sense, he was the victim of the same holocaust that had engulfed his fellow countrymen at Auschwitz, but forty years later. Although he had existed since "liberation", to "survive and tell", the burden of his own atheism — "If there is an Auschwitz, then there cannot be a God"; the weight of being a witness as the years passed, and the guilt of survival, and ongoing depression—added him to the tragic list of the survivors-who-would-not-survive or find final liberation. His was another testimony to the blackness that overwhelms, and which is the product of evil human intent. The image of God appears to have been obliterated there.

Occasionally, as a family, we like to visit a city or place of great significance. Two years ago we visited the house of Anne Frank in Amsterdam, made famous by the extraordinary diary that she kept whilst living there for two years in the attic during the Second World War, fearing arrest by the occupying German forces. Eventually the family was discovered and sent to a concentration camp, where Anne tragically died, shortly before the end of the war. Her diary displays a courage, humour and perception which have made it one of the world's greatest bestsellers. It is a story that, once again, displays the paradox of our human existence in which the good and the evil in man are in deepest contention.

Some of our best known correspondents have both witnessed and struggled with the evidence of human evil around the world. Fergal Keane wrote *Season of Blood,* an account of the Rwanda genocide in which, in one hundred days, up to one million people were hacked, shot, strangled, clubbed and burned to death. Keane emphasises that figure of one million. He tells of an incident in Nairobi, which took place before he began his journey with others into that stricken land. He recalls meeting a man in the old colonial hotel in Nairobi, who had just arrived from Rwanda. Surrounded by tourists, he movingly speculates as to whether the carefree visitors even knew of the genocidal killing which was taking place such a relatively short flight away.

Many who have seen such things have noted the sad fact that, when the normal restraints of civilization are absent, very many people prove to be capable of terrible evil.

The same paradox is, so to speak, strewn over the battlefields of the First World War; a war which has increasingly fascinated the reading public in the West through books like *Birdsong* and films like *Regeneration*, which gave an insight into the terrors of trench warfare and the struggle of the war poets respectively. One private in the British army wrote of the remarkable comradeship displayed in appalling conditions; "To live amongst men who would give their last fag, their last bite, aye, even their last breath if need be for a pal, that is comradeship; the comradeship of the trenches. The only clean thing borne of this life of cruelty and filth. It grows in purity from the very obscenity of its surroundings."

If, as Christian and Jewish doctrine put it, we, as a race, were made in the image of God but now we are this walking paradox, displaying either appalling evil or great altruism, how did we become what we are, and how might we become again what we were meant to be —that is, properly and fully human? This is the underlying question of this book, which addresses this human dilemma and charts a way whereby the fractured image of God in us humans may be repaired, so that the image we were meant to project can once more be glimpsed.

Notes

1 John Calvin, *The Institutes* Book I.
2 Acts 17:22–23.
3 Genesis 1:26.
4 Genesis 1:27.
5 Ecclesiastes 3:11b.
6 See Os Guinness, *Time for Truth* (IVP, 2000), p. 76; and Baker Book House, USA.

2

The Right Diagnosis

A friend of mine was seriously ill in hospital, having
contracted some unspecified disease whilst working abroad.
He spent some weeks there before a proper diagnosis was
made and treatment could begin. Eventually the problem
was diagnosed and the treatment began; soon he was on his
way to a full recovery.

The diagnosis was essential to the cure, and finding it is
the particular skill of the physician. As we look at humankind
there are few people who are in any doubt that we have some
kind of dis-ease. The questions at issue are: what is the right
diagnosis, and what should be the treatment?

A doctor will make his diagnosis through various means:
a blood test will be taken, there may be other laboratory
tests, symptoms will be carefully studied, a case history
involving painstaking research into the patient's previous
medical history and recent past will be made, there will be
discussions with other doctors and specialists, and then a
diagnosis will, hopefully, be forthcoming. It can be a difficult
and uncertain process. But until the diagnosis is properly
made, treatment is a shot in the dark.

To most thinking people there is a self-evident problem in

33

our human existence. There cannot be many who believe that our human condition is as it should be. But there are two ways of approaching what we observe in human relations. **Either** we can come at it from the point of view that there is no root cause of the problem, no virus or bacterium to be treated, so to speak, which has invaded our being, and so think that the problem can be satisfactorily relieved by simply alleviating the symptoms, **or** we can take the view that something has invaded our lives which in a sense was a foreign body —in that it was not originally there, and has taken up a parasitic residence in us. The former view assumes that we have not **fallen** from a previous state of goodness, whilst the latter view is that we have done so. How are we to know which is the right approach to this self-evident problem of human folly? The answer to this question is that either we can try and reach our own conclusions or we can accept an explanation that is practicable, capable of being tested and has been revealed.

Christianity gives us a clear answer to our human predicament, and it has been echoed by some of the greatest philosophers. The basis for this diagnosis is to be found in the account in Genesis chapter three, to which we must turn for the explanation that both Judaism and Christianity provide. Even if the reader is not committed to the literal details of the narrative recorded here, there is little doubt that the human authors of the Bible regarded the story as recording a space–time event. In reading the text, the crucial question is: what is the main idea that the author wants to convey? Whilst we may feel that the early chapters of Genesis do not wholly answer all our scientific questions about **how** life began, they show **why** what happened happened, and they set before us the moral and spiritual consequences. The narratives convey wisdom about our relationship to God. So much of the language is symbolic. The snake signifies the presence of evil and the existence of the devil; the fruit represents moral knowledge, and Adam is both depicted as an individual (as in Genesis 3:17) and referred to by a collective noun as representing the human

34

family (as in Genesis 1:26 and in 2:7).[1] This switching by the author from the personal name to the collective noun is surely deliberate, to show that this account is both the personal tragedy of an individual man and a collective disaster for humanity. As many theologians have pointed out, Adam's action was both representative and individual. It serves both as a record of why the human race is what it is, and it is the story of us all. We are both meant to understand from it why we are as we are and to see ourselves as having transgressed with Adam. Let us read through the passage:

Now the serpent was more crafty than any of the wild animals the LORD God had made. He said to the woman, "Did God really say, 'You must not eat from any tree in the garden'?"

The woman said to the serpent, "We may eat fruit from the trees in the garden, but God did say, 'You must not eat fruit from the tree that is in the middle of the garden, and you must not touch it, or you will die.' "

"You will not surely die," the serpent said to the woman. "For God knows that when you eat of it your eyes will be opened, and you will be like God, knowing good and evil."

When the woman saw that the fruit of the tree was good for food and pleasing to the eye, and also desirable for gaining wisdom, she took some and ate it. She also gave some to her husband, who was with her, and he ate it. Then the eyes of both of them were opened, and they realised that they were naked; so they sewed fig leaves together and made coverings for themselves.

Then the man and his wife heard the sound of the LORD God as he was walking in the garden in the cool of the day, and they hid from the LORD God among the trees of the garden. But the LORD God called to the man, "Where are you?"

He answered, "I heard you in the garden, and I was afraid because I was naked; so I hid."

And he said, "Who told you that you were naked? Have you eaten from the tree from which I commanded you not to eat?"

The man said, "The woman you put here with me— she gave me some fruit from the tree, and I ate it."

Then the LORD God said to the woman, "What is this you have done?"

The woman said, "The serpent deceived me, and I ate."

So the LORD God said to the serpent, "Because you have done this,

> Cursed are you above all the livestock
> and all the wild animals!
> You will crawl on your belly
> and you will eat dust
> all the days of your life.
> And I will put enmity
> between you and the woman,
> and between your offspring and hers;
> he will crush your head,
> and you will strike his heel."

To the woman he said,

> "I will greatly increase your pains in childbearing;
> with pain you will give birth to children.
> Your desire will be for your husband,
> and he will rule over you."

To Adam he said, "Because you listened to your wife and ate from the tree about which I commanded you, 'You must not eat of it',

> Cursed is the ground because of you;
> through painful toil you will eat of it
> all the days of your life.
> It will produce thorns and thistles for you,

and you will eat the plants of the field.
By the sweat of your brow
you will eat food
until you return to the ground,
since from it you were taken;
for dust you are
and to dust you will return."

Adam named his wife Eve, because she would become the mother of all the living.

The LORD God made garments of skin for Adam and his wife and clothed them. And the LORD God said, "The man has now become like one of us, knowing good and evil. He must not be allowed to reach out his hand and take also from the tree of life and eat, and live for ever." So the LORD God banished him from the Garden of Eden to work the ground from which he had been taken. After he drove the man out, he placed on the east side of the Garden of Eden cherubim and a flaming sword flashing back and forth to guard the way to the tree of life.[2]

At the traditional Nine Lessons and Carols service which began during the First World War in 1918, and is broadcast every year by the BBC from King's College Cambridge, there is a Bidding Prayer which includes these lovely words, "Let us read and mark in Holy Scripture the tale of the loving purposes of God from the first days of our disobedience unto the glorious redemption brought us by this Holy Child." The story of that disobedience is read, beginning with this chapter in Genesis. It is a story which explains the paradox of our human nature, our great destiny and our tragic Fall. Reflecting on it and explaining the inner workings of salvation, St Paul, with his formidable analytical skills, gives a vital gloss to the elements of the Genesis story when he writes in his greatest exposition of the Christian faith, the Epistle to the Romans, these words:

Therefore, just as sin entered the world through one man, and death through sin, and in this way death came to all men, because all sinned—for before the law was given, sin was in the world. But sin is not taken into account when there is no law. Nevertheless, death reigned from the time of Adam to the time of Moses, even over those who did not sin by breaking a command, as did Adam, who was a pattern of the one to come.

But the gift is not like the trespass. For if the many died by the trespass of the one man, how much more did God's grace and the gift that came by the grace of the one man, Jesus Christ, overflow to many! Again, the gift of God is not like the result of the one man's sin: the judgement followed one sin and brought condemnation, but the gift followed many trespasses and brought justification. For if, by the trespass of the one man, death reigned through that one man, how much more will those who receive God's abundant provision of grace and of the gift of righteousness reign in life through the one man, Jesus Christ.

Consequently, just as the result of one trespass was condemnation for all men, so also the result of one act of righteousness was justification that brings life for all men. For just as through the disobedience of the one man the many were made sinners, so also through the obedience of one man the many will be made righteous.

The law was added so that the trespass might increase. But where sin increased, grace increased all the more, so that, just as sin reigned in death, so also grace might reign through righteousness to bring eternal life through Jesus Christ our Lord.[3]

Once again Paul displays the interplay and interaction between two ideas: on the one hand the corporate and personal nature of our sin and on the other hand the power of Christ to reverse all its effects. George Carey has pointed out, in regard to our human predicament, that Paul is combining these ideas.[4] Humanity's condition is inextricably linked with the disobedience of Adam.

THE CAUSE OF THE FALL

The cause of the Fall is spelt out in the account in Genesis. At the end of the Creation narratives, God is satisfied with his work, all is well, and the final pinnacle of his creation has been brought into being. Adam and Eve enjoy an open and warm relationship with their Creator and find in each other the companionship they need. In the Garden they find delightful and rewarding work. Their sexual relationship is hallowed by marriage, and in that state they are both blissful and innocent. The closing words of Genesis chapter two are full of contentment: "The man and his wife were both naked, and they felt no shame."[5]

Enter the snake, a symbolic picture of the Devil, "that great serpent", who pervades the human story in the Bible. What is clear from the account in Genesis three is that he is a creature, he is crafty and he is intent on ruining the paradise that God has created. We will have time to fill out his curriculum vitae later, but here we can watch him in devastating action.

The essential causes of the Fall of Adam and Eve are not hard to find. The possibility of the Fall is related to three things. Firstly, there is the existence in the world of a malevolent power who had his own history of rebellion and banishment from heaven and who was determined to take creation with him.[6] Secondly, we observe the creation of humans who have the capacity for true love both towards each other and their Creator, necessitating the existence of free will. Thirdly, there is a connected order in which the choices of these humans had a profound effect not only on themselves but also on their relationship to God and their relationship to their environment. It is into such an existence that the crafty serpent insinuates his corrosive thought, couched as a question, to provoke doubt.

The question at first sight looks remarkably bland, but that is its craftiness; "Did God really say, 'You must not eat from any tree in the Garden'?" You can almost hear the emphasis being put on the word 'really'. It is a question directed at Eve, who supposedly is more susceptible to the blandishments of the serpent's logic. The woman in a sense is being wooed by the excitement of evil, and in particular she is being led in her mind to doubt the goodness of God who, it is insinuated, has withheld some exciting opportunity of self-improvement (namely eating from the Tree of the knowledge of good and evil) from her and her husband. The purpose of the serpent's question is to make her doubt the goodness of God, to make her doubt that he has her best interests at heart, and finally to make her doubt that the knowledge from this tree would be harmful to her and her husband. Initially, Eve holds her ground, repeating to the serpent the command that they have been given by God verbatim. But the serpent presses his attack with a more outright assault on her. She is encouraged to believe that she may eat the forbidden fruit as she is told, "You will not surely die." Once again, he sows the thought in her mind that God is withholding something from her which will benefit her. In fact, the serpent's words suggest that God is withholding from her that which will make her great or *like him.* So the serpent has made Eve doubt God's goodness, by focussing her mind on the one prohibition that they have been given, rather than the permission to enjoy the paradise they have been granted and all the many blessings they were enjoying.

Disobedience like that depicted in this familiar account has been evident on countless billions of occasions in the annals of human temptation. Again and again, we humans, like our ancestors Adam and Eve, fail to be content with what God gives and to operate in line with his rules, which are for our own good. Although we may have much to enjoy, just because one thing is lacking or not granted we are tempted to deny God's goodness and disbelieve that he really has our best interests at heart. So, in an act of defiant rebellion, we seize what we think is really what we need.

If the serpent wanted Eve to doubt God's goodness, and so to be persuaded to eat the fruit, an act which signified disobedience, he also wanted her to doubt God's holiness. He simply said, "You will not surely die"; [7] meaning by this: not only will you become more powerful, but God will not punish you, the pinnacle of his creation. Instead he will find some way round the penalty attached to his prohibition. Or to put it another way, God will find some way of accommodating his standard to your action. It was implied that God's standards are flexible, and could be compliant with human wilfulness. This was a deliberate attempt to undermine God's holy standards, and to deny the reality of the penalty God had attached to breaking them.

Eve was persuaded by these crafty insinuations, swallowing these specious arguments. Although they were not convincing in themselves, perhaps they were enough for her to say to herself: they will be arguments that I can use after the act of eating, both to convince myself that I acted rightly and to give an account of why I did it. They were excuses to do something which, on the face of it, looked exciting. After all, the fruit looked good, was nourishing, and, she thought, conferred wisdom. The fruit appeared to have many virtues which the woman no doubt found attractive, but eating it would be an act of rebellion. In short the fruit itself was appealing and did not appear dangerous; and she was deceived.

Adam, in contrast, seems to have been a total pushover! —He acts like a man who has switched off his critical mind and is willing to accept anything his wife says! His behaviour puts one in mind of the proverbial man who, when anything faintly religious comes to the door, sends his wife to deal with it and puts up with the consequences! Adam appears remarkably passive, even lazy, in his acquiescence in eating the fruit. Defending his action subsequently, he has nothing more to say than that, "She gave me and I did eat!" One wonders what conclusions the writer expects you to come to about Adam! It looks as though Adam, in the face of this assault both on his lifestyle and marriage, abdicated all responsibility as his way of complying with the conspiracy that the serpent had set before them.

So the causes of their fall are not hard to find: a willingness to doubt both God's goodness and his willingness to carry through the penalty that he had attached to disobedience; a desire to become like God, not content to be a subordinate creature; and a willingness to risk all on the illusion that somehow it would all turn out alright and things would not change, or, to put it bluntly, they would simply get away with it and not be found out. All these thoughts were sown in the minds of our ancient forbears by the serpent which, as the writer says, was craftier than any other creature. But the consequences were immediate, disastrous and almost irreversible.

THE CONSEQUENCES OF THE FALL

The consequences were essentially twofold or, as the theologians would tell us, they were man-ward and God-ward. Adam and Eve had broken a relationship of love and trust and the consequences were incalculable.

Imagine a trivial incident by comparison. You invite some friends to stay while you are away for a number of months and leave them in charge of your home, which has in it a priceless picture, left to you by an ancestor. The picture, by a French impressionist, hangs in your main room overlooking a spectacular view. The room in which the picture hangs has extensive glazing and so the temperature of the room needs to be finely controlled. The only instruction you give them before leaving is to maintain the room temperature at eighteen degrees centigrade, especially when the sun shines directly into the room. They know little about art and decide to ignore your instructions, failing to maintain the room temperature and taking other less trustworthy advice. Consequently, you discover on your return that the picture is damaged; it will need restoration but, more importantly than that, your relationship with your friends is spoilt. You feel that they ignored your advice, did not care for your property and hardly showed appreciation for the lengths to which you had gone to make their stay pleasant and comfortable. You are hurt; and the image in the picture has been damaged. It is still recognisable, but both an artist and even an average connoisseur can tell that it is not what it had been.

By comparison with the account in Genesis three , this is trivial but it does serve to show the effect on the relationship; and it suggests in a limited way something of the consequence of such wilful disregard. The consequences of the cosmic disobedience depicted in Genesis are huge for the human race. Innocence has departed. Adam and Eve make themselves clothes of leaves to hide their nakedness and they feel ashamed, no longer feeling at ease in their nakedness before each other and before God; now they are trying to hide from his presence. For the first time in their lives they are afraid at the appearance of God.

Then God demands of them, "Who told you that you were naked?" It is not, as some psychiatrists suppose, that Judaism or Christianity actually planted the germ of sexual shame in the psyche of humanity, but rather that, at some moment, a real—and not suggested—sense of shame about ourselves entered our psyche.

A further consequence of the Fall was that a blame culture began. Adam blamed both God and Eve for what happened: 'The woman you put here with me—she gave me, and I did eat.' Whereas earlier he had exulted in his God-given partner, now both God and Eve were to blame. Eve blamed the serpent who, as the preacher's old gibe goes, 'had not, or would not have, a leg to stand on!' But blaming others—whether for actions taken or not taken—is an evasion of moral responsibility. It is an attitude that is very prevalent today, but its origins are beyond carbon dating!

Furthermore, pain in fact touched every party involved in this tragedy —and to a degree that is beyond comprehension. It touched both the innocent and the guilty. Adam's work would be transformed from delight to a combination of fulfilment and drudgery. Whereas, before the Fall, creation itself was in harmony with his intentions, now Adam would earn his bread through "painful toil" and the "sweat of his brow". Pain would enter Eve's life, too. Her pain in childbirth would be greatly increased and her relations with Adam would no longer be purely harmonious; she would desire her husband, but he would reciprocate by seeking to dominate her. Pain would enter their family life, with bitter jealousy, leading to the murder of Abel. Grief would also be experienced both by the Creator God as well as in the created order. Only a few chapters later, God would express his grief at the wickedness by now prevalent in human society: "The LORD was grieved that he had made man on the earth, and his heart was filled with pain."[8] There was now disorder in the environment itself, which had been affected by dislocation caused by Adam's disobedience. Adam and Eve, being representative of their descendants, the whole human race, did not suffer these judgments alone, but in a mysterious way the human family of the future was caught up in their loss and trauma.

Finally, mortality would replace immortality. It is beyond our understanding even to contemplate a life that did not end in death, but presumably that was God's original intention for human beings. It is said by some commentators that Jesus wept at the tomb of his friend Lazarus because he felt the full ignominy of death and the full force of its destructive power and intrusion into life, robbing Jesus of a friend he dearly loved. But now God himself passes a sentence of mortality on man. Adam had come from dust and to dust he would now return. Added to this, both Adam and Eve would be banished from God's presence and prevented from returning. It is a picture of devastating bleakness.

The image of God in man is now fractured like a broken mirror, so that the likeness it is supposed to convey is hard to see clearly. Worse still, the image has a corrosion caused by a contagious infection, which now spreads across the image of God in man.

THE CONTAGION OF SIN

The apostle Paul's summary of the story of Genesis Chapter three is stark:

> Therefore, just as sin entered the world through one man, and death through sin, and in this way death came to all men, because all sinned....[9]

Paul's argument is simply that Adam, being the representative of the human race, became the source of a deadly infection, which spread throughout humanity.

In February 2001, a vet making an inspection of animals at an abattoir in Essex saw the symptoms of a disease he had hoped he would personally never witness. It was the beginning of a "foot and mouth" epidemic in England, Scotland and Wales. The last time it had occurred was in 1967. The source of the disease was soon traced to a small farm where swill containing the virus had been fed to the pigs. The epidemic necessitated the slaughter of over six million cattle and sheep. The epidemic began from a single source.

Epidemiology was not a science with which many of us were familiar, but scientists who were expert in this area were nightly on our news, showing the spread of the disease and its likely course, outlining the action taken by the government, and telling us what was being done to trace the path of infection. The treatment of the disease was both uncompromising and contentious. The preferred option of the farming community was slaughter, entailing huge suffering to the animals themselves, the farmers and their families, but thereby ensuring that the herd would eventually be free of the infection, and the meat capable of being sold internationally.

There are obvious parallels between the spread of this disease in a national flock or herd and the spread of a fatal infection in the human race from a single source.

Genesis gives us an explanation of how an infection spread throughout the human family. It shows that it began from a single source, one in which we all have a personal involvement. Although much of the detail is symbolic, it nevertheless records, in narrative form, a space-time event. What is undeniable is that the symptoms of that infection are to be found wherever the human family exists.

A vet diagnosing foot and mouth disease will know what signs to look for: the animals' lameness, coughing, running nose and loss of weight. The clincher will be the results of a blood test. The symptoms will be obvious and the diagnosis clearly follows.

The human infection, which spread from Adam, bringing in its wake fear, blame, guilt, pain, alienation and mortality, has tell-tale signs of its presence. The technical word for this infection or disease is "sin", which now is a largely misunderstood word. In popular culture it is widely taken to mean sexual misdemeanour, but of course its scope is far wider and more serious. Like a disease, it has its obvious presenting symptoms, some of which showed themselves immediately following Adam and Eve's act of rebellion; but also, like a disease, it has a structure and a pathology.

The structure of sin is a complex one. It has many facets and exhibits itself in many ways, but the Bible most frequently speaks of it as "falling short" or "erring". This, in turn, stems from rebellion and pride; man prefers to be master of his own destiny rather than be subject to the just and gentle rule of God. It is acceptance of this view of ourselves which is both so contentious and so resisted today by modern man. On the one hand, it seems to some unscientific, although it is, as we have already said, the one doctrine of man which may be empirically proved from history; and, on the other hand, it appears to many so bleak. Yet, it is the diagnosis which can lead to a cure. Pascal put it well when he wrote, "Certainly, nothing offends us more rudely than this doctrine and yet, without this mystery, the most incomprehensible of all, we are incomprehensible to ourselves."[10] Paul, at the end of the early chapters of Romans, in which he has been proving the sinfulness of man, concludes in his famous statement, "..for all have sinned and fall short of the glory of God."[11] The common experience of humankind is that we all do fall short of God's ways and standards as perfectly expressed to us in the two great commandments: "Love the Lord your God with all your heart and with all your soul and with all your mind and with all your strength..." and, "Love your neighbour as yourself."[12] The question for us is whether we will admit it.

Only when the right diagnosis is made can the treatment really begin. When a patient goes to a doctor he does not want to be told "all is well" if he suspects something is amiss, for that will only store up further trouble for the future. What he hopes for is correct diagnosis and news of a cure. As we said at the outset, Christianity has offered a diagnosis and it has been more than corroborated by Jesus himself, who said,

> "For from within, out of men's hearts, come evil thoughts, sexual immorality, theft, murder, adultery, greed, malice, deceit, lewdness, envy, slander, arrogance and folly. All these evils come from inside and make a man 'unclean'."[13]

Too often we would rather hear something more flattering about ourselves than this sobering and bleak description of our hearts. If we are ready to accept it, then the gospel is good news of a cure.

It was only when my friend in hospital had been given the correct diagnosis that treatment could begin. Of course he could have refused to accept it and discharged himself from the hospital saying they were a load of incompetents. But he trusted their conclusions and the diagnosis they had made from the evidence they had gained from tests and examination. From that point a cure could begin, and it did.

The Genesis account, when understood in the light of Paul's clear explanation that Adam was the source of our human disease, shows us that Jesus is able to reverse the process: Paul writes:

> For if, by the trespass of the one man [Adam], death reigned through that one man, how much more will those who receive God's abundant provision of grace and of the gift of righteousness reign in life through the one man, Jesus Christ.[14]

Jesus overcame sin and death for all who believe. It only remains for us to receive "God's abundant provision of grace and gift of righteousness", which we can do through accepting the diagnosis, admitting our own involvement and complicity with Adam's disobedience, and receiving the provision of grace offered through the sacrificial death of Jesus Christ. This will radically change us, giving us forgiveness and a new nature. The penalty for past failure has been removed completely from that "new creation", and the power of the self-life may be broken, although the presence of sin is still around. It is only when that step of faith has been made that we can start on the path of becoming fully human. In case these ideas still seem opaque and unreal, hopefully they will become clearer as the book develops; all we need to know for now is this Christian diagnosis, and that God in Christ has made abundant provision for our pardon and acceptance.

Finally, consider some words of Augustine:

> Adam lies now scattered on the whole surface of the earth. Formerly concentrated in one place, he has fallen; having broken to pieces, as it were, he has filled the universe with his debris. However, God's mercy has gathered together from everywhere his fragments and by fusing them in the fire of his charity, has reconstituted their broken unity.[15]

Our hope is that by accepting the diagnosis and the treatment of Christ's grace, the shattered image of God in each one of us might be restored. Although we may have this image of God in us re-activated by his grace instantly, it still entails a process thereafter, in which we become what he wants us to be —which is *fully human*. This process involves us in a struggle and a fight, which we hear about at baptism.

Notes

1   See George Carey, *I Believe in Man* (Hodder & Stoughton, 1977), p. 52.
2   Genesis 3:1–24.
3   Romans 5:12–21.
4   Ibid.
5   Genesis 2:25.
6   See Isaiah 14:10ff.
7   Genesis 3:4.
8   Genesis 6:6.
9   Romans 5:12.
10   Pascal, *Pensées* 131.
11   Romans 3:23.
12   See Mark 12:30–31.
13   Mark 7:21–23.
14   Romans 5:17.
15   In *City Of God.*

3

The Infernal Opposition

When taking a service of baptism, a declaration and prayer that takes place before the actual baptism increasingly strikes me. After the minister has signed the candidate with the cross, the congregation says, "Fight valiantly as a disciple of Christ against sin, the world and the devil, and remain faithful to Christ to the end of your life." In the new Anglican *Common Worship* service, the minister then prays, "May Almighty God deliver you from the powers of darkness, restore in you the **image** of his glory, and lead you in the light and obedience of Christ."[1]

Compressed into those few sentences of exhortation and prayer are assumptions about life and discipleship which are vital for us to understand and appreciate. They distil essential truths which are now in danger of being so diluted that we may miss them. In fact, unless we are careful, elements of the baptismal service could become so perfunctory that we empty the event of much of its meaning. To understand this short piece of liturgy, we have to see that the process of restoring the image of God in us is inextricably linked with the valiant fight (echoes of Pilgrim from *Pilgrim's Progress*). A fight against what I call the "infernal opposition" rages, which has three sources: the world, the flesh and the devil. In baptism we affirm that, on the one hand, our salvation is a gift granted to us through faith and celebrated in this sign, but on the other hand we commit ourselves, with the help of God's people, to work out our salvation "with fear and trembling", as Paul puts it.[2] So restoring this image, which was fundamentally damaged in the Fall, involves both receiving the gift of eternal life and taking part in a fight against the infernal opposition.

Gazing into the eyes of a delectable baby (in the case of infant baptism), who has his whole life before him and is surrounded by the prayers and hopes of his family and church, you can only guess at the ways he will face this opposition —whether he will fight valiantly, and whether family and church will continue in the prayer that he may be delivered from the powers of darkness, restored in the image of God's glory and led in the light and obedience of Christ. It is time to look more closely at this opposition with which every Christian soul must contend.

THE WORLD

As part of my sabbatical, during which most of this book has been written, I journeyed by car with a friend from Bath, where I live, to Amman in Jordan, passing through, amongst other countries, Yugoslavia, Turkey and Syria on the way — a journey of around four thousand miles. The last part of the route took us past Aleppo in Syria, near to which is the site where St Symeon Stiletes lived on top of his pillar. What remains of the pillar is just a short knob of stone. But for years he sat on his pillar, from where he shouted advice and counsel to all the pilgrims who came to see him and hear his teaching. It is now surrounded by a beautiful but ruined Orthodox church with commanding views over the Syrian landscape. I only mention St Symeon because he is an exceptional example of what is sometimes called a world-denying faith, that is a faith that turns its back on the world in order to seek God.

As so often happens, there are two extremes or polarities for Christians to wrestle with. In relating to the world, we may adopt either a world-denying or a world-affirming approach. Symeon, seated on his pillar, had embraced a world–denying way. He had withdrawn from it, and was indeed 'up' above the world! Although such a form of discipleship would court ridicule in our modern age, it does nevertheless beg questions about what it means to live unworldly lives. Is this the kind of expectation that we should have for a child at baptism, whom we exhort to fight valiantly *against the world*? I expect not. To unravel what is meant by this baptismal exhortation, we must enquire more deeply about what should be the Christian's relation to the world as mapped out by Scripture.

There are three distinct ways in which the term "world" is used in the Bible. The first denotes the world as planet earth, of which the Psalmist says,

> The earth is the LORD's, and everything in it,
> the world, and all who live in it.[3]

The second is the "world" of humans; it is in this sense that John writes, "For God so loved the world that he gave his one and only Son...."[4] The "world" God loved was the human family he had created but which rejected him: "He was in the world, and though the world was made through him, the world did not recognise him."[5] The third use of the term, again especially by St John, is to denote the spirit of the age. This is behind what John says repeatedly to his readers in his first letter; as, for instance, in his command "Do not love the world or anything in the world. If anyone loves the world, the love of the Father is not him."[6] It is this third sense in which the term "world" is used which creates both the challenge and the tension for the Christian.

Why is love for this world so antipathetic to love for the Father? How is it that love for the world cannot be held in tandem with love for the Father? At root, love for the world means prizing above all else the values, attitudes and lifestyle of the world, and it is this which cannot live alongside love for the Father. John spells out what the determining attitudes of the world are: "..the cravings of sinful man, the lust of his eyes and the boasting of what he has or does...."[7] To put it more bluntly still, the ruling principles of the world's life are sex, power and money! As to the latter, Jesus explicitly taught that you cannot serve God and mammon! But what is true of money is equally true of sex and power; you cannot **serve** them and Jesus Christ! Each of these things—sex, power and money—has a proper place in our lives, but each should be subservient to the authority of God. We should not make idols of any of them.

The reason why the world is hostile to the Father is because it is under the power of the evil one. As Jacques Ellul wrote in his important, post–Second World war book entitled *The Presence of the Kingdom*, "The fact of living in the world, from which we ought not to escape, is a stumbling block to our faith. It ought to be so, and so it must remain. We have no right to accustom ourselves to this world, or to try to hide it from ourselves with Christian illusions. Living in the world we are living in the domain of the Prince of this world, of Satan, and all around us we constantly see the action of this Prince, and the result of the state of sin in which we are all placed without exception, because in spite of all our efforts and our piety we share in the sin of the world."[8]

As Jesus himself said, only hours before his crucifixion, "Now is the time for judgment on this world; now the prince of this world will be driven out."[9] This meant that his death on the cross would constitute a judgment of the 'prince of this world' and the way the world operates. It would demonstrate that humility, righteousness, purity, justice and mercy would finally reign, and that the ways of the world would be shown up to be tawdry and hollow, and far from what God had intended. We constantly have to choose between the way of his kingdom and the way of the world;

the two are opposed to each other.

It has often been observed that although evil is, in reality, boring and dreary, the good in fiction is often depicted as boring and flat, though fictional evil is misleadingly portrayed as being attractive. We continually believe the fiction rather than the reality, so all too often choose to believe the lie of fantasy and fiction.

We also need to be aware that the ways of this world, and worldly desires, are passing away.[10]

So how should we react and fight valiantly against the world and its influences? As already said there are two distinct reactions to the world and its powerful influences: either we can withdraw from it or we can become indistinct from it. To put it another way, either we can fight its influences by removing ourselves from its culture or we can take the risk of living amid its corrosive pressure. In fact most of us are forced, by the need to earn a living, to live in the world and so learn to withstand its pressures. Those pressures are almost always ones to make us conform to the standards and attitudes around us. It is worth trying to identify what those particular pressures are, and how to live amongst them without being overwhelmed.

Jesus' prayer to the Father, in John 17, helps us to understand something of the place of the Christian in the world. He said, "I am not praying for the world, but for those you have given me, for they are yours."[11] The guiding principle that Jesus gives us in relation to the world is to live in the world but not to become of (like) the world. The mark of the disciple is obedience to the word of God.[12] Christians are to see themselves as sent into the world to be envoys of the kingdom of God, in the same way that a citizen of one country might be sent to live as an envoy in another country with which it was in dispute. It could well be uncomfortable for that person. Sometimes he might feel real hostility from the local population, but he would be there to convey the message of his government and would not be at liberty to change it. The sending country often calls such a role a "mission". Christians are to live in the world, to convey a message about God's kingdom by both their demeanour and their words, and to retain a distinctiveness without which they would be simply assimilated into the culture of the people to whom they have been sent. However, in order to truly affect those people to whom they have been sent, envoys need to be both sensitive and well-orientated, understanding their "language" and ways.

As Paul wrote in his famous teaching about the Christian and the world:

> Do not conform any longer to the pattern of this world, but be transformed by the renewing of your mind. Then you will be able to test and approve what God's will is — his good, pleasing and perfect will.[13]

The only way to withstand the continual pressure of the world to make us into **its** own likeness, is to be constantly and continually renewed by worship, prayer, fellowship and teaching. We need the continual action of the Holy Spirit, for we have, "...put on the new self, which is being renewed in knowledge in the image of its Creator."[14]

So, as the congregation exhorts the baptismal candidate to fight valiantly against the world in his Christian discipleship, he will need the earnest prayers of the church if "the image of Christ's glory" is to be restored in him as in all who follow "the Way". But our struggle is not only with the world but also with the flesh!

THE FLESH

The apostle Peter was adamant that, although everyone else would desert Jesus at the time of Jesus' arrest and trial, he would not. But Peter did not yet appreciate the weakness of the flesh. For, as Jesus said to him, although "the spirit is willing, the flesh is weak." In fact, anyone with any self-knowledge knows the weakness of the flesh, but what does this term mean and how do we deal with it?

The Greeks knew all about the flesh and, as so often, they give a particular twist to its meaning compared with the biblical authors. Greek civilisation quarried ideas like the builders of the city of Bath quarried stone in the late 18th century: they analysed them, and invented meanings with extraordinary intellectual energy. They quarried, chiselled and fitted together ideas as builders might precious stone or marble. When it came to defining the term "flesh" (sarx in Greek), they gave it a particular definition.

In Hellenistic thought, flesh meant our bodily life and appetites, which came to be regarded as inherently evil, or at least degrading, and were at odds with the aspirations and destiny of the soul. Much of Western thought, and so subsequent attitudes to the flesh, were tinged, to a greater or lesser degree, with this attitude. In fact you could say that the gnostic heresy, which denigrated all material existence and therefore the humanity of Christ, found much of its basis in this type of Hellenistic thought.

However, Hebrew thought, as expressed in the Old Testament, had various meanings for the single term "flesh" ("basar" in Hebrew). At its most basic it simply meant the tissue or flesh of an animal or person. So in Leviticus the flesh of the animal offered as a sin offering was infectious in terms of holiness. "Whatever touches any of the flesh will become holy."[15] Or the term could denote the whole person or self. Here, "body" is synonymous with "flesh":

> O God, you are my God,
>   earnestly I seek you;
>   my soul thirsts for you,
>   my body longs for you,
>   in a dry and weary land
> where there is no water.[16]

Or again the term could denote the whole human family, as in Psalm 65:2:

O You who hear prayer,
To You all flesh will come.[17]

So we could say that the use of the term "flesh" in the Old Testament generally refers to our whole human existence, either our bodily tissue or the human race as an entity. But a further development of meaning takes place when we consider the teaching of Jesus and then of Paul.

Jesus heralded the main **new** definition of meaning in the New Testament in conversation with Nicodemus in John Chapter three. Here we see the contradistinction between flesh and "the Spirit" for the first time. Nicodemus came by night to discover both who Jesus was and what this kingdom, which Jesus had come to inaugurate, was all about. Jesus surprised Nicodemus by saying that it was not possible to enter this kingdom without being born of both water and the Spirit. The reason for this new birth into the kingdom was simple in the mind of Jesus, for, "Flesh gives birth to flesh and Spirit gives birth to spirit." At a stroke, Jesus defined the two worlds that he had come to bridge: the world of the flesh, which was a purely human existence, without reference to God or without experience of his power and salvation, and the world of the Spirit, which could only be experienced through forgiveness of sins and receipt of the offered Spirit. All Jesus was saying was that the world of the flesh or human existence, without true knowledge of God, was shackled to the frailty, mortality and ephemeral passions of our earthly and fleshly life. The flesh was not therefore essentially and inherently evil, but it was circumscribed, limited, and weak, and bound to see human life from a restricted vantage point. As someone has said, it is the landing port of the enemy or the airstrip for his attacks. But it was Paul who further developed the idea of the flesh being in opposition to the Spirit, in the life of a Christian.

For Paul, his own life was the most powerful illustration of what he sought to explain to others. In a passage of great clarity, he demonstrated the sheer limitedness of the life of the flesh, and its innate tendency to selfishness.

If anyone else thinks he has reasons to put confidence in the flesh, I have more: circumcised on the eighth day, of the people of Israel, of the tribe of Benjamin, a Hebrew of Hebrews; in regard to the law, a Pharisee; as for zeal, persecuting the church; as for legalistic righteousness, faultless. But whatever was to my profit I now consider loss for the sake of Christ.[18]

What Paul is saying is that whatever human achievements, honour and privileges he had, they may have elevated him in human society and his own particular Jewish circle, which prized these things, but he nevertheless remained shackled to a form of existence which was earth bound, self-centred and self-important. He was rather like a person in a lift or elevator. No doubt he was going higher in the building, but he was still stuck in the same old office block and restricted by its walls, while a whole world outside in which he would truly find his destiny was beyond his experience.

The bridge from one form of existence, which was confined, restricted and man-made, to the other which was free, fulfilling and heavenly, was Jesus Christ. Only through relationship with him could he find the fulfilment he sought. He summarises his new aspiration as wanting, "to know Christ and the power of his resurrection and the fellowship of sharing in his sufferings."[19]

If Paul, on the one hand, recognised that he needed a transfer from the world of the flesh to that of the Spirit, he also realised that it was an ongoing battle to live in the Spirit and not according to the flesh, and we shall look more in depth at this struggle towards the end of the book, in the chapter entitled "The Way we Live Now." Suffice it to say that the flesh can lead us in either of two directions, each as debilitating to true Christian living as the other. One way is termed legalism and the other libertarianism. Although they appear poles apart in their presenting characteristics, they both spring from the weakness of the flesh.

For example, what connection would you draw between

two such different people as these? One is a pillar of the community, a successful businessman who readily gives to charities, who is hardworking and morally upright but who sees no need to open his life to belief or trust in God; and the other is a man who inherited a great fortune, but through boredom and a surfeit of luxury, took up a habit of drug abuse that consumed him as well as his inheritance. In many ways there are no outward connections between these two people; but according to the principles in Paul's teaching, both would be seen as shackled to the way of "the flesh". To use the same analogy as before; one is travelling up in a metaphorical lift to a high level within his office block but nevertheless is trapped. Although enjoying the view and the dizzy height he has reached, he is still trapped within the building, while the other is, metaphorically, at the bottom of the stairwell in the basement, surrounded by syringes and debris, with no view, but he is equally trapped. Both need to be freed from the world of the flesh and enter the world of the Spirit, for as Jesus said to a successful man, Nicodemus, "Flesh gives birth to flesh, but the Spirit gives birth to spirit."[20]

So our baptism candidate not only faces the world, with all its temptations and lures, but the flesh as well. That would seem enough to contend with, but there is a further member of this unholy alliance, against whom we must fight valiantly, who uses the other two as allies in his devilish designs.

THE DEVIL

"Fight valiantly", the congregation says "against the world, the flesh and the devil, and continue Christ's soldier and servant to the end of your life" —to the about-to-be-baptised individual. There should be little doubt that the Christian life will remain a struggle for all of our earthly life. However much you say this to yourself and others, it still comes as a surprise.

In fact, there is more than enough evidence around us today to show that we are caught up in a spiritual conflict, and this appears to be recognised as much by the secular world and its writers as by the church, although they would probably not see this conflict in quite the same way as the New Testament.

In the last few months alone there have been plenty of reminders. J.R. Tolkien's epic narrative, *Lord of the Rings*, visualised in a powerful, if disputed, film version of the novel, shows an almost unrelenting battle between forces of good and evil. J.K. Rowling has enthralled children and adults the world over with tales of Harry Potter and his power to use magic to combat evil in the unlikely setting of an English boarding school. Philip Pullman, in a much more provocative and self-conscious attack on the tenets of the Christian faith, has given his readers what he describes as a "Paradise lost for teenagers", except the paradise lost is a story in which the protagonists, Lyra and Will, kill off God and create a "republic of heaven" to replace a kingdom of heaven revealed as corrupt and morally bankrupt. Although some Christians have wanted to put various health warnings on these works and continue to discuss their implications, it is quite clear that the seam of good and evil, darkness and light, provides inexhaustible material for literary invention and the engagement of human imagination.

What is increasingly obvious is that there is a public pre-occupation with fantasy, and with the latent struggle between good and evil; that dark forces are at work in the world; that supernatural power and the paranormal are real, and that individuals may be aligned with one or other. It is ironic that, hand in hand with an age that is exploring the furthest reaches of outer space and has completed the genome project, tabulating the thirty thousand genes that make up the human being, we have a fascination with darker forces at work in human life, a revival of paganism, and a growing and sometimes violent interest in the occult. But such pendulum swings between scientific materialism and fascination with myth and magic have been seen before.

At the end of the nineteenth century, following the period of scientific advance marked by Darwin and Huxley, there was renewed interest in the paranormal, as evidenced by Fraser's *Golden Bough* and the searchings of a poet like W.B.Yeats. What seems clear is that in generations when scientific materialism makes rapid progress, often denying any need for a faith-centred explanation of the world, there seems to be a corporate reaction in society —so that people go in search of anything "spiritual". In the absence of a truly supernatural Christian faith, this search becomes all the more widespread. But Christianity, properly understood, is all about the working of God's supernatural power, and any reading of the Gospels tells us so. The liberal position, working from a world view that has excised the possibility of an open world in which God may intervene to fulfil his purposes by subordinating normal physical laws to the interests of his will, has left Christianity stripped of its power and despised by a population increasingly in search both of meaning and miracle. This search is part of our human longing; as the ever-modern writer of Ecclesiastes puts it: "He has also set eternity in the hearts of men...."[21]

In what must be one of the best loved descriptions of Jesus' ministry in Acts, we are told by Peter whilst in the house of Cornelius, the first official Gentile convert:

> You know what has happened throughout Judea, beginning in Galilee after the baptism that John preached —how God anointed Jesus of Nazareth with the Holy Spirit and power, and how he went around doing good and healing all who were under the power of the devil, because God was with him.[22]

The ministry of Jesus could be seen as a campaign to bring freedom to the captives of the devil. In the Gospels there is an astonishing sense of how obvious and unremarkable this is. On the one hand, every first century Jew had a world view in which it was to be expected that God would destroy the works of the devil —but what was amazing was the authority with which Jesus did this as a sign of the presence of his kingdom, and that the same authority was conferred upon his disciples. But the starting point of the Gospels is a long way from the starting point of modern Western man.

The starting point of most in the modern West today is one of denial that "the devil and all his works" exist. It appears too fanciful, medieval or even pre-historic for them. The feeling is that we have outgrown such crude ideas, that there are other explanations for the paranormal, for structural evil in societies and communities; and that there may be psychological reasons why people are predisposed to get involved in occult practices or cannot take any move in life without consulting their astrological guides.

But it could be quite reasonably argued that it is unscientific to rule out such a large body of evidence which suggests that more and more people are strongly influenced in their lives by what is traditionally and biblically described as "the works of the devil". In fact there are four plain and simple truths presented to us in the Bible about the devil. They are: that he exists; that he is evil personified; that he is powerful; and that he has been overcome.

Surprisingly, perhaps, it is the "apostle of love", St John, who records both the most vehement denunciation of the character of the devil and the clearest statement about Jesus' intention to destroy him. St John records Jesus' character reference on the devil in the following terms:

He was a murderer from the beginning, not holding to the truth, for there is no truth in him. When he lies, he speaks his native language, for he is a liar and the father of lies.[23]

Later, in one of his Epistles, John says simply that, "The reason the Son of God appeared was to destroy the devil's work."[24]

Throughout Jesus' ministry he was in more or less constant warfare with the devil. Immediately after his baptism, he was led by the Spirit into the wilderness, where he was tempted by the evil one. In the opening chapter of St Mark's Gospel, he freed a man who had an evil spirit. The people were astonished not so much by the existence of such things as by the spirits' obedience to the authoritative word of Jesus. Again and again, it is the subservience of the spirits to the authority of Jesus which is a hallmark of the coming of the kingdom of God amongst them: "..If I drive out demons by the finger of God, then the kingdom of God has come to you."[25] Despite Jesus' own authority over the powers of darkness, he enjoined constant vigilance and prayerfulness on his disciples, as expressed in this warning: "Simon, Simon, Satan has asked to sift you as wheat. But I have prayed for you, Simon, that your faith may not fail."[26]

So his disciples are to pray "deliver us from the evil one"; they need to pray and fast if evil is to be cast out those whom it has occupied;[27] they must make sure those who have been cleansed from an evil spirit are then filled with his presence and Spirit;[28] they must beware the evil one's sowing of "tares" within the church, and his snatching of the good seed that has been sown.[29] The combination of Jesus' own personal confrontation with the devil, his deliverance of others who were under that power, his conferring of authority upon his disciples to do likewise, and his exhortation to prayerfulness and vigilance, make up the ongoing battle with Satan in the Gospels, but all this was to come to crisis and resolution at the cross.

Again, it is in John's Gospel that this moment is at its most vivid and intense. As his crucifixion grew closer, so Jesus' awareness of the final great battle with Satan became more intense. On the last night of his life he said, "The prince of this world is coming. He has no hold on me, but the world must learn that I love the Father and that I do exactly what my Father has commanded me...."[30]

The cross is, amongst other things, a final disarming of the power of Satan. As Paul said, "And having disarmed the powers and authorities, he made a public spectacle of them, triumphing over them by the cross."[31]

Christians are now to live in the light of that victory, putting on spiritual armour to defend themselves, using the word of God as an attacking weapon, praying at all times in the Spirit, avoiding places of fierce temptation, being alert to the wiles of Satan in their lives, and recognising both that our flesh is the place he loves to make his playground and that the world remains the theatre of his operations and where he is still far from dislodged.

Mindful of this ongoing struggle with the world, the flesh and the devil, Christians in the early years of the faith were robust in their declarations at baptism. So baptismal candidates, in the rite of St Cyril of Jerusalem, were called upon to say: "I renounce you, Satan, you wicked and most cruel tyrant.... I renounce you most cunning and vicious serpent. I renounce you, you plotter, who under the guise of friendship have worked all manner of wrong and caused our first parents to secede from God. I renounce you, Satan, author and associate in every evil!" A tad more emphatic than our own dear Anglican rite that exhorts us to fight valiantly against the world, the flesh and the devil, in a typically English and Anglican understated way. In our rite, if you blink you will miss this exhortation, or if your thoughts wander for half a minute you will have not noticed that it was there!

In these opening chapters we have set the scene. We have considered the effect of "man's first disobedience"; the diagnosis of his condition; his need of salvation, and have begun to consider the fight that working out that salvation involves us in. The content of this fight is well expressed at our baptism. Before we consider the resources at our disposal in fighting this good fight, and so becoming more fully human, we shall look more closely at this theatre of conflict, both in our lives and in our interaction with the world around us. Traditionally, Christians have given a certain construct to this spiritual battlefield, and have described these endless skirmishes in the continuing campaign as "The Seven Deadly Sins". They still represent a succinct and readily identifiable classification of these well known assaults upon our souls, even if they are not a fully comprehensive classification of what used to be called the process of sanctification, or being made like Christ, in whom we see the Father.

Of course, the process of becoming fully human cannot get underway without a beginning, and that beginning is being born into the kingdom of God by the Spirit, believing Christ as Lord, and receiving the gift of eternal life after repentance and faith. The New Testament is rich in its vocabulary in describing this essential beginning, of which baptism is the outward sign. But having made this beginning, we find there are what I call "soul assaults", in the form of continuous choices to be made between good and evil. We shall try and see how these assaults arise in the context of modern Western society, for that is the culture for which I am writing. Increasingly in the West there is a culture, or lifestyle, in which we live and move and have our being, which is constantly pressing us into its own mould. That mould or shape is one which predisposes us into becoming either more or less human. We need to be aware and discerning as to what is happening. We can see these forces powerfully at work, making us humans increasingly the arbiters of life, apparently extending our range of choice so that we could, if we so desire, choose the sex of our baby, determine when life is no longer for living and switch it off, and decide who enters life if it is convenient. I say apparently, because our ever increasing fixation about choice and creating a better quality of living is probably, in part, an illusion —does being in charge of gene selection, birth control (I mean birth control and not conception control), and death control, really make us more fully human?

For the moment, having seen some of the Christian framework of understanding in relation to man: his creation in the image of God; his fractured being after the Fall; the paradox that he has become part–wonderful, part–horrible; the struggle in which he is engaged, wittingly or unwittingly, with the world, the flesh and the devil; it is time to consider those soul struggles which we have, and the choices they throw up.

If we are to become fully human, then we are bound to be involved with these choices, more or less, at most stages of life. So we need to recognise their existence, see the choice for what it is, and in the context of our modern Western society. In the third section of this book we shall see those resources that God has made available to us, in order for us to become what he wants us to be.

Notes

[1]   Extract from *Common Worship: Pastoral Services* is copyright © The Archbishops' Council, 2000 and is reproduced with permission. [My emphasis.]

[2]   Philippians 2:12.

[3]   Psalm 24:1.

[4]   John 3:16.

[5]   John 1:10.

[6]   1 John 2:15.

[7]   1 John 2:16.

[8]   Jacques Ellul, *The Presence of the Kingdom* (Colorado Springs, CO: Helmers & Howard), 1989.

[9]   John 12:31.

[10] See 1 John 2:17.

[11] John 17:9.

[12] See John 17:6.

[13] Romans 12:2..

[14] See Colossians 3:10.

[15] See Leviticus 6:27.

[16] Psalm 63:1.

[17] Psalm 65:2 *NKJV*

[18] Philippians 3:4–7.

[19] Philippians 3:10.

[20] John 3:6.

[21] Ecclesiastes 3:11b.

[22] Acts 10:37–38.

[23] John 8:44b.

[24] 1 John 3:8b.

25 Luke 11:20.
26 Luke 22:31–32a.
27 See Matthew 6:13 and Mark 9:29.
28 See Luke 11:24–26.
29 See Matthew 13:39 and Mark 4:15.
30 John 14:30–31a.
31 Colossians 2:15.

Part Two

STRUGGLING SOULS

4

Gluttony or Health

The soul struggles which comprise this part of the book are in no special order; the sequence simply reflects that of a series of Lent talks entitled, "The Seven Deadly Sins". The first, neatly and appropriately, co-incided with Shrove Tuesday, that pre–Lent festival when medieval Christendom used up all the fat in the larder before embarking on its annual fast. But the issue of "fat" or, as we now call it, obesity, is not for most of us identified with a single day each year; rather, in our overfed and super abundant culture, it is a daily struggle —I am speaking for myself, too! For most of us, it is not so much that we *feel* that we are gluttons, but that we now have a lifestyle which makes it all too easy for it to *appear* that we are. Many struggle with genuine difficulties in this area, which have become more widely recognised, and for which help is more forthcoming nowadays.

It has been reported that a rare form of obesity-linked diabetes has been on the increase, and *Diabetics UK* has expressed particular concerns about the trend indicated by this development. The discovery of such a link has alarming implications for the health service in Britain. The authors of a report entitled *Archives of Disease in Childhood* have warned of the impact on healthcare systems which could occur if the incidence of this disease continues to increase in the UK.

A Zambian priest, from a diocese with which we have a link in the Diocese of Bath and Wells, was staying in an ordinary home in England; he could not get over the quantities of food that we consume!

Some years ago, Mother Teresa was in a television studio, preparing for an interview on commercial television. Immediately before her programme was broadcast, there were some advertisements, one of which was for a new slimmers' sliced bread. The chief selling point of this bread was that almost all the calories had been extracted from the bread, so that the eater could eat without being nourished! She was astonished at the advertisement and could not get over the irony that in Calcutta she spent all her waking energy procuring food and care for the dying beggars of that city whilst we, in the West, used our ingenuity and science to remove the calorific nutrition from this staple of our diet. Although there is malnutrition due to famine or scarcity in the developing world, there is another form of malnutrition in the West in which we eat too much of things that do us no good for a whole variety of reasons. For instance, on average we eat our body weight in sugar every year, whilst in 1900 the average annual per capita consumption was 10lbs!

In his intriguing book *What Would Jesus Eat?*,[1] the American doctor Don Colbert warns of the consequences of excessive reliance upon processed foods, of which a huge number of new lines come on to the market annually. He regards this as the principal explanation for the increases in many degenerative disorders, and especially cancer, heart disease and diabetes. It is much better to consume local produce from farmers' markets and what Dr. Colbert and others describe as a "Mediterranean" diet, such as Jesus would have eaten!

Obesity, we are now told, is not the preserve of the overfed West but is becoming more prevalent around the world. The spread of sedentary lifestyles and fast food is leading to spiralling rates of obesity in developing countries which have never before experienced that problem. Approximately eighteen per cent of the world's population is clinically obese —the proportion having increased from twelve per cent in seven years, according to World Health Organisation figures. Whilst most of those people live in the industrialised countries such as Britain and the United States —where 61 per cent of adults are overweight—the problem is being seen for the first time in parts of Africa and Asia. We are facing what seems like a typically modern situation, in which childhood malnutrition and stunted growth co-exist in the same communities as growing rates of obesity.

What soon becomes clear is that obesity is not the result of gluttony alone, but a complex web of lifestyle and other causes. There are issues of economics, environment, genetic predisposition (some would argue); and, occasionally, psychological disorders. Before we look more specifically at dealing with the failing of gluttony and what it is, we shall consider some of the issues relating to food in our society and reflect on Jesus' own attitude to food.

FOOD FOR THOUGHT

There is little doubt that food has become a preoccupation of our society —both its production and consumption. Eating out ranks just behind watching television as a leisure activity, and some say it is not just a hobby but an obsession amongst the middle classes. This increase has occurred as home cooking continues to decline in our urban society, and with it the family meal as a regular event. This is partly the result of the fact that more and more people live on their own, so it is more sociable—and sometimes easier—to eat out with others in the evening. If, on the one hand, family eating is on the decline, overtaken by the twin assaults of fast food and television (and the average person in Britain watches twenty six hours a week), on the other hand, ironically, there has never been greater interest in cooking. Self proclaimed "super chefs" are household names and celebrities, their programmes are watched by millions, and their books are invariably at the top of best-selling lists. In a generation, the eating expectations of the public have been transformed —especially in higher income groups, but changes in eating habits have affected every part of society. If one part is more interested in "cuisine" than ever before, another is more dependent on junk and fast food. Cookery is a common "lingua franca", second only to sport. The enjoyment of good food is something for which we should be thankful, but there are latent dangers.

Beneath the shimmering surface of some exotic dish produced by one of our super chefs, and perhaps emulated in an average kitchen, there is a deep unease running through the communities which produce our food. The pressure exerted by the consumer, through the supermarket, on the producer to provide cheap food has led to farming practices which have been the breeding ground for new diseases. The classic case was BSE, leading to the tragic incidence of CJD in humans. I saw the effect at first hand when counselling and then baptising a young adult who was suffering from CJD. What we are latterly discovering is that we cannot break into natural patterns of feeding and caring for stock without endangering another species further up the food chain.

Living in Somerset, where the effects on the farming communities have been considerable, I have observed the stress inflicted on our farming communities by the ensuing policies which sought, quite rightly, to eradicate BSE. As we all know in Britain, as soon as we had dealt with that disease, foot and mouth followed all too swiftly and tragically. This was another onslaught on the beleaguered farmers, but in this case both the cause of infection and the reason for slaughter were very different.

What we must recognise is that the demand for cheap, good quality, safe food—exerted by the consumer through those giant retailers, the supermarkets—has created a downward pressure on the primary producer, the farmer.

Incomes of farmers in the UK have plummeted over the past few years. They, in turn, face the pressure of producing what is needed at lower costs to themselves, because they are being offered less and less for their product in the market place, thereby (in the past) being tempted to use methods of feeding or care which are both injurious to the stock and hazardous—indeed lethal, as in the case of CJD—to the consumer. The economics of the farming industry are now immensely complex. Subsidies to farmers in the West have been called into question by global summits, like that held in Johannesburg in 2002, since they prevent free trade and a market for the developing world's agricultural products. But even with these subsidies, tens of thousands of farmers in Britain are giving up the struggle to survive on incomes that have more than halved in recent years. It seems patently unfair that the farm gate price of lamb is twenty times lower than the price at which the supermarket sells it, and the cost of rearing lamb is greater than the price obtained for it; and, equally, that despite the huge upsurge in coffee drinking in the West, some 30,000 coffee growers are currently going out of business worldwide. The effect of continuing losses amongst stock farmers is to drive them from the land with which they are so intimate and about which they have a unique knowledge.

So we have here a structural problem, the root of which is society's understandable desire for more, better, and cheaper food. Cheap food for the consumer has spelt redundancy for the farmer, and one farmer's subsidy in one part of the world is another farmer's tariff barrier! The complexities are enormous. The debate is now underway, huge vested interests are at stake, and politicians' careers depend in some countries on how they treat their farming lobbies.

A further matter for reflection is that despite our general abundance of food in the West we are beset by problems relating to it. We have already touched on some of the problems that we have faced in relation to food production; other debates rage on in relation to GM crops, and whether all or any genetically modified crops should be proscribed.

What seems right is that there should be rigorous testing of modified crops, wherever they are grown, and that such testing should not be bypassed in poorer countries, where commercial interests can exert greater leverage on governments through "sweeteners". I see no theological prohibition of the use of science in the genetic development of crops, provided we can properly ascertain that they really are an improvement and that proper licensing follows. Given the build up of huge commercial pressures to buy into new genetic food technologies, governments will need to be both rigorous and resistant to the blandishments of companies seeking to commercially exploit their science. The dangers of destabilizing the environment through the wrong introduction of GM crops are huge.

But if there are big issues relating to production, we face equally formidable ones over consumption. Despite the availability of a vast array of food unknown to previous generations, we face growing issues in relation to healthy eating. Articles on diet and exercise scream from the pages of every glossy magazine; these topics have now become a national obsession. If we think of food in terms of everything and anything that we take into our bodies, including non–nutritious substances, then the scope for trouble is further extended. In fact, the way we eat, what we eat and drink, how we see ourselves, how we use those gifts in our life, becomes both a physical and a spiritual issue —as all these habits reflect on our inner state of being. We must turn to Jesus for some answers.

JESUS THE LIBERATOR

It might seem strange to give Jesus the title "liberator" at this stage of our discussion, but it is absolutely necessary. As so often happens with God's gifts, we take what is good and sometimes abuse it! At the outset in the creation narratives, we are told:

"...I give you every seed-bearing plant on the face of the whole earth and every tree that has fruit with seed in it. They will be yours for food."[2]

A little later, Noah is told:

"Everything that lives and moves will be food for you. Just as I gave you the green plants, I now give you everything."[3]

Some of the greatest pictures of contentment in the Bible are of humans being well occupied and well fed, like the proverbial Israelite under his vine and fig tree, finding rest, satisfaction and contentment! The writer of Ecclesiastes puts it well when he says:

I know that there is nothing better for men than to be happy and do good while they live. That everyone may eat and drink and find satisfaction in all his toil —this is the gift of God.[4]

But to arrive at this picture of ease and contentment we often need both liberation and healing.

To enjoy what God has given us, in terms of food and drink, we do have to be liberated from gluttony or excess, from abuse or addiction, and from false asceticism or legalism. Freedom to enjoy rightly God's rich creation is a hallmark of true Christian discipleship, and this may involve us in struggle to overcome previous fears, scruples or abuse. The good news is that Christ is able to bring liberation, albeit through some hard fought battles along the way.

Although Jesus, as an orthodox Jew, submitted himself to the Jewish food laws, which had originally been given to the Israelite people through Moses, he inaugurated a kingdom in which all food would be declared clean. The apostle Peter had it spelt out to him in a vision in Joppa that all food was clean, and that no longer would the Gentiles, who ate differently, be excluded from the kingdom of God. Paul was to teach the divided church in Rome (where conscience prevented some Jews from eating all food, and some Gentile Christians from eating any meat previously used as a sacrifice to a pagan idol) categorically that, "I am fully convinced that no food is unclean in itself."[5] So the kingdom of God was one in which all restrictions on what may be eaten were abandoned. Whereas, in the Old Testament, dietary regulations gave the Israelites part of their distinctiveness, now in the kingdom of God the distinctiveness was not a matter of food and drink: "For the kingdom of God is not a matter of eating and drinking, but of righteousness, peace and joy in the Holy Spirit."[6] This may seem unremarkable to us who gather all or anything from the shelves of our supermarkets, but it was a remarkable act of liberation, which proved too revolutionary for some Jewish Christians. It means that there are no food laws in the Christian faith, except the ones we care to impose on ourselves! In essence, Jesus gives an *à la carte* menu to choose from; we must do what proceeds from conscience, enhances peace, joy and righteousness, and is in step with the Spirit. So Jesus firstly sought to free us from regulations, when it came to eating, or rituals that surrounded the meal, making us focus more on what comes from our hearts than goes into our stomachs.

Secondly, Jesus can release us from fear when it comes to eating. This may seem strange but there are some 165,000 people with eating disorders in Britain, and many of these proceed from fear, anxiety, guilt or a false self-image. It is probably hard to overestimate the role that the media play now in forming our ideas of what is an acceptable shape. Once again, we veer from a general increase in over-eating in Western countries to an obsession—where, oftentimes, none need exist—over either weight or shape, because of unhelpful or downright misleading role models in either the media or advertising. Numerous complaints have been lodged with the Advertising Standards Agency over the use of waif-like models by clothing retailers or fashion houses; they sometimes look as if they have just appeared out of Belsen! However, the root problem of these eating disorders is often emotional, and healing of those emotions is needed for normal eating to resume. Otherwise, people use eating or not eating as a way of damaging themselves. Those emotions may be related to broken relationships in the home, or personal anxieties of one kind or another. Skilled counselling, together with prayer, in the context of ongoing support, should become a therapy that every church ought to work towards, but in the case of severe disorders, specialist help should be sought as well.

The liberation that Jesus can give us is essentially twofold. First and foremost, a relationship with him, and experience of his love in our lives, should diminish anxiety, even if that sense of his love dawns slowly; in turn, this will develop into a greater self-acceptance, and lead to healthier eating. Secondly, every true Christian has the Holy Spirit living within him, and the Spirit is at work in our lives to bring wholeness and health. Knowing that we have this person of the godhead living within us, means that we should listen to his help and encouragement in this as in all departments of our lives; for, as we shall say repeatedly in this section of the book, growing into what we are truly meant to be as humans requires the continual help of the Spirit. Becoming fully human is not possible without the aid of the Spirit!

But, someone says, there has been little practical help in this chapter on dealing with the gluttony; and anyhow, what is it? It is a craving for food which is not satisfied by more! It craves either quantity or quality of food, and sometimes both, in increasing measure. It makes the consumption of food or drink or drugs the motive force for living, without which, life itself would become unbearable. In this sense, gluttony could be seen as an addiction from which the individual needs liberation. As with most addictions, it most probably stems either from an emotional weakness or a cycle of desire and satisfaction, which becomes an habitual pattern. Indeed, the word "vice", often interchangeable with sin, is an apt one; since the pattern of behaviour takes a vice-like grip upon the order of our lives, driving everything else to the periphery. The pattern becomes a "vice" in the sense of gripping the individual's life so that he or she cannot be free of it. The failing of gluttony takes what is a good and wonderful gift of God, turning it into a curse. Instead we are to enjoy the food provided in creation in a balanced and thoughtful way; to eat fresh food rather than processed food, to eat at leisure and not in a rush, to eat with others and not with the television! Jesus, as Dr Don Colbert has pointed out, would have eaten a Mediterranean diet including whole grain cereal, fish, a little meat, figs, grapes and olives—especially olive oil, vegetables, herbs, yoghurt, honey, nuts and seed and red wine. It doesn't sound like a bad diet to me, and we could do much worse than following something similar. It may mean clearing out our larders and re-educating our tastes, but the benefits could be great.[7]

In parenthesis, it is worth saying quite simply that a person who is fat is not necessarily greedy; rates of metabolism, genetics, childhood experiences and illness all have their effect, and may well account for our shape. Humanity does not come only in one size, but all of us should be seeking a balanced, nourishing intake which produces a reasonable standard of physical fitness.

So food is a gift from God to be enjoyed, celebrated and experienced —with others, for the most part. Gluttony or addiction may have its root in a spiritual and emotional problem, of which the addiction or compulsive overeating is simply a manifestation. In that case, the healing of a person's emotions or inner life will be needed —as in the case of the woman who admitted: "I used food as a comfort, like an alcoholic uses alcohol. I binge on chocolate, cake, sweets, often driving for miles to buy it because I am embarrassed to keep going back to the same shop. I'll buy a dozen bars of chocolate and eat them as soon as I get back in the car."

But for most of us gluttony, if that is what it is, is simply eating more than we need, or to put it more scientifically, taking in more calories than we expend in activity. The proverbial extra cream cake, the fry-up we don't need, the third or fourth pint of beer, the second bar of chocolate, the second helping! The solution, in these more day-to-day cases of overeating, is not far to find: less intake, more exercise, and more resistance! It has been pointed out that Jesus walked many thousands of miles in his lifetime—not least because he would have made the journey from Nazareth to Jerusalem for the chief Jewish festivals—and that regular walking remains the most natural form of exercise —now, just as it was in those days. As a non marathon runner, I am inclined to agree!

But if resistance to overeating, and under–exercising, has become hard because we have let things go, then specific strategies maybe required, whether it is weight watchers or the gym. Learning to say "no", especially when no one else is looking, will be a test of our resolve and spiritual discipline, but we should remember that the fruit of the Spirit includes "self-control"! But the most inspiring way to deal with gluttony, if it is an issue, is to recall and follow the example of Jesus.

JESUS THE "BON VIVEUR"

As a teenager, I was taken to see *Godspell* in the West End of London when it was first performed. The supreme impression, which I remember from that musical, was the sheer zest, brio, energy and infectious joy of Jesus. We would certainly have enjoyed being in his company during his earthly ministry. I can almost hear the theologians and churchmen lining up to qualify such a remark, and for sure Jesus was also "a man of sorrows and acquainted with grief", but his basic disposition was joyful, as indeed his followers should be. This was reflected in his eating. He was not a vegetarian —eating both fish and meat, like his contemporaries. His closest friends were fishermen, who fished both for pleasure and for their livelihood.

Jesus' catering arrangements were always interesting, and food and meals played a vital part in his ministry. He chose a number of fishermen, who were continually surprised by his fishing methods and food provision. His most famous miracle, repeated, it seems, on more than one occasion, was the feeding of thousands from very little. Three of his resurrection appearances were centred around meals. One occurred in the upper room in Jerusalem, when all the disciples were locked away, and he came and stood amongst them, and took some fish and ate it, proving that he was not a ghost. Another appearance was around breakfast on the beach at Galilee. Moreover, he had given us a meal by which to remember him and his death, and in which we look forward to his return. In short, in the ministry of Jesus, there were times for fasting or going without, and times for feasting.

The most famous feasting occasion was the wedding at Cana, where Jesus was called upon to deal with the crisis of a wine shortage at the wedding feast, and save the blushes of the host or the catering company who had under-ordered. Jesus, it is estimated, produced from water no less than 360 litres of wine of the very best quality! By any standard that was an abundant provision. Repeatedly, Jesus went to parties and dinners given either by his followers or by those who wanted to cross-question him. His reputation for "eating and drinking" was such that the Pharisees sought to smear his name through it. In fact, Jesus took issue with his detractors by comparing them to contrary children:

"To what, then, can I compare the people of this generation? What are they like? They are like children sitting in the market–place and calling out to each other:

'We played the flute for you,
and you did not dance;
we sang a dirge,
and you did not cry.'

For John the Baptist came neither eating bread nor
drinking wine, and you say, 'He has a demon.' The Son
of Man came eating and drinking, and you say, 'Here is
a glutton and a drunkard, a friend of tax-collectors and
"sinners".' But wisdom is proved right by all her
children."[8]

Jesus showed that you could not please people who in their hearts were resolved to despise you. Whether you fasted or feasted, they would continue to find fault with you. Jesus both fasted and feasted with a passion. Like King David in the Old Testament, he would dance or weep, feast or fast, celebrate or mourn. As the writer of Ecclesiastes put it in his famous poem, there is:

> a time to weep and a time to laugh,
> a time to mourn and a time to dance.[9]

Equally, Jesus fasted. It was one of the principal devotional disciplines of the Jew, and Jesus endorsed its practice in the Sermon on the Mount. He said,

"When you fast, do not look sombre as the hypocrites do, for they disfigure their faces to show men they are fasting. I tell you the truth, they have received their reward in full. But when you fast, put oil on your head and wash your face, so that it will not be obvious to men that you are fasting, but only to your Father who is unseen; and your Father, who sees what is done in secret, will reward you."[10]

Fasting lay at the basis of his ministry. He fasted at the outset of his public ministry, in the temptations. Fasting was a discipline to sharpen spiritual perception, to accompany intercession, to strengthen spiritually the combatant in spiritual warfare and to prepare a person for a new phase of ministry. For all these purposes, Jesus fasted and enjoined the discipline on his disciples. So Jesus knew by the leading of the Spirit when to fast and when to feast. His life oscillated between the two. Before leaving the example of Jesus, there is one more aspect of Jesus' understanding about food which we must grasp.

Jesus had invisible means of support. On one occasion, recorded in St John's Gospel, the disciples had gone off shopping to a Samaritan town called Sychar, leaving Jesus, tired after the journey, outside the town at a well. While he waited there, he fell into conversation with a woman who was evidently intrigued that he knew so much about her, without being told. He offered her a gift of eternal life, saying,

> "...but whoever drinks the water I give him will never thirst. Indeed, the water I give him will become in him a spring of water welling up to eternal life."[11]

On their return, the disciples were surprised to see Jesus talking to a woman, and urged him to eat: "Rabbi, eat something." Jesus then enigmatically replies, " I have food to eat that you know nothing about." This obviously foxes the disciples, since they say, "Could someone have brought him some food?" Jesus explains, "My food is to do the will of him who sent me and finish his work." Such a concept is similar to the statement quoted by Jesus in the temptations, that, "Man does not live on bread alone, but on every word that comes from the mouth of God"[12]

Implicit in both these responses of Jesus—firstly to the temptation of the devil to turn stones to bread, and secondly to the urging of his disciples to eat—is the truth that for Jesus there was sustenance of a kind in both **knowing** and **doing** the will of his Father. Although we are not meant to conclude from this that Jesus did not need normal physical nourishment, he gained, and his disciples would in time gain, deep satisfaction from knowing that they were fulfilling their heavenly Father's purpose for them. The diet of Jesus was to do his Father's will, and whilst this same diet may not guarantee a good figure, as that may depend on each person's metabolism, circumstances and genetic coding, it will nonetheless keep us from gluttony! The disciples were to discover that commitment to the kingdom and its work meant that on occasions there was not even time to eat![13]

So the example of Jesus in the Gospels included feasting and fasting. He ate to live, rather than living to eat. He appreciated the companionship of a meal shared, the quality of food and wine, and the provision by his Father of food in creation, for which he always expressed thanks. Undoubtedly, for Jesus, there was a strong link between food and prayer. The provision of food was never assumed; it was always a gift to be appreciated. Eating is, in a sense, a sacramental act, a sign of our dependence on God. Jesus ate food so that he might do his Father's will. Although eating was important, above all, because of the human contact it gave, the urgency of his ministry and the opportunities before him meant that there was another "food" he needed, which was to finish the work set for him by the Father.

There are danger signals in regard to food in our modern Western society, and they are obvious. We are in danger of divorcing eating from human companionship, as people eat alone or grab fast food to eat alone. We are in danger of being overwhelmed by surfeit, so that a sense of dependence and gratitude for food is overtaken by ever increasing expectations of what we should be able to have. We are in danger of divorcing our consuming from the complexities of production, turning a blind eye to the effects of what we have come to expect. We are in danger of making food our first comfort stop, rather than feeding that underlying appetite for what Jesus called "the bread of life". We can learn from the example of Jesus in this aspect of living, which so perplexes us in modern society. Becoming fully human does involve a healthy approach to eating. As one wise proverb (which has more than once been spoken in our kitchen) says:

> Better a meal of vegetables where there is love
> than a fattened calf with hatred.[14]

Or again,

> If you find honey, eat just enough—
> too much of it, and you will vomit![15]

—a salutary word on which to conclude the first assault on our souls and bodies in this generation so prone to excess.

Notes

1.   See Don Colbert MD, *What Would Jesus Eat?* Thomas Nelson, Nashville, 2002.
2.   Genesis 1:29.
3.   Genesis 9:3.
4.   Ecclesiastes 3:12&13.
5.   See Romans 14:14.
6.   Romans 14:17.
7.   Op. cit.
8.   Luke 7:31–35
9.   Ecclesiastes 3:4.
10.   Matthew 6:16–18.
11.   John 4:14.
12.   See Matthew 4:4 (and Deuteronomy 8:3).
13.   See Mark 3:20.
14.   Proverbs 15:17.
15.   Proverbs 25:16.

5

Greed or Contentment

An American farmer was trying to impress a fellow farmer
from Somerset with the size of his place "back home". He
was attempting to explain how large his farm was, so he said
"I can drive all day in my tractor and still not get around my
farm, it's so big!"

The farmer from Somerset thought long and hard and
eventually said in a broad and laconic accent, "aaarhhhhh,
yes; I used to have a tractor like that!!"

There is a deep-seated desire in all of us to impress; to
build higher, to do better, to have more, and much of this is
fuelled by greed or covetousness. Our capitalist society, now
termed a consumerist society, is set up to foster such
ambitions. It is substantially based on the need to make us
require its products. Many commentators have observed
that along with the growth in consumerism and individual-
ism, morality has, in effect, been privatised.

Advertising which is often amusing, banal or predictable
must be effective otherwise it would not go on! Nor would
companies continue to spend huge sums on it unless they
knew their products sold better. Commercials are enor-
mously expensive to make, and their purpose is to keep their

brand or product somewhere in the consciousness or subliminal thought of the public; influencing our choice in its direction, even if we are not aware of it! Once again, the aim is to implant an image in our minds, which, if we like it, we are then tempted to live out ourselves; by buying the product, and so putting ourselves **into** the image which we have come to admire.

So, for instance, when we watch an advertisement, say for a car, we imagine ourselves driving **that** car along the Riviera with everyone else looking on and being impressed, looking as svelte as the delectable model in the advertisement. Of course, most of us are far more practical when it comes to buying! —Or are we?

Greed and covetousness are slightly different things. Greed simply wants more without having a proper need for it; covetousness has a more personal or relational flavour to it, in part at least: it wants what someone else has got! This is brought out in the commandment where we are forbidden to covet our neighbour's wife, servant, ox or donkey (transport!)[1] We sometimes want something precisely because someone else has it and we do not! This covetous desire borders on envy, which we shall look at later.

Nowhere is this clearer than in sibling rivalry amongst young children. A brother or sister craves what the other has, not because they especially want whatever it is, but because they resent their sibling, whom they perceive as a rival, having something they have not got! If that describes a facet of covetousness, then the action which often follows such a desire is one of trying to satisfy it, whether legally or not, until we get what we want! There is usually any number of examples in the press of people who have gone to extraordinary lengths to get what they want. Some may be quite spectacular and tragic.

An accountant earning over £50,000 p.a. set up several ghost companies to bill his employer for bogus work. Over the course of five years he billed his employer for almost three million pounds. He used the money to establish himself as a key player in the motor-racing world, buying three

Aston Martins, a Ferrari 348TV, a Benetton F1 racing car, a Ferrari 550, a Jaguar XJR, two Ducati motorbikes, three Mercedes and his pride and joy, two McClaren F1 racing cars, one of which he entered with a team of drivers for the 1999GT championships. He launched his team with a champagne reception, and hired a supermodel to pose in front of the McClaren. He was found out and convicted. What had happened? He presumably had a picture of himself as a successful racing-car team owner. He yearned to fulfil the image, so he committed fraud on a grand scale to realise his own inflated picture of himself.

None of us can underrate the power of greed, and most of us will have fallen into its clutches on occasion, but we must get beneath its skin, see where its appeal lies and how to combat it in our lives. What is greed or covetousness?

A DICTATORIAL DESIRE

Many passages in the Bible teach us that sin brings slavery and Jesus brings freedom. He himself made this clear, saying: "...everyone who sins is a slave to sin," and, "If the Son sets you free, you will be free indeed."[2] And yet the normal, worldly view is completely the other way round. A person is free, we are told , when he or she is free to do what he wants. But that is a tragic lie, and one of the greatest deceptions there is. Equally, the world looks at the Christian with his vocabulary of sin and says to itself, "Call that freedom? All that praying; drawing guidelines-for-living from the Bible; taking part in acts of worship; listening to sermons; upholding the standard of the Ten Commandments —no, that is a curtailment of freedom!" But all this begs the question: what does it mean to be free?

When is a fish most free? —surely, when it is in the element for which it was made; when it is in either fresh or salt water, unless it is a salmon, which lives in both. Freedom comes when we are in the element for which we were made. I know this begs all sorts of other questions, not least concerning the proposition that we were intentionally created. But if we accept that fundamental presupposition for a moment, then consider this: when might we be free? The answer must be: when we are doing those things which best suit the purpose for which we were made. And how are we to find out what that is without reference to the One who created us and purposed our existence? When we find relationship with him, and follow the pattern of life he intended for us, *then* we shall be free. But for as long as we are driven by desires which do not suit our true well-being, we are driven by an oppressive, interior "dictatorship", one feature of which is greed or covetousness.

Covetousness, at its most extreme, can become an aching desire to have, to own, to possess, or simply to have under our control. Its power only seems to be temporarily allayed once that-which-I-want has become mine. I say "temporarily" because if we have become generally covetous we find that as soon as we have what we previously had wanted, we find there is something new to want! So it becomes a desire for more, only to find that the more the desire is fed, the less it seems to be satisfied. All of us will have been aware of moments when we have been gripped by a desire to have something, and the effect that has on us. A husband wants a particular car, for which he is prepared to sacrifice the family budget. A gardener desperately wants first prize in the proverbial "marrow" competition, and is prepared to damage, in some night raid, a rival's plant! An athlete yearns for a medal in a competition and is prepared to risk taking an illegal substance to get it. An employee wants promotion and is prepared to rubbish a colleague who might get it instead of him. A man wants a particular woman, about whom he becomes obsessed. All these yearnings drive people on to other actions which only diminish their true humanity, demeaning them. So covetousness can lie at the root of theft, cheating, slander, lust or negligence as well as a host of other tawdry actions.

The trouble with this "deadly sin" is that we can observe

its corrosive effect in others, but often we cannot see it in ourselves. One character in the Old Testament in whom the desire of covetousness wreaked awful and pitiable havoc was Ahab. He was a king, but he was reduced to a whimpering wreck by the sheer dictatorship of covetousness in his life. The writer of Kings tells us that when he was refused what he wanted—Naboth's vineyard, which adjoined his property and which he wanted for a vegetable garden! —he became, "sullen and angry and lay on his bed sulking and refusing to eat!"[3] You might have thought he was a two-year-old child in the grip of a terrible tantrum, but he was a grown man, a king and an owner of considerable assets, yet he was overwhelmed with desire when he saw this piece of real estate—in which he hoped to grow vegetables—evade his grasp! So with the aid of his notorious and scheming wife, Jezebel, he permitted conspiracy, murder and theft, until he got what he wanted! His petulance was only relieved by possession. This deep-seated desire in all of us to control, to own and to dispose of, seems to lie at the root of our fallen humanity. It is in striking contrast to Jesus, who divested himself of the glory of heaven, giving up privileges and position for a season, to take on his redemptive work.

But the apostle Paul has a still more serious and puzzling charge to lay at the feet of a covetous person, which is that if such a desire grips us, then we fall into idolatry. This needs further explanation.

DESCENT INTO IDOLATRY

"Idolatry" is one of those familiar biblical words which is often misunderstood. When idolatry is mentioned, it probably brings to mind particular forms of worship in which primitive idols or images are central to a cult as in pagan or animistic religions in Africa or Asia, but the idea of idolatry in the Bible is far wider than that.

Idolatry means the worship of something or someone other than the true Creator who has revealed himself finally and fully as the God and Father of Jesus Christ.

The apostle Paul is quite clear about this in the opening chapter of the Epistle to the Romans. Here, he teaches that one of the main pieces of evidence that man is by nature sinful is that he suppresses the truth, which is evident to him, and chooses to worship an idol rather than God himself. Paul writes:

> For although they knew God, they neither glorified him as God nor gave thanks to him, but their thinking became futile and their foolish hearts were darkened. Although they claimed to be wise, they became fools and exchanged the glory of the immortal God for images made to look like mortal man and birds and animals and reptiles.[4]

Paul teaches not only that this worship of something or someone which is both a creature and mortal is futile, but that it is wholly inconsistent with the common or general revelation given to humans, which is, "...that since the creation of the world God's invisible qualities—his eternal power and divine nature—have been clearly seen." Apart from anything else, such worship of idols or created things is illogical. How could such things have been responsible for making the world, as they have no intrinsic power or intelligence, and are obviously part of creation (or, at the very least, existence) rather than responsible for it?

The prophet Isaiah put it powerfully when he demonstrated the stupidity of worshipping an idol made by a man, in this passage of prophetic invective and ridicule:

> The blacksmith takes a tool
> and works with it in the coals;
> he shapes an idol with hammers,
> he forges it with the might of his arm.
> He gets hungry and loses his strength;
> he drinks no water and grows faint.
> The carpenter measures with a line
> and makes an outline with a marker;

94

he roughs it out with chisels
and marks it with compasses.
He shapes it in the form of a man,
of man in all his glory,
that it may dwell in a shrine.
He cuts down cedars,
or perhaps took a cypress or oak.
He let it grow among the trees of the forest,
or planted a pine, and the rain made it grow.
It is man's fuel for burning;
some of it he takes and warms himself,
he kindles a fire and bakes bread.
But he also fashions a god and worships it;
he makes an idol and bows down to it.
Half of the wood he burns in the fire;
over it he prepares his meal,
he roasts his meat and eats his fill.
He also warms himself and says,
"Ah! I am warm; I see the fire."
From the rest he makes a god, his idol;
he bows down to it and worships.
He prays to it and says,
"Save me; you are my god."
They know nothing, they understand nothing;
their eyes are plastered over so that they cannot see,
and their minds closed so that they cannot
understand.
No–one stops to think,
no–one has the knowledge or understanding to say,
"Half of it I used for fuel;
I even baked bread over its coals,
I roasted meat and I ate.
Shall I make a detestable thing from what is left?
Shall I bow down to a block of wood?"
He feeds on ashes, a deluded heart misleads him;
he cannot save himself, or say,
"Is not this thing in my right hand a lie?"[5]

If idolatry is the worship of the creature or created thing rather than the Creator, and such worship is based on a suppression of the truth, as Paul has explained, covetousness is a particular desire for something or someone which becomes central to our existence, and so itself becomes idolatrous. The consequence may then be that we simply live for whoever or whatever it is. Presumably this is why Paul says to the Colossian Christians, "Put to death, therefore, whatever belongs to your earthly nature: sexual immorality, impurity, lust, evil desires and **greed, which is idolatry**."[6] Greed, in this list of sins, is specifically attached to idolatry; Why is this? Presumably, greed or covetousness lead to idolatry because they contain a desire to put the possession of something, or a whole range of things, at the centre of our existence. So, in this sense, idolatry is not simply the primitive worship of an idol, which the Old Testament contemptuously tells us is quite powerless to help us, but it can also be the desire for, or worship of, something which then becomes central in our life.

Such covetous desires can range from a desire for wealth, status, fame, power, a particular lifestyle to more specific desires, perhaps for a car, clothes, an apartment or house. Isaiah would be equally ridiculing of trusting in (or worshipping) any of these things. For instance, a car, which may be an efficient mode of transport, but which grows old and may be crashed, is also the product of human skill, and so can no more be worthy of human worship than the piece of wood—which was both used to cook with and shaped into an idol—that Isaiah spoke of.

Although none of these objects is wrong or evil in itself, when such a desire becomes the object of our life, it can become an "idol" or, to put it another way, the thing we live for. It is not that we should not enjoy such things in their proper place, but that if they come to *control* us then they have usurped God's rightful place in our lives. As Hartmut Kopsch says in his excellent book *The Struggle*, "The covetous person does not become an idolater by valuing and enjoying earthly possessions, but by making a God out of them; in the sense that he seeks not only to derive pleasure from them, but through them to gain security, peace of mind and meaning."[7]

However, there is a deeper spiritual outcome which arises from the presence of covetousness in our lives that takes us back to the whole issue of image. The simple spiritual truth is that we become, in a profound sense, *like* that which we truly worship. The New Testament tells us that we reap what we sow, and we shall look at this in greater detail later.[8] The truth of this can be seen in several of the characters in the Gospels. For instance, we are told that Judas loved money and was prepared to steal from the common purse of the disciples of which he had been appointed treasurer! He appeared to want to use money to relieve the needs of the poor whilst in fact he wanted to steal it for his own use. You could say, therefore, that he loved money (and was certainly greedy for it), with the result that he was prepared to sell Jesus into the hands of the chief priests for thirty pieces of silver. In his case, his greed had distorted his entire spiritual vision so that he was prepared to betray Jesus to gain what he craved: more money.

This general principle of becoming like the thing that motivates us, whether it is greed, pride or for that matter any of these "seven deadly sins" can be further seen in another bit part player in the narrative of the New Testament.[9] Her name was Herodias and she was the wife of Herod the tetrarch, who ruled over the area of Galilee where Jesus extensively preached and healed. Mark tells us that she nursed a grudge against John the Baptist, who had criticised the validity of her marriage to Herod. When her daughter, Salome, who had moved Herod to offer anything she asked for—up to half his kingdom—through her captivating dancing before his court, consulted her mother, Herodias, as to what she should request, Herodias suggested the head of John the Baptist on a platter! What more macabre prize could there be! In effect, Herodias desired more than anything else revenge for John's criticism of her marriage, as she had married her previous husband's brother, which was against the Jewish law. And she was prepared to go to any lengths to get what she wanted, even abusing her daughter's relationship with Herod. Her desire for revenge fuelled her life, and she increasingly **became like what drove her.** A bitter and twisted woman!

As we have already observed, man was made in the image of God, having been given certain attributes and abilities, and is distinguished from the rest of creation by being made in this image. That image was marred but not eradicated by the Fall, but through faith in Christ may be restored by the work of the Holy Spirit in us. However, if we humans take a different route and decide to put created objects or other human ambitions at the centre of our desires, and so begin to worship them, then we will become like those things we worship; we will take on their image in our lives, further corroding the true image of God in us. Our true humanity is then either imprisoned or degraded. Conversely, to become fully human we must worship the One in whose image we are made —then we shall become increasingly as we were meant to be. The truth is simply that we become like what we worship with the passage of time.

The effect of greed or covetousness is therefore to distort our lives, diminish our humanity, and underline our separation from God. It exerts a growing dictatorship in our lives, until it takes up an unchallenged position of command; it plunges us ever increasingly into those things that inflame our desires, so ensnaring us in the pursuit and even worship of the created things that have become idols. Paul teaches that we have exchanged worship of the God who has generally revealed his power and deity (as Creator) for the worship of creatures instead. This descent into false worship further diminishes our true humanity, and increases our misery as we realise those things, which promise so much, satisfy so little. At this point we may well ask, "How do I escape from the grip of such powerful desires?"

DEADENED BY A GREATER PASSION

I always remember an incident, which typified the wisdom of a grandparent when it came to the care of children. Such childcare was not surprising since, I imagine, she had learnt such tricks as a parent. Think of a child vehemently holding onto a toy or object, which you want to remove from their grasp either because it is not good for them or you yourself want it. You know that if you seek to remove it from the child's grasp forcibly, you run the risk of terrible screaming and tears, which you hope to avoid. So what do you do? At this point, Granny stepped in and, with the wisdom of years, simply found something more interesting, more colourful and more fascinating than the object in the tightly gripped hand of the child. As soon as she sees the proffered "goodie", then the other object is dropped without a moment's hesitation; you have what you want, peace reigns and wisdom has prevailed! —for a while....

In many ways, we must look to God like that tense, anxious and defensive child, holding on grimly to those things we have set our hearts on and, by ourselves, are quite incapable of releasing our grip upon. As with the child, only a greater passion will make us let go of that something or someone, which has come to dominate our life.

Paul spoke of being in the grip of covetousness as he said,

I would not have known what sin was except through the law. For I would not have known what coveting really was if the law had not said, "Do not covet." But sin, seizing the opportunity afforded by the commandment, produced in me every kind of covetous desire.[10]

Although Paul's chief point in this passage is to show that the moral law brings to the surface, indeed exacerbates, our innate sinful tendency, he also shows that left to ourselves we are powerless to combat this or, for that matter, any other selfish tendency. The only way to deaden this self-centred passion is to know the Holy Spirit's power to help us and to set our mind and heart on a greater passion, which will release the grip (in this instance) of wanting. The advertisers promise to take the waiting out of wanting by purchase schemes, invariably based on various degrees of credit; the New Testament promises that God can so work in us that our wants themselves can be changed! That is nothing short of a supernatural change in our hearts, birthed by the Holy Spirit, and we shall look at the nature of this transformation later in this book.

In a sense, what God is doing is releasing our grip on a way of life that is doing us no good, birthing in us a whole new set of values, aspirations and priorities, and replacing our old passions with a new one which is essentially the growth and extension of the kingdom of God in us and in the world. In his teaching on the Sermon on the Mount, Jesus dealt with many false trails which we are prone to follow as humans, which include parading an image of ourselves which is simply not true, to gain the applause of others; imposing our selfish will on others by thought or deed; or being driven by anxiety in our lives about those things we crave, such as health, material prosperity or clothing. Jesus issued his followers with a challenge, which was to, "...seek first his kingdom and his righteousness, and all these things will be given to you as well."[11] "All these things" meant food, clothes and security. Here was the new passion that was to replace all others, and would deaden the grip of greed or covetousness; for how could you be greedy for yourself if you were really passionate about the advance of the kingdom of God? How could you be fixated on some clothes, or a home or car, if you realised that these were really passing possessions compared with the eternal nature of the kingdom of heaven? However, to actively "seek first the kingdom of God", to the exclusion of other personal aggrandisement, does need a revolution in the heart as well as the ongoing help of the Spirit of God, without whom it would be impossible!

So becoming human—for most, if not all of us—means wrestling with the desire to want more, to own more, to set about getting more. There are plenty of warnings in the teaching of Jesus to beware of saying, like the fool in the parable of the Rich Fool,

> ...'This is what I'll do. I will tear down my barns and build bigger ones, and there I will store all my grain and my goods. And I'll say to myself, "You have plenty of good things laid up for many years. Take life easy; eat, drink and be merry."'
>
> But God said to him, "You fool! This very night your life will be demanded from you. Then who will get what you have prepared for yourself?"[12]

It is a hard lesson for us to learn, that life does not consist in the abundance of possessions; and often, having learnt it once, we have to learn it all over again. To learn it, we both need a revolution in the heart and then a continual renewal of our minds. As Jesus said in introducing this parable:

> "Watch out! Be on your guard against all kinds of greed. A man's life does not consist in the abundance of his possessions."[13]

THE SECRET OF CONTENTMENT

Writing from a Roman gaol whilst chained to a soldier from the Praetorian Guard, Paul wrote warmly to the Philippian church, which he had established in such eventful circumstances ten and more years before. Perhaps he was especially mindful that he had ended up in gaol in their city, too. Imprisoned when a riot had taken place after his deliverance of a slave girl from an evil spirit of divination (or fortune telling), which had earned her owners a great deal of money, he had been freed, following an earthquake that had thrown open the prison doors. The gaoler and his family came to faith and were baptised in the early hours of the morning. In such extraordinary circumstances the church at Philippi had grown. And now, years later and from another gaol, Paul wrote of his joy, love and hopes for the Philippian church. At the end of his letter he wrote of the contentment he had found:

"I know what it is to be in need, and I know what it is to have plenty. I have learned the secret of being content in any and every situation, whether well fed or hungry, whether living in plenty or in want. I can do everything through him who gives me strength."[14]

The clue to the secret of which he speaks, which in turn is the key to his contentment, surely lies in the final words of this paragraph; "I can do all things through him who gives me strength." The point for Paul is that his contentment did not reside in any outward circumstances of life —having good food or clothing or adequate housing or having career prospects—it resided not in having possessions but in being, in the best sense, possessed by Christ. Since nothing and no-one can remove that fact from his existence, then the secret of his contentment will never disappear, and the experience of contentment, which does not rest on outward circumstances, will never go way. In the knowledge of Christ dwelling in him by faith he is content. This sort of "contentment" does not, of course, mean *complacency* in the face of evil and injustice against others; it refuses to attend to and elevate the insistent desires and demands of the self, the flesh, and it is all about trust in God.

So whether or not a person is content as Paul was depends absolutely on the subsidiary question: what is it that makes you content? For most of us, if we are honest, our contentment all too often seems to depend on the outward circumstances of life and upon the well being of our nearest relationships. But we are encouraged, by Paul's example, to move from a position of dependence on those outward circumstances of life, and anxiety about our nearest relationships, to a position of trust in God concerning *every aspect of life.* As we move to that position of trust, we gradually embrace the secret, which Paul had come to grasp himself, that we can do all things through him who gives strength — and the strength to which Paul refers was to face *all circumstances* with true contentment. Contentment will then truly replace greed; and avarice will be defeated in our lives. As that change takes place in us, we will also find that we become more fully human.

Notes

[1]   See Exodus 20:17.
[2]   See John 8:34–36.
[3]   See 1 Kings 21:4.
[4]   Romans 1:21–23.
[5]   Isaiah 44:12–20.
[6]   Colossians 3:5, my emphasis.
[7]   Hartmut Kopsch, *The Struggle* (Terra Nova, 2000).
[8]   See Galatians 6:7.
[9]   See Mark 6:14–29.
[10]   Romans 7:7b–8a.
[11]   Matthew 6:33.
[12]   Luke 12:18–20.
[13]   Luke 12:15.
[14]   Philippians 4:12–13.

6

Lust or Love

There can be little doubt that the sexual ethic as taught in the Bible and traditionally held by the church is now held only by a small minority in the UK. In a recent survey, 63% of 18–24 year olds saw nothing wrong in sexual relations before marriage and 43% of 25–34 year olds saw nothing wrong in two people of the same sex having sexual relations. This survey is over two years old at the time of writing, and it is probable that these percentages have now increased rather than diminished. The orthodox Christian sexual ethic or standard can be simply put as follows: celibacy outside marriage; faithfulness in marriage.

Just because society generally has moved so far from this exacting standard does not mean that this ideal must now change to keep in step with our culture. At the same time, we must realise that the gap between the standard of this ideal and our own shortcomings is covered by God's compassion and forgiveness whenever it is truly sought. This surely reflects Jesus' own attitude to the woman caught in adultery whom he did not condemn but whom he told to go and sin no more.[1] This balance, between compassion and purity, is one that the church must keep; neither excluding the sinner nor condoning the falling short of this gold standard of sexual conduct. It is a real tightrope to walk, for overbalancing on one side or the other can seem either like self-righteous prudishness or cold exclusiveness on the one hand, or unprincipled laxity on the other. The starting points when it comes to thinking about our sexuality are, firstly, that God's standard is clear—if impossibly high, were we left to attain it for ourselves—and, secondly, **all** our sexual conduct is flawed compared with this standard; and, thirdly, God's grace and strength are available to cover the yawning gulf between the two. But the standard nevertheless remains: celibacy outside marriage; faithfulness in marriage!

If that seems rather an old fashioned way of putting it, and greater explicitness is required in our 21st century culture, then how about this as a basic sexual ethic: genital acts between people should be confined to heterosexual marriage. Yes, heterosexual marriage. Because although there may be as many as 5% of the population who are homophile, through either nature or nurture, there is no God-given mandate in the Scriptures for same sex marriage.[2] So in our "postmodern" society, in which most terms need to be defined anew, we need to define marriage, otherwise people assign their own private meaning to a word (or, in the case of marriage, to an institution) rather than holding to an agreed public description of what it is.

Marriage is a public covenant, witnessed by others, made by a man and a woman voluntarily to love each other faithfully for the whole of their life together. It is a relationship entered into freely by each party; that is to say, without coercion. Our society, based on Judaeo-Christian principles, has given marriage legal status, and ensured thereby that a father and mother, generally speaking, raise children. The basis of this relationship is love. Law protects this relationship when constituted in marriage. This relationship born out of love, protected by law, creates the social bedrock for society. Although there have been attempts to give other relationships an equivalent status, such as a private arrangement of co-habitation which is sometimes given the title of "common law marriage", or the attempted registration of same sex partnerships, in fact the only sexual relationship protected by law in the United Kingdom at the time of writing is marriage. However, there is a growing movement to liberalise this position, as such a privileged arrangement for marriage is increasingly cast as unjust or discriminatory to other so-called "stable" sexual relationships.

Such charges of injustice take us back to the basic question as to who is to define what is just or unjust or, to use the associated biblical terms, righteous or unrighteous? Law itself is an expression of values and customs, and is necessarily founded either on accepted codes of conduct, or human rights, or on religious belief. The biblical view of marriage, which is simply expressed in the opening chapters of Genesis, is summarised in this way by its author inspired by the Spirit of God:

> For this reason a man will leave his father and mother and be united to his wife, and they will become one flesh.[3]

In this short statement, which forms the bedrock of marriage, and describes what it is, are enshrined the essential principles of marriage which are leaving, cleaving and becoming one flesh. As much of our law is tethered to the Judaeo-Christian understanding of sex and marriage, the law has understandably given marriage this unique position amongst all our human relationships. The gift and enjoyment of sex is thereby clearly set within the context of marriage.

The trouble in the past has been that the church has conspired with some contemporary attitudes in society to portray sex as either defiling or itself sinful. St Augustine, who had famously enjoyed the favours of many women before his conversion, suggested that King David's penitential Psalm 51, which contains the line "In sin did my mother conceive me", literally meant that sexual intercourse even in marriage was sinful; in fact, David meant that, with the rest of humanity, he shared in a sin-infected nature from the very origin of his life which is dated from conception.

Such an Augustinian view had a profound influence on the way the church generally related to the gift of sex. It has been noted that in medieval times Yves of Chartres recommended refraining from sexual relations between Thursdays and Mondays (inclusive) for various religious commemorations. His counsel, if observed, must have resulted in some quiet weekends in north west France!

But, as with other appetites implanted in man by God, sex has endless potential for joy or despair. The fact is that there appears to be much obvious despair about it; and sex, as we shall see, has become a panacea for so many of our modern ills. For some it has almost become a religion —the only piece of mystery in our all too materialist life. But it cannot be treated as such without grave damage to our humanity. It is a means and not an end: a means to companionship; a means of celebration; a means of having children; a means of helping continuing love. But once it becomes an end it changes from being fertile to being sterile, from being nurturing to being damaging, from being a celebration to being funereal!

It happens that, as I write this chapter, one of the original porn stars of America has just died in a tragic car accident. She was used to make a notorious blue movie in the 1970s. Later in life she became a campaigner against the exploitation of women in roles such as she had taken, insisting that she had been forced to take the part in the film against her will, and reminding others that, each time someone watched that film, they were watching her being raped. But what was begun in the 1970s has not stopped; that era of filmmaking has yet to end.

Pornography is a vast industry, bigger in the US than the national game; in fact, £2.75 billion is spent annually on pornographic videos in the States. Underlining how invasive sexual abuse has become, in the same week that Linda Lovelace died, the Pope summoned to Rome all the US cardinals, to confer about what to do about the 56 cases of child abuse by Roman Catholic priests that have emerged in the first few months of 2002.

The most commercially lucrative part of the internet is porn sites. The Online Computer Library Centre's annual review found 74,000 websites last year, accounting for 2% of the sites on the net. It is a massive, lucrative industry and it is based on the exploitation of a God-given gift —in a way which can only diminish our true humanity.

In 1998, Project Cathedral, a combined operation in twelve countries to tackle internet child pornography began. It has identified 300,000 images, through which the police can find offenders. One officer of the Swedish National Criminal Intelligence Service, who works on tracing hard-core child pornography, despite spending eight hours a day examining that demeaning material, bravely said that knowing even one child had been rescued would be enough.

So what is it about our present society that has allowed this explosion of lust, exploitation and abuse? It seems that a number of factors have come together to enable such an explosion to take place. The first is the possibility of conveying sexually explicit images between people in relative secrecy, thus enabling the possibility of a double life in which the "consumers" may not be found out. Another is the availability of huge numbers of videos with equally explicit material. In short, there is now a technology, which conveys visual images to the watcher, which only deepens his dependence on receiving more of the same, and forms what is in reality a pornographic addiction, which is dangerous, damaging and, sometimes, deadly. It is also extremely widespread.

Another factor is the breakdown of ordinary human intimacy. It is one of those ironies of human behaviour that the very deprivation of affection, security and intimacy in relationships, particularly in childhood and in family life, leads to an aggressive acquisition of that which has been missing, in a way which is damaging both to the person and the one who is the subject of their attentions. It is the absence of such secure intimacy in relationships within families that, in part at least, has led to such a growth in teenage sexual activity. The break-up of so many relationships or marriages creates an emotional deficit, which an early sexual relationship promises to erase, but does not. It has been observed by many commentators and experts that children who are valued and affirmed within stable families are much less likely to engage in premature sexual activity.

In other words, the greater the security and intimacy in family relationships the greater the possibility of forming a permanent relationship of marriage in which sex may be freely and fruitfully enjoyed. But of course there is no such thing as a guarantee, because of the third main factor at work in our sexual culture in the West.

This other factor, which has done so much to influence and develop our sexual culture in the post–war (and now postmodern) society, is the separation, even divorce, that has taken place between sexual activity and personality, or the depersonalising of sex. In one sense, this is as old as the hills, or as old as the oldest profession, where sexual gratification is bought without any expectation or requirement of relationship. But the separation between personality and sexuality has reached a new level in Western society, as the visual image has become supreme. This development is also intricately bound up with the ethics of our consumerist society.

As we all know, one of the most powerful ways to sell any product is to associate the product with a "beautiful" person, male or female; that is, of itself, quite understandable: in fairness, you are not going sell anything by associating the product with (or by showing it with) someone who is unattractive or even repellent —but there is a border which the advertisers can intentionally cross, in which the product is associated with suggested, subliminal or quite overtly sexual behaviour. At this point we are going down the slippery slope in which the projection that is made is not in any way **personal**, in the truest sense of that word, but is only sexual. The model, most often female, does not speak, nothing of her character is conveyed, and her sexuality is conveyed in a powerful and memorable way, with the single purpose of selling the product. This is just one modern example of the way in which personality can be subsumed totally in sexuality in order to sell a product.

The reason why this separation is so insidious is that it sows the seed of a lie, which we are all too ready to buy into, given our general predisposition to self-gratification. The lie is simply that we can detach our sexuality from our personality: that sex can become a "recreational activity", or another "commodity" that we can offer or get, and from the effects of which we can shield ourselves by contraception, the morning after pill, or, in the worst scenario, abortion. This view has become generally accepted in Western culture, so that to even question it appears eccentric, bizarre or medieval, but it is at complete variance with the biblical view of humankind. This view, which we have already looked at, is that we are, as humans, a psychosomatic unity—so that what we do in our bodies affects our souls in the deepest way. It is this thinking that drove Paul to write to the Corinthian Christians in the following terms:

> Shall I then take the members of Christ* and unite them with a prostitute? Never! Do you not know that he who unites himself with a prostitute is one with her in body? For it is said, "The two will become one flesh."[5]
> [*Christians]

The underlying argument here is that we cannot detach our sexual activity from the core of our being; to unite our body with another is tantamount to uniting our whole being with her, which is fundamental to "becoming one flesh". To do anything less is to devalue, diminish, trivialise the gift of sex.

So sexual intercourse, far from simply being a recreational activity which we can be turned off or on like a tap, is in fact a profound joining of our **whole being**, which is both an expression of love and commitment and, potentially, literally life-giving. So what we have achieved in our society, as with so much else, is the trivialising of God's gift of sex: extracting from it the juices of sensation, and leaving out the substance of commitment and total self-giving.

These three factors, which are so powerfully at work in our Western culture, provide a climate in which what the old Anglican marriage liturgy calls "the natural instincts and affections implanted by God in us" may *not* be hallowed, as they are not being "directed aright". The combination of ever–increasing volumes of pornography, available often in a secret way, the lack of true and secure intimacy in family relationships, and the increasing separation of personality and sexuality in the context of commerce, are amongst the reasons why there exists a sexual climate which, far from creating well-being, further diminish our true humanity. However, we cannot blame our environment for the prevalence of lust in our society. For Jesus, it was part of that nexus of sins that proceeded from the human heart. We would be foolish to explain it away simply in terms of social change, new media technologies and family breakdown; they simply remove various barriers of protection, leaving man more exposed than ever to the powerful onslaught of this damaging failure. The damage which lust can produce was never more powerfully illustrated than in the life of King David, and none of the prevailing conditions we have looked at existed in ninth century BC Israel. David's experience simply shows the reality of what Jesus taught, even in a man who had an extraordinary relationship with God.

THE SECOND LOOK

The author of Samuel tells us, in a few terse phrases, that David was in the wrong place at the wrong time, and he looked more than twice at Bathsheba.

> In the spring, at the time when kings go off to war, David sent Joab out with the King's men and the whole Israelite army. They destroyed the Ammonites and besieged Rabbah. But David remained in Jerusalem.

One evening David got up from his bed and walked around on the roof of the palace. From the roof he saw a woman bathing. The woman was very beautiful, and David sent someone to find out about her....[6]

As we have already observed, the sexual climate in the twenty first century may have few restraints, and there may be a cocktail of reasons for the sexual revolution Western society has been through in the last forty years, but none of these things excuses us from individual responsibility in this area of our lives. Society now may make the struggle to maintain a Christian ethic in this area all the harder, but the difficulties do not constitute a revoking of the original standard laid out in Genesis 2:24–25. However, no-one should underestimate the strength of sexual desire or lust, a word of which we are probably shy, because it describes too baldly that which dogs our steps.

For a moment it is worth pausing and asking ourselves the question as to what is or is not lust. Lust is a distortion of sexual love. But lines must be drawn between admiration, erotic love and lust; and one must not be confused with the other, else we sell a dummy on the gift of physical sex. Beauty is unashamedly admitted and acknowledged in several descriptions of women in the Bible, Bathsheba amongst them. Acknowledgement and admiration of beauty or good looks is distinct from lust, and may be an antidote to it.

Once, while a mechanic at a local garage changed a punctured tyre on our car, a beautiful woman walked by. We were both aware of her beauty, so I remarked to the mechanic what a beautiful woman she was! He was surprised and said, knowing I was a clergyman, that he did not think I should think like that! So I said I thought there was a difference between admiration and lust! He probably thought that was a piece of semantics or casuistry, which was simply camouflage for sin. It could be; but presumably only the individual or God would know the intentions of heart and mind. But it is worth making two points before returning to King David's predicament. The first is that there *is* such a thing as eros, to use the Greek word for sexual or romantic passion. The Bible is no stranger to it, and is in fact far more candid and plain about sexual love than the church has been. If Genesis, in its description of the creation of men and women as sexual beings, affirms sex, then the Song of Songs celebrates it! Too often, I have heard commentators speak of the Song of Songs primarily as an allegory of Christ's love for the church, and although it may be read in that allegorical way, it is not its first and plain meaning, which is the best hermeneutic for the interpretation of Scripture. The plain understanding of it is as a passionate love poem, which celebrates the total infatuation of two lovers in physical, emotional, mental and spiritual commitment to each other. Their love is permanent, as the following extract suggests:

> Place me like a seal over your heart,
> Like a seal on your arm;
> for love is as strong as death,
> its jealousy as unyielding as the grave.
> It burns like blazing fire,
> like a mighty flame.
> Many waters cannot quench love;
> rivers cannot wash it away.[7]

But their love is intensely physical and erotic. The language is not body–denying, but affirming and celebratory, and within the confines of commitment. The passion for each other is only heightened by previous restraint. The bridegroom says, in Hebrew hyperbole, that he could have had, "sixty queens... eighty concubines, and virgins beyond number; but my dove, my perfect one, is unique"; the bride is described as "a garden enclosed... a fountain sealed."[8] She has waited for her lover and so says, "my own vineyard is mine to give."[9]

But eros, although the most intense, physical and sexual desire of what has been described as the four loves, can nevertheless make fools and knaves of us all. Presidents and prime ministers have had their reputations mired by the sheer power and folly of their sexual encounters. It is like a mighty river, confined in its proper stream or riverbed it flows by degrees majestically, in rapids or in long slow reaches, but if it should overflow its banks, it can damage, flood and destroy all that is in its path. It is at once both brilliant and banal! So we are back to our paradox of human existence, to put in crude Lutheran language, soaring but farting; heavenward yet earthbound! In the case of David, he looked at Bathsheba not once but twice and then again, and then summoned her to his palace. He had not been able to read what would be written in his son Solomon's reign:

> Do not arouse or awaken love
> until it so desires.[10]

In this case the love was illicit and was not love but lust, for he did not even know who she was. And what, you ask, is the difference?

At what point does fleeting admiration for the obvious beauty of a woman's body, seen not by design as in this case but by chance, turn from natural admiration into driving lust? We cannot be held responsible for every fleeting sexual fantasy which passes through our minds in our sex sodden Western world, but we can be held responsible for the motive that precipitates the second look or the fantasy which we allow to develop until it becomes the platform for action. Jesus gave unmistakable and uncompromising teaching about adultery, in which he upbraided the Pharisees for confining adultery to the sexual act. Jesus extended the scope of adultery to our thoughts as well;

> "But I tell you that everyone who looks at a woman lustfully has already committed adultery with her in his heart"[11]

But what is a lustful look? It is that look which in the first instance reduces an individual to being an object for gratifying our own sexual appetite, often through sexual fantasising; and, in the second instance, wants to possess that person sexually, indeed to dominate them rather than to know them, which **together** constitutes what St John calls "the lust of the eyes". All of these thoughts must have been part of King David's desire for Bathsheba. He looked, in this case, on her already naked body; no need for imagination here. His admiration quickly passed from wonder to lust, which in turn precipitated a plan whereby he could possess what he yearned for.

> Then David sent messengers to get her. She came to him, and he slept with her. (She had purified herself from her uncleanness.) Then she went back home. The woman conceived and sent word to David, saying, "I am pregnant."[12]

The rest, as they say, is history, but of a very painful kind.

THE FABRIC OF PAIN

There is no airbrushing of failure in the Bible. There are heroes, but they are always recorded warts and all. In the Old Testament, many, for various reasons, are portrayed both in their greatest moments of faith, courage and obedience and in their bleakest periods, when in despair, shame and anguish of heart. Abraham, Elijah and, above all, David, soared to heights of spiritual greatness uncharted by most; but, by contrast, the latter also sank to depths that most have not fathomed. David would have agreed with the later prophet Jeremiah, who said, "...the heart is deceitful above all things...."[13] In the New Testament, Paul wrote of his own struggle, "I do not understand what I do. For what I want to do I do not do, but what I hate I do."[14] We shall return to Paul's famous description of the moral struggle later, but suffice it to say now that David would have more than empathised with that description of the struggle.

116

There could not have been a more painful moment in his life than when the prophet Nathan said to him, whilst uncovering his sin, "You are the man!" That is, you are the man who, although God had given the throne of Israel, military strength, innumerable victories, and other wives, snatched what was not his. In a few brief weeks, David was ensnared in adultery, conspiracy to murder, murder, involving others in his sordid cover-up, and deceitfulness! And although the inner desire that had initially landed him in all this trouble was his craving for Bathsheba, it had led him to commit one injustice after the other: injustice towards Uriah on two counts —taking his wife while he was away fighting the nation's battles against the Ammonites, and then, having failed to get him to sleep with Bathsheba after his summons to Jerusalem by the king, conspiring to and succeeding in taking Uriah's life. It is interesting to trace how lust has been transformed into injustice. For although lust begins as a desire to satisfy an inner private craving, it almost invariably ends in the unjust treatment of others, whether it be by propping up an industry that relies on the exploitation of others, or the use of another person for no other reason than our own gratification, or duplicity towards another whom we end up deceiving. In Nathan's famous story that implicates David as the culprit, it is the injustice that makes David angry; we are told David burned with anger against the man in Nathan's story who, though having many lambs of his own, had taken the single pet lamb of the poor man.

If David's lust had led to injustice it had also brought in pain. It is a spiritual truth as old as the world that sin and pain go hand in hand. Of course, pain is not always explained by the presence of sin, there are many other causes of pain. We can often experience pain by being the victim of others' sin, but we can also bring pain onto ourselves by entering into wrongdoing. David's folly brought consequences, which affected the whole community he lived in: his family, his court, the nation. We know from his penitential psalm how profound was his repentance, but nonetheless there were deep and lasting consequences to his life from that point on. Just as Adam and Eve were faced by a sentence, which affected the whole human race, David's sentence would affect the rest of his life and the national life of Israel. "The sword shall never depart from your house," said the Lord through Nathan. "Out of your own house I will bring calamity upon you,"[15] Nathan predicted. Civil war, rebellion, family division, rape and enmity appeared to have been sown in the family and kingdom of David, following this denouement.

Yet alongside this tragic course of events, which would unravel over the succeeding years, there is more than a thread of redemption and grace. David remains devoted to Bathsheba, their second son is none other than Solomon — the most munificent of all Jewish kings and the builder of the Temple; victories in the field are still granted to David and, supremely, the covenant made by God with him holds good, and from his line the Messiah will come. Once again it is the faithfulness of God to his word that will triumph, even if, in the darkest patch of his life, David had "despised the word of the Lord".

These Old Testament stories are written for our instruction and training in righteousness or in the just ways of God. They are not there so that we can sit in smug self-righteousness about the lives of others, but to provide both a warning as to what can happen to us and a hope that the grace of God can take us at our worst and restore us, even if damage and pain persist.

I remember a long time ago when a junior government minister "fell from grace" in what used to be called a "call girl" scandal in those rather less explicit days. The newspapers were full of his misdemeanour. I was helping with an event for young people and happened to fall into conversation about it with the elderly clergyman and previous leader of these "camps". I asked for his reaction, and without any censoriousness or cant he simply said, "Poor man". It was a fitting epithet. The minister knew the pain. It was the end of his career. He was sorrowful about it, and now no account of his life would be complete without the inclusion of this affair.

With David, we should say,

> Have mercy on me, O God,
> according to your unfailing love;
> according to your great compassion
> blot out my transgressions.
> Wash away all my iniquity
> and cleanse me from my sin.[16]

Or, as the Orthodox Church's "Jesus prayer" puts it, "Lord Jesus, have mercy on me, a sinner." Although repentance after the fact is always more constructive than trying to justify our actions, is there a prescription for dealing with lust? What does becoming fully human in this area of our broken sexuality really mean? It is a huge question, and one that deserves far greater reflection than this all too cursory treatment. But perhaps a few things can be usefully said to map out a way forward.

THE PRESCRIPTION FOR LUST

It may seem too much like a clever aphorism, but the prescription for lust is love. In that sense, the title for this chapter is exactly right: lust or love? They cannot co-exist. As we have already seen, erotic love must be trained, disciplined, allowed only to flow in the channels in which it was pre-ordained to run by its divine Creator. It may cascade, tumble, foam and rush there, with safety and satisfaction; but elsewhere it may only diminish and damage its "actors". A responsible way of controlling sexual passion, rather than simply denying its powerful existence, is for a relationship in courtship to develop in a synchronised way: that is, for the relationship to move forward in intimacy **only** as it moves forward in commitment, so that the final act of commitment in marriage, made public in a wedding, is also the shelter in which full and unashamed sexual union can take place. But however wonderful such love in marriage may be, this too has an end, but not a cessation, in its absorption into a greater form of love, which is already present in Christ.

Some Sadducees, who intended to discredit the hope of bodily resurrection, once accosted Jesus. They recounted an absurd, fictitious story in which a woman was married in turn to seven brothers. Each died in turn and successive brothers, fulfilling Jewish inheritance laws, married the widow to provide the previous brother with an heir. All of them failed to do so. The question was, "Whose wife was she in heaven?" Such a nuptial muddle-up in the afterlife surely disproved the existence of it, they smugly believed. Jesus replied that they knew neither the Scriptures nor the power of God; and anyhow, he said, in an explosive one liner, there was no marriage in heaven! Presumably, the need for marriage—to avoid loneliness, or to populate heaven, or to order sexual passion—would not be present. So erotic love is a temporary pleasure. It will be supplanted by a love which endures eternally, which has been supremely demonstrated in Jesus, which is his greatest gift to the human family, which is received through the Spirit, and which transforms our humanity with an infusion of his grace. As Paul said, in introducing the greatest single piece of sustained exposition of what kind of loving this is, to the Corinthian Christians who were high on gifts and short on love, "And now I will show you the most excellent way."[17] This type of love is agape love, a love that called for a new word in the Christians' vocabulary. At its centre is the idea of giving, and it is supremely demonstrated in the life of Jesus.

On the night of his betrayal, Jesus had eaten the Passover meal with the disciples. At the beginning of the meal, there being no household servant present, he had taken off his outer garment, wrapped a towel around his waist, and with a bowl of water proceeded to wash his disciples' feet. St John, who is described as the apostle of love, tells us, in introducing this foot washing narrative:

> ...Jesus knew that the time had come for him to leave
> this world and go to the Father. Having loved his own

who were in the world, he now showed them the full extent of his love.[18]

The full extent of his love is shown by his sacrificial death on the cross, and it is essentially giving, indeed life-giving, love.

As we know, again from St John, "God so loved the world that he **gave** his only Son that whoever believes in him should not perish but have eternal life." This agape love is both self-giving and enemy–embracing. Another distinctive characteristic of this Christ–love is that it can love those who hurt it, who are indifferent to it, or who are implacably opposed to it. This is the love that can be impregnated by the Holy Spirit into our lives, so that our loving resembles Christ's love, both giving and forgiving, both compassionate and holy.

So we face a choice, or, to put it another way, a struggle — to choose love rather than lust; to supplant our own gratuitous desires for another's body with a love which seeks the interests of our neighbour in all her being. In making the right choice we become truly human. It is a choice, which elects to do what does not come naturally to us, but only supernaturally. In an interview just minutes before he was assassinated, the Dutch politician Pim Fortuyn was asked: "Should sexuality be flaunted?" He replied, "No, but sexuality is so important and everyone should be able to do what comes naturally to them." The trouble is that what comes naturally does not bring the freedom we desire. At the centre of lust comes a wanting for yourself, gratifying yourself; but the centre of love is giving and not withholding. It is in the latter that we find dignity, integrity, happiness and peace.

If we choose agape love, then it must firstly be received as a gift in Christ —that is, not apart from him but *in* him. As in the case of the prodigal son, it means coming to our senses, returning from whatever far countries we have got ourselves into, and from what ever filth (like the pig swill) we have fed on, back to a Father's embrace and love, which gives us new clothes and good food. Having received that embrace and experienced that love, we set out to love, too, in that way which Paul describes. Of this love, he says,

> Love is patient, love is kind. It does not envy, it does not boast, it is not proud. It is not rude, it is not self-seeking, it is not easily angered, it keeps no record of wrongs. Love does not delight in evil but rejoices with the truth. It always protects, always trusts, always hopes, always perseveres.[19]

It is a love which outlasts all other loves, and is open to all: the single and the married, the homophile and the heterosexual, the divorced and the bereaved, the child and the aged. It will be the language of heaven but it must first be learnt, however falteringly, on earth. As Joshua said to the Israelites: choose this day whom you will serve.

Notes

[1]   See John 8:1–11.

[2]   See Lance Pierson, *No Gay Areas? Pastoral care of Homosexual Christians*. Grove Booklet No. 38.
This is a very helpful introduction to the subject, covering scriptural teaching and encouraging a healthy response to the homophile Christian.

[3]   Genesis 2:24.

[4]   See R. Foster, *Sex, Power and Money* (Hodder, 1985).

[5]   1 Corinthians 6:15b–16.

[6]   2 Samuel 11:1–3a.

[7]   Song of Songs 8:6–7a.

[8]   Song of Songs, see 6:8–9 and 4:12.

[9]   Song of Songs, see 8:12.

[10]   Song of Songs 8:4b.

[11]   Matthew 5:28.

[12]   2 Samuel 11:4–5.

[13]   Jeremiah 17:9.

[14]   Romans 7:15.

[15]   See 2 Samuel 12:10–11.

[16]   Psalm 51:1–2.
[17]   1 Corinthians 13:1.
[18]   John 13:1.
[19]   1 Corinthians 13:4–7.

7

Sloth or Rest

The prophet Micah had a fabulous vision of contentment, which he described as follows,

> Every man will sit under his own vine
> and his own fig tree,
> and no-one will make them afraid,
> for the LORD Almighty has spoken.[1]

In this vision we see people resting from their labours, in touch with their Creator, at ease with the environment and at peace with themselves, without fear or anxiety. It is a far cry from the picture of modern man trying to juggle three things at once and never being really satisfied with the results of any of those activities. One of the most used words in our modern, Western vocabulary is "stress". We recently received a letter from the mother of a French girl with whom one of our children was to do an exchange; in her introductory letter she spoke of the stress that she and her husband, a hospital manager, were under, and this was our first contact with them!

A few years ago, stress was a word mostly used by

engineers, but now it is common currency. According to the Health and Safety Executive, stress is the second most common work-related illness. Signs of stress include inability to make small decisions, deterioration in punctuality, working long hours, aggressiveness or passivity, lack of concentration, inflexibility, and change in appearance or posture. People who suffer from stress linked to depression sometimes find the mixture overwhelming. Depression affects one in ten people at any one time, and one in four in their lifetime. Stress can have awful consequences.

It probably should not fall to a clergyman to write on either rest or sloth. I am frequently asked by members of my congregation, "What do you do all week?"

"Clergymen", I have replied, tongue in cheek, "are six days a week invisible, one day a week incomprehensible!" There was a grain of truth in this. In Victorian or Georgian days in England they frequently appear in literature as having a more than gentle lifestyle, which afforded ample time to associate with their patrons in a sociable way and spend quantities of time catching rare species of butterflies around Lake Como! Indeed, I have an ancestor who became a bishop in what is now the Church of Ireland, who spent much of his time travelling along the route of the Grand Tour and building munificent buildings, which have long since become derelict, to put in them all that he had collected! Perhaps my own parishioners are more than tempted to say, "What has changed?" But stress now takes its toll on my own vocation.

A friend of mine, also a clergyman, once told me that he saw a table of occupations ranked in order of stress. Clergy, he told me, came near the bottom, with market gardeners! Perhaps the proof of that was when the actuaries of the Church Commissioners found that they had miscalculated the length of life of the average clergyperson, who lives, on average, not to 78, as they had previously thought, but to 83 years old! The effect of this miscalculation was that a further substantial sum was needed to adequately fund Church of England pensions.

However, whatever work we do, the aim must be to find a

balance between work and rest; this has become a pressing need in Western society, and this is the issue, which we must address in this chapter.

SLOTH

Sloth is not a word that we use today very much; the word which we would probably use to describe the same thing is idleness. Laziness gets a bad press in the Bible. One of the most graphic and memorable passages describing the effects of idleness is found in the Book of Proverbs:

> Go to the ant, you sluggard;
> consider its ways and be wise
> It has no commander,
> no overseer or ruler,
> yet it stores its provisions in summer
> and gathers its food at harvest.
> How long will you lie there, you sluggard?
> When will you get up from your sleep?
> A little sleep, a little slumber,
> a little folding of the hands to rest —
> and poverty will come on you like a bandit
> and scarcity like an armed man.[2]

The ant was certainly not prone to spend large quantities of time slouched before a small screen with insect like antennae! Idleness comes in many forms, but in our society it is mostly encouraged by that ubiquitous small screen, a television or monitor, which has come to dominate more hours than any other leisure "activity" except sleeping —if that can be properly described as an activity! One of the caricatures of our society is someone slumped in front of the television set, channel–changer in one hand (normally held by the male, apparently!), lager in the other and take-away meal nearby. The average Briton, we are told, watches 26 hours a week, has on average 3 television sets in the house with as many as 30% of children having their own in their bedroom. The effect on personal fitness, mental ability, and voluntary groups—which find it increasingly hard to find leaders—must be considerable.

Indeed, there are now television programmes about watching television, such as *The Royle Family*, a BBC sitcom which more than adequately exemplifies the quip that a family is a group of individuals held together by a television! The "policing" of the television by parents in the interests of homework, sport or even conversation, must be one of their most arduous and demanding tasks. Having four children at home, we know it is a daily challenge!

But idleness is hardly confined to any particular age group. Indeed, you can now make the case that from 14 upwards in the UK, young people have more pressure on them to work for exams than any other nation on earth! Equally, once the need to earn presses in, the ever rising cost of living, fuelled by the ever increasing rise of material expectations, means that work becomes literally a new religion; that is, *the* thing that binds us.

The apostle Paul, in uncompromising teaching, makes us embrace the challenge of work. He writes at some length to the Thessalonians, who were in danger of chucking in their normal day-to-day occupations in the expectation that Jesus would soon return and end their daily grind:

In the name of the Lord Jesus, we command you, brothers, to keep away from every brother who is idle and does not live according to the teaching you received from us. For you yourselves know how you ought to follow our example. We were not idle when we were with you, nor did we eat anyone's food without paying for it. On the contrary, we worked night and day, labouring and toiling so that we would not be a burden to any of you. We did this, not because we do not have the right to such help, but in order to make ourselves a model for you to follow. For even when we were with you, we gave you this rule: "If a man will not work, he shall not eat."

We hear that some among you are idle. They are not busy; they are busybodies. Such people we command and urge in the Lord Jesus Christ to settle down and earn the bread they eat. And as for you, brothers, never tire of doing what is right.

If anyone does not obey our instruction in this letter, take special note of him. Do not associate with him, in order that he may feel ashamed. Yet do not regard him as an enemy, but warn him as a brother.[3]

So to fulfil our purpose on earth we must not shrink from work, nor shirk its demands, whether physical or mental; for idleness will only atrophy our gifts, diminish our self-respect and, at worst, possibly imprison us in poverty. But it is the responsibility of the whole community to provide a society in which work may be found, and the blight of idleness and unemployment avoided.

One Two-Thirds World project, with which our church has been in partnership over several years, is Chisomo, a charity to help street children in Blantyre, Malawi. The process of rehabilitation for these abandoned children invariably involves friendship, Christian love, shelter, accountability, education and the provision of work. Part of this holistic mission throughout the world means engaging not only with the spiritual needs of the individual but also the conditions of their environment, to improve them. High on the list of such improvement must be the provision of work, for few things are more likely to produce depression and despair than enforced idleness.

GOD'S CALL TO WORK

As with marriage, so with work; both these fundamental human activities are rooted in the original mandate given by God to humanity. As God himself said:

"...Let us make man in our image, in our likeness, and let them rule over the fish of the sea and the birds of the air, over the livestock, over all the earth, and over all the creatures that move along the ground."

> So God created man in his own image,
>   in the image of God, he created him;
>   male and female he created them.

God blessed them and said to them, "Be fruitful and increase in number; fill the earth and subdue it. Rule over the fish of the sea and the birds of the air and over every living creature that moves on the ground."[4]

Intertwined with Adam and Eve's creation was their role as vice-regents over the earth, to act as stewards of the world that God had wonderfully and beautifully made, and to populate and enjoy this planet. Horticulture, agriculture and the procreation of children were the original activities of humankind! At first, work was a sheer delight but, after the Fall, work took on an element of drudgery as Adam suffered the curse of those words: "By the sweat of your brow you will eat your food."[5] Equally, Eve heard that, "I will greatly increase your pains in childbearing."[6] So horticulture and having a family were invaded with hardship. Work was no longer a romp in the garden but a necessity, at once both wanted and hated. Just as relations between man and woman oscillated from desire to enmity, as might be inferred from the sentence, "Your desire will be for your husband and he will rule over you",[7] so man's relationship with work became equally ambivalent, on the one hand needing it for finding dignity and purpose, and on the other hand longing to be free from it and the toil that was involved.

This same paradox is evident in our working lives in the West, where huge quantities of money and time are spent in preparation for retirement, yet when it comes to it, the very work we so wanted to be rid of is sometimes missed! By contrast, last week I read of an Indian hotelier who built up a successful chain of hotels in the Indian sub-continent and was still working at 102! So what should be our attitude to work?

"Work," wrote John Stott, "is the expenditure of energy (manual, mental or both) in the service of others which brings fulfilment to the worker, benefit to the community and glory to God."[8] Fulfilment, benefit and glory: this three-fold definition shows that in work there are three parties to be satisfied: ourselves, who may be fulfilled; the community, which is served, and God who is glorified. The third part of this definition of work, the glorifying of God, needs a little more explanation or exposition. God is glorified in our work not only when our gifts, which he has granted us, are used (as demonstrated in the parable of the talents) but also when our activity is an extension of his creative activity, and honours his purpose in creation.

As we have already seen, work, in essence, is more than paid employment. It is the expenditure of energy in the service of others, so it applies as much to the father bringing up children at home as the mother who works in a retail business at what we have come to term a "place of work". But a "place of work" is as much the kitchen as the boardroom, the playroom as the factory floor! What is clear from these examples, is that the patterns of work are changing fast, and it is necessary to have as fundamental a definition of work as possible. Equally, we are being constantly challenged to distinguish between what is a purely cultural understanding of work and what is a God-given understanding. So we need to acknowledge and value any work that is done which is the expenditure of energy in the service of others, ascribing to it value and significance in our human family.

Quite apart from financial reward, work gives dignity and fulfilment to the worker. A farmer who was deprived of his herd of cows because of foot and mouth disease wrote of despairing after they had all been slaughtered: "Financially we were unemployed. The cows were producing £600 worth of milk a day. How do you make that sort of money? But I don't want any money. I want my cows back, please. I want to be out there, getting shitty!" The fact is that work, however menial, bestows a sense of dignity, worth, purpose and significance to life. To be without it can spell depression, dissolution and sometimes despair; whereas once this may have been confined to the manual worker, now, since the 1980s, it has afflicted the middle-classes in the West too. Very few have escaped the pain of unemployment.

On the way back on the bus from central Bristol to the "park and ride", I overheard the conversation of a fellow passenger to a friend on her mobile; she was obviously distressed and angry. It did not take too much eaves-dropping to hear that the cause of her anger and distress was that that afternoon she had been sacked. That was distressing, but what had made her angry was that it was all so impersonally done: she had been informed on her email, and had been asked to leave that afternoon! It reminded me of an occasion many years before, when I had by chance met a friend from college days; he was a brilliant individual with, unusually, degrees in law and theology, and was working in a senior post in the telecommunications industry. He had just heard that that he was no longer needed, but no-one told him personally —he had been sent a message on his pager! We all know of many who have suffered the sudden loss of work in our market economy, so we will have witnessed at first hand that our well–being is related to having work, which is both a service to others and a fulfilment of our own gifts and training.

The writer of Ecclesiastes has a high view of work. Although his style may seem a little cynical or morbid at times, he writes with refreshing candour and modernity. He concludes his famous section beginning ,"There is a time for everything and a season for every activity under heaven" with this telling statement, "So I saw that there is nothing better for a man than to enjoy his work, because that is his lot."[9]

So we are to avoid idleness on the one hand, and respond to God's call to work on the other. This call is not an optional extra but is part of our very humanity. Preachers often exhort their hearers, quite properly, to find all their security in God, to the point that even without human and material props, we should remain perfectly at peace and felicitous. Of course we are to trust that all our needs will be met. Indeed, Jesus reminded his hearers that even the birds of the air or the lilies of the field have their needs met by God; and we should learn from creation. But work and relationships are the very stuff of our humanity, so rather than pretend that these essential characteristics of life are inessential, we need to provide for them and allow them to be irradiated with the presence of God. For this to happen, our work needs to be encompassed by our prayer! Our work needs to be a place where we find the presence and purpose of God, and the ministry of the church should aid that discovery. Indeed, it is my experience that our congregation has never been more grateful for biblical teaching than on the subject of work. A vital part of this teaching today is how to avoid stress!

AVOIDING STRESS

As part of my sabbatical, a privilege which only some clergy seem to enjoy, and during which I am writing this, as I mentioned earlier I travelled overland to the Middle East, so providing some background to this book. The journey to Jordan was about 4000 miles, and one of our most southerly destinations was the hidden city of Petra, built by the Nabataean people around 100BC. Many have visited this extraordinary city, which at its height housed some 35,000 people living in caves in the sandstone rocks. After a short climb up to what is called the "high place", where the Nabataeans sacrificed animals, we had a tea break. One of the Bedouin got out his simple, one-stringed musical instrument, and before singing what we were told was a love-song, tuned his simple, primitive instrument. Tuning simply meant moving the bridge under the single wire to the right place, until the appropriate tension was created on the string to play the exquisite notes. In fact, he was doing what every musician does before playing. Without the right amount of tension or stress on the string, nothing beautiful will emerge. What is true for music making is also true for our well–being: the right amount of tension or stress is needed so that, on the one hand, our lives are not either unproductive or flaccid, and on the other hand, neither strident or squeaky! The issue is: how are we to be restful in a culture that seems to be ratcheting up the levels of stress?

The warning signals are now very evident. We are increasingly living in a culture of suspicion, in which people may be thought guilty until proven innocent, causing considerable stress. The testing of children and young people has reached an all time high, in which pupils feel that their destiny turns on marks awarded in their teens. For three years, from 16 upwards in the UK, we examine young people: a process in which it is all too easy for schools to trade the long term objectives of education—namely training pupils to think and choose for themselves—for the short term gain of good statistics. League tables, once the preserve of football clubs, now quantify every aspect of living. So we have become obsessed by measuring, without having put in place the fundamental yardstick by which we are to measure; and what we are left with is endless tables of comparison. No wonder, therefore, people are constantly looking over their shoulders to compare themselves with others and are now exhibiting greater signs of stress.

In pastoral ministry we face congregations in which the teachers long for the end of term or early retirement; nurses are recruited from abroad to fill the gap between need and supply; young couples are burdened with huge mortgages, and commuters face the uncertainties of daily travel. In this context, in which the opportunity for sloth is minimal, the challenge is, in fact, to find rest for our souls. All too often we are confronted daily by the language of anxiety and stress as phrases cascade from the lips of our neighbours such as: "There is never enough time"; "There is never a spare moment"; "We are always on the go"; "I need it by yesterday"; "There are never enough hours in the day." To cap it all, we have made a virtue out of busy-ness, so that the busier you are, the more important you feel you have become! Understandably, given all this, one of the most attractive sayings of Jesus is, "Come to me, all you who are weary and burdened and I will give you rest."[10] When first spoken in the rugged and physically demanding days of the first century, they must have appeared like an oasis in the desert of political uncertainty and religious controversy. In our own day they are equally attractive, as so many feel battered by the demands of modern living. What is this rest which is on offer, that will allow us to reach our potential as human beings?

SOUL REST

Of course the full quotation of Jesus' invitation is:

> "Come to me, all you who are weary and burdened, and I will give you rest. Take my yoke upon you and learn from me, for I am gentle and humble in heart, and you will find rest for your souls. For my yoke is easy and my burden is light."[11]

What more wonderful invitation could there be? But for it to be taken up, a number of assumptions must be agreed. The first, which is utterly basic, is the assumption that we have souls. The opening chapters of Genesis show that we are a mixture of material and spiritual. We are taken from the dust of the earth, but imbued with the image of God, so that we are described as living souls. Although—to use the Russian novelist Gogol's title of his famous novel—we have become, through the Fall, "dead souls", we need to be raised to newness of life and have the image of God re-created in us. We still have a residual awareness that we were created for an eternal destiny. So, as is well–known, Augustine wrote that, "our hearts are restless till they find their rest in you." The offer of Jesus Christ is rest for our souls. As we know, much of modern life is marked by a profound restlessness. To be left alone with our own thoughts can be unbearable; to have little in the diary, or few mobile phone calls, a cause for concern; to have little or no inner peace, a spur to generate more activity; and, for those of us who are prone to addiction, this restlessness is like a black hole that sucks in our fears and offers only temporary satisfaction — a bleak picture, you might say, but all too true. Although I have had my own season of rest, or sabbatical, the cries of the human heart can never be so neatly laid to rest.

On returning from the Middle East, I was summoned to the bedside of a dying man, who had a life as a successful and well known actor, but who now feared the approach of death. I have talked on the telephone with a young man who has an awful sense of worthlessness, although he comes from a loving home; and I have shared in the tragic news of the loss, soon after birth, of the baby of a couple I married last year. No wonder we need rest for our souls!

If we are to succeed in finding rest for our souls in all the uncertainties of life, there are two instructions that Jesus gives us here: the first is to come, and the second is to take. We need to come to him as the Lord and Saviour, and take his yoke upon ourselves. Coming to him is a matter of prayer; of saying in our words that that is what we are doing, in response to his invitation, and then deliberately, and most probably in fellowship with others, taking his yoke upon ourselves.

A yoke is a wooden harness that sits over the shoulders of a working animal, normally either a horse or bullock. It should fit well, and it enables the farmer to direct and control the creature. When a person has responded to Jesus' invitation to come to him, then the exchange that is made is *his* yoke for *our* restlessness. We are left with a choice —to continue with our restlessness or put on this yoke of Christ, which is well made, and lovingly placed on us, because he is "gentle and humble in heart". It is a yoke that is present in both times of joy and sorrow.

A number of years ago we were given a teapot with the corny quip on the outside: "Life is one long strain." It may be. Or, as Dr. Johnson is reported to have said, "Life is one long process of getting tired"; but the offer which is, so to speak, on the table, is to come to the rest-giver, find soul-rest, and take the yoke that is offered from the gentle and humble Son of God.

SABBATH REST

A Californian Christian surfer is said to have put on the back of his car the slogan, "And on the seventh day God went surfing." If he didn't, then he must have seen the surf and said that looks good!

The concept of the Sabbath is all too often mired in legalism. It was in Jesus' day, when the religious leaders watched out to see whether Jesus would do any work of healing or deliverance on the Sabbath, so that they could upbraid him. Jesus taught that, "...the Sabbath was made for man, not man for the Sabbath."[12] The fourth commandment, to keep the Sabbath holy, is essentially a provision for our welfare and not one for our impoverishment. But, as so often with God's commandments, they are wrongly depicted as being killjoy rather than life-enhancing. But if someone came to you and simply said, "I want you to have one day a week of rest, don't do any work", then most of us would receive that gladly. This is what God says: get a day's rest each week! The purpose behind this is significant. It is both to help us to rest and also to provide space in which God can renew his image in us—the image which, as we have seen already, is the defining aspect of our humanity—and so we are refreshed and re-focused; or, to put it in the context of the theme of this book, this is to help us become more fully human; truly be ourselves, and meet our potential.

To twist a well-known proverb: all work and no play makes the image of God in us duller still! To be made in the image of God is to be spiritual, social, creative, thoughtful and moral. The day of rest, which is whatever day of the week that works for you, although ideally it is a Sunday, is the day when these aspects of the image of God can be renewed in each of us.

SEASONAL REST

The first kind of rest, soul rest, is essential, for without it there is no inner peace, no sense of the presence of God, no leading and guiding of your life. The second kind of rest, Sabbath rest, is part of God's wise provision for our humanity and its renewal and re-creation. A third type of rest consists of what I call a seasonal approach to life.

In these northerly Islands called the British Isles, the seasons are marked out by changes in the weather and natural changes in the landscape. They are protracted periods of change from one type of weather to another. Except now, in these times affected by global warming, the boundaries between one season and another are becoming more and more blurred and indistinct. Indeed, in one day it seems that we can have three seasons of weather wrapped up in twenty-four hours! Nevertheless, we are used to seasons, even if it takes a while longer to decide which season we are presently in! A skill which we need to acquire is to understand the season of our life and ministry, or Christian service, that we are in; like the men of Issachar in the Bible, who were gifted to know the times and seasons.[13]

The biblical author who gives us this way of thinking is, once again, the writer of Ecclesiastes. He tells us that there is "a time for everything, and a season for every activity under heaven." He then identifies those seasons as follows:

A time to be born and a time to die,
A time to plant and a time to uproot,
A time to kill and a time to heal,
A time to tear down and a time to build,
A time to weep and a time to laugh,
A time to mourn and a time to dance,
A time to scatter stones and a time to gather them,
A time to embrace and a time to refrain,
A time to search and a time to give up,
A time to keep and a time to throw away,

A time to tear and a time to mend,
A time to be silent and a time to speak,
A time to love and a time to hate,
A time for war and a time for peace.[14]

It is our task to identify the season that we are presently in, and to make the most of it. Some seasons are all too obvious. Having recognised which season we are in, we are to give ourselves to fulfil it until it is time to move on again. Just as in the natural seasons, we would not expect corn to ripen in January or snow to fall in July (in the Northern hemisphere at least!) so in our personal lives it is worth discerning at what stage of life we are, and acting appropriately. There will come a time when what is not possible now will be appropriate later, and vice versa. Although, in one sense, this may not of itself sound restful, this acknowledgement of life's seasons can in fact be a liberating insight. For by recognising the particular "time" we are in and giving ourselves to it, we can free ourselves from those other demands which we need not meet now.

But it may also be possible for us to create special times of rest. This may vary from annual holiday, a short break, a weekend retreat, or a planned break from work with your employer's blessing. In the Old Testament there was a cycle of rest built into the agricultural pattern (see Leviticus 25). Every seven years the land was to be rested and left fallow, and after 49 years there was to be a year of Jubilee in which people would return to their own clan, and land could be redeemed by those who had lost it. The principle in both the year of Jubilee and the year of Sabbath was to allow for the restoration of the people—and the land, after a period of use—and to provide an opportunity of redemption for that which had been alienated. The purpose of this particular cyclical rest was to restore that which was depleted, alienated or lost. If that was true of land in the Old Testament, surely it is even more important that people who belong to the new covenant should have the opportunity of having restored to them what, in personal terms, has been depleted, alienated or lost. Although this will probably not refer to material assets, it can surely mean the restoration of body, mind and spirit, through the grace of God, in a season of deliberate rest.[15]

Provision of such a season of rest must be a counterpoint to the incessant demands of modern living. There is little danger that, generally speaking in Western society, we will be overtaken by sloth (unless it is a particular personal challenge), but for many of us it may be a far greater challenge to find rest for our souls, refreshment and recreation on a weekly basis, and seasons of renewal for the whole of our lives. But in finding rest we find an opportunity for God to renew his image in us.

Notes

[1]   Micah 4:4.
[2]   Proverbs 6:6–11.
[3]   2 Thessalonians 3:6–15.
[4]   Genesis 1:26–28.
[5]   See Genesis 3:19.
[6]   See Genesis 3:16.
[7]   Genesis 3:16.
[8]   In *Issues Facing Christians Today* (Zondervan).
[9]   Ecclesiastes 3:22a.
[10]   Matthew 11:28.
[11]   Matthew 11:28–29.
[12]   See Mark 2:27.
[13]   See 1 Chronicles 12:32.
[14]   Ecclesiastes 3:2–8.
[15]   See Hebrews 4:9–11.

8

Anger or Forgiveness

We come now to one of the most difficult choices that we may ever face; although it is not by any means a straight choice between anger or forgiveness, as life is not that simple. But before launching into this most difficult area it may be worth pressing the "rewind" button to reflect briefly on where we have come from.

Orthodox Christianity holds that two individuals, Adam and Eve, both historical and representative of the human race, in the mists of time, took a choice, which has profoundly affected us all. They chose to rebel against their good and loving Creator in a bid to become more powerful. In doing so they chose to listen to a malevolent voice, which was close at hand and who suggested that, in this act of disobedience, they would become like their Creator. However, they found that far from becoming what they thought they would become, namely more powerful and more splendid, they plunged instead from their harmony and peace into discord, pain, death and alienation from the source of life. They found, too, that their original likeness and image had been impaired, and that they must now do battle —with an innate tendency to care mostly for themselves, and with this malevolent force, which continued to make empty promises in which it was all too easy to become ensnared, and with a culture around them that became increasingly distant from the original environment they had been given. Ever since then, humans have been involved in a struggle, and we have come to describe it in various ways. The description of the struggle, which we are following here in these central chapters of this book, was made long ago by some of our medieval forbears who had a penchant for classification. They called it the struggle with seven deadly sins. In fact, as far as our Creator is concerned, all sins are deadly to his pure eyes, whereas we sometimes think that one class of sin is more deadly than the next! One (no doubt, kindly) Victorian clergyman wrote a book, to be found in our vestry library, entitled *Respectable Sins*!

So we are involved in a struggle, which in turn involves us in choices between things that are either beneficial or harmful. Except we soon discover that **left to ourselves** we cannot make the right choices, and cannot easily change our patterns of behaviour which are affected by what we inherit from the past and the influences from the present. The biggest choice is whether we will accept help from our Creator to remake the shattered image, impaired and disabled so long ago, and be remade inwardly so that we can become what we were truly meant to be; to become, in fact, fully human. But that is to jump ahead of where we are now, which is considering another of life's choices.

These choices are neither exhaustive nor definitive. We are simply following a system of classification which has been with the human family for many hundreds of years. The choice which we are considering here is not always a straight one, but it is nevertheless one between anger and forgiveness.

The first thing to say here is that anger, *per se*, is not uniformly wrong. In fact, on occasions, it is good and just. For what we must initially come to terms with is that God himself is capable of anger.

GOD'S ANGER

Some people have such a view of God that anger does not enter into the picture. They conceive of him as an all-absorbing force, duty bound to take all the moral muck and filth we throw at him. They think, with Voltaire, that he is bound to forgive, for that is his business. But this emasculated view of God, shorn of all affection and feeling, is not the one presented in either the Old or New Testament. What we find there is a God who is loving and holy, merciful and just, compassionate and jealous. In fact we could say that, although it seems a paradox, his anger is simply one response of his just love to the events and actions that confront him in the world. On numerous occasions in the Old Testament, God shows his anger towards either an obdurate individual who refuses to trust him, or towards a nation whose practices offend his standard of justice and righteousness, and above all towards Israel, who repeatedly squandered the revelation given to them by turning her back on his faithful love towards them. Instances of such anger for such causes are not far to seek.

Moses was to become the friend of God who, we are told, spoke with him face to face; but it was not always so. Although he was rescued from almost certain infanticide, brought up in the luxury of Pharaoh's palace, given sanctuary in Midian after he killed an Egyptian, he found it hard to believe that God had called him to go to Pharaoh and bring the Israelites out of Egypt. Time and again, he demanded reassurance from God that his presence would go with him in this great task. And, although he was given repeated signs, he eventually said, "O Lord, please send someone else to do it!" At this we are told, "Then the Lord's anger burned against Moses!"[1] It is not a surprising response. Such an unwillingness to trust and obey after so much reassurance was bound to precipitate this eventual response of anger. As anyone in a loving relationship will know, we incur no less disfavour when we repeatedly refuse to believe the one we say we love, and fail to take him or her at their word. It is quite probable that they would get angry with us!

More frequent was God's expression of deep disappointment and anger with the Israelite nation. They had received so much but had rejected his ways. Perhaps there is no greater insight into the anger and sadness that God felt over Judah and Israel than in the love song he sings over them, through the prophet Isaiah in chapter five of his prophecy. Despite all the care and attention lavished over their destiny, they spurn his love. They were like a vineyard to him, which he had protected and cared for, but which then yielded only bitter fruit:

> The vineyard of the LORD Almighty
> is the house of Israel,
> and the men of Judah
> are the garden of his delight.
> And he looked for justice, but saw bloodshed:
> for righteousness, but heard cries of distress.[2]

No wonder that this love song turned lament should conclude on such a different note, as disappointment and despair turns to anger:

> Therefore, as tongues of fire lick up straw
> and as dry grass sinks down in the flames,
> so their roots will decay
> and their flowers blow away like dust;
> For they have rejected the law of the LORD Almighty
> And spurned the word of the Holy One of Israel.
> Therefore the LORD's anger burns against his people;
> his hand is raised and he strikes them down.
> The mountains shake,
> and the dead bodies are like refuse in the streets.[3]

As on so many occasions, God's anger literally wrestled with his compassion until it is finally resolved in the agony of the cross; this struggle is no more vividly shown than in his cry over Israel in the words of the prophet Hosea:

> How can I give you up, Ephraim?
> How can I hand you over, Israel?
> How can I treat you like Admah?
> How can I make you like Zeboiim?
> My heart is changed within me;
> all my compassion is aroused.
> I will not carry out my fierce anger,
> nor will I turn and devastate Ephraim.
> For I am God, and not man—
> The Holy One among you.
> I will not come in wrath.[4]

However, despite the incessant pleadings with the Northern kingdom, Israel, and the southern kingdom, Judah, the warnings and entreaties of God to return to him, in both their hearts and ways, fell on deaf ears. Disaster came to them both. Israel was overrun by the Assyrians, and Jerusalem by the Babylonians. Both events are seen as the outworking of the anger of God —an anger which we are repeatedly told in the Old Testament is slow to come about. Nowhere is this more poignantly put than when the psalmist declares,

> The LORD is gracious and compassionate,
> slow to anger and rich in love.
> The LORD is good to all;
> he has compassion on all he has made.[5]

Nor is it right to contrast the Old Testament as being full of punishment and anger with the New Testament, full of compassion and love. Both are present in each. Jesus repeatedly showed anger towards his religious opponents in Israel who sought to discredit and then destroy him. He also showed disappointment, bordering on exasperation, with the disciples who were slow to catch on to the nature of the kingdom of God. Lastly, he showed rage with those who turned the Temple into a money exchange with a "bureau de change" crowded into its many corners.

So anger was the inevitable response of God's just love towards evil, injustice, ingratitude or lack of trust, which he so often found in the world. It was an anger, which literally struggled with his mercy and compassion, and found its final outworking in the cross. But it was an anger which arose for two reasons: either his love was spurned or his righteous standards ignored. His anger was not capricious, moody or sullen. It abated quickly and this sometimes happened when there was repentance or change on man's part. His anger was slow to arrive and could be quick to go. It was the outworking of his holy love in the life of humankind. As the apostle Paul shows, in his opening chapter of Romans, God's righteousness was demonstrated in two ways. On the one hand, his righteousness was shown through his anger working in judgement, giving man up to the results of his choices; and, on the other hand, it was shown through his mercy and grace, offering a new way of restoring his broken image in man through the gospel. If God's anger is always righteous and directed, this cannot always be said for our anger.

HUMAN ANGER

The Bible tells us that the anger of man does not always work the righteousness of God. This means that God may not always be impressed with our protestations of indignant rage, because he knows our hearts and actions too well. Although there may well be just cause for human anger at some dereliction of responsibility, some great injustice or abuse, we must be wary lest the blaze of anger transmutes to another settled attitude of revenge, hatred or vindictiveness. We are told, "In your anger do not sin."[6] The trouble with human anger is that we may be too quick to be angry and too slow to cool, which is the exact opposite of God's anger. But human temperaments vary greatly when it comes to being angry, and we do well to know ourselves in this respect, so that we can mature in the way we deal with anger.

The Greeks divided humankind into four temperaments. Firstly there are the sanguine, who are optimistic, warm-hearted, outgoing and relaxed, mostly looking on the bright side. Then there are the phlegmatic, who are cool, detached laid-back, unemotional, and indeed a little apathetic. Next there are the choleric, who are quick, active, and impatient, with a relatively short fuse. Finally, there are the melancholic, who are pessimistic, inward looking, and inclined to cynicism and depression.[6] Often, our personality may be a mixture of these. When it comes to anger, one person may hardly ever be angry, but for another it is a daily occurrence. The issue, for most of us, is when is (or is not) anger appropriate? And secondly, how do we handle anger in a society which seems to be becoming more and more angry?

Before thinking about how to handle anger, it is worth charting why anger is on the increase in our society, for we now have new names for different types of rage! There are road-rage, air-rage, and computer-rage, to name but a few. Aggression has always been part of life. It certainly appears to be on the increase, and it is worth seeking the reasons for this. Indeed, aggression, which is a characteristic of preservation in most species, may be transformed in humans from being a warning to "keep your distance" to becoming violent. It is this all too common and frequent mutation of anger into violence which has become one of the banes of our Western society. There are a number of reasons why this instinct for self-preservation or aggression may mutate into anger, which in turn may mutate into violence. Some of these reasons are pragmatic, like boredom or alcohol abuse, others are psychological, and others rooted in our new expectations of living.

One reason for greater aggression and, consequently, anger, is simply that there is less living space. People are crowded together in confined conditions. The living space per individual may still be more in Europe than in, say, parts of India, China and the Far East, but less living space will only work where family and neighbourly relations remain good. Where the neighbour's dog, music, rubbish and friends are a cause for concern, then levels of anger quickly rise! Not only that, but there is less space on the roads, on the train, and on the pavement. It is one cause for the pressure rising in the cooker of modern living.

Another pressure is the revolution in communication. Although the web brings the great benefits of being able to be in touch frequently, easily and cheaply with people around the world, it has produced a technology which needs to be properly managed and used. It also imposes new pressures upon the user, and requires new disciplines to manage this communication overload. An executive may well have150 or more emails to deal with each day. Huge amounts of information are available on the net, which we need to learn how to deal with. Computers have a habit of crashing just when we need them most, or not functioning as we expect. The more we make ourselves dependent on them, the more vulnerable and anxious we are when they malfunction or we do not use them correctly. An illustration of the information overload we have reached is that one copy of the *New York Times* is said to contain as much information as a seventeenth century American would come across in his whole life!

Our expectations of living have also grown immeasurably. We want it, and we want it now! As has often been said, we have learnt to take the waiting out of wanting. We expect to have something to entertain us. We expect to get instant access to the web, to get fast food fast, to communicate across the globe, and travel wherever we will!

A woman was travelling by plane to the United States when the pilot came on the intercom to apologise that the flight would be half an hour late because of a strong headwind. She turned to her neighbour and uttered one word: "Typical!" It is just a small indication of an attitude that is so prevalent today in Western culture: that we should be always in control; and if someone lets us down, then we are legitimately angry, even if the "problem" is caused by a natural force —in this case the weather, which is beyond human control! There is a real danger that the quality of humility, so integral both to the Christian faith and being fully human, is going to be mistaken for weakness. When that happens, our society becomes a place in which the Beatitudes become completely incomprehensible to many.

What often fuels anger is not one thing but a mixture of causes which, added together, may provoke a surprisingly combustible reaction. We now have such a cocktail of causes. We have declining resources, with an increasing number of people buying or claiming them. We have a philosophical change, in which my rights are more important than my obligations. We have greater expectations of life. We have a dictatorship of feelings, so if we feel we need or want something, then who is to deny us? Not least, we have increasing numbers of people who have experienced rejection, guilt and separation in their closest relationships. Put this all together and we do have a lethal brew, which can easily explode. The question we must now consider is how may we control anger and, at times, abandon it.

HANDLING ANGER

On at least two occasions, when being interviewed for a job as leader of a local church, I have been asked how I deal with conflict, or what makes me angry. Both are good questions, though slightly different. Churches are communities of people who are in the process of becoming fully human and, precisely because they are in that process and have not arrived (nor should they pretend that they **have** arrived), there are bound to be moments of anger, conflict and confusion. Anyone who has just a passing familiarity with Paul's letters to the churches in the New Testament will know that the situation was exactly the same then. There were many heated disagreements over doctrine; differences of opinion over what was permissible or not in the church; personal falling out between different members of the church; and actions that needed to be confronted and challenged by

Paul. I can remember a few "moments of conflict" as surely every pastor can, but what helps to resolve conflicts in a mature way is both a proper understanding of ourselves, a humble knowledge of God's will, and some strategies for dealing with our own anger and with conflict where we find it. Handling conflict and dealing with anger is a vital aspect of any relationship. Jack Dominian identifies four ingredients for growth in our married love: availability, communication, demonstration of affection and resolution of conflict.[7] As a first step towards resolving conflict we need to understand ourselves—what makes us angry, and what strategies we have for handling anger and resolving conflict.

If we take the basic Greek definition of personality type, we may feel that one or more of the categories seems to fit best. Then there are more contemporary attempts at categorisation, such as the Myers Briggs approach. A cautionary note is called for, though. One must beware of treating such analyses as absolute. On the Greek scale, I know I am somewhere between the sanguine and the phlegmatic, so that I probably require either considerable provocation or must see an act of blatant injustice or unfairness for there to be a reaction of anger at all! But whatever place we occupy on the temperament scale we need to know some ways in which we will control or handle our anger. Unthinking angry reactions may seem the very stuff of the hours of soap opera on all our television channels, but such drama cannot be the daily diet of our households without risking our health and the health of our nearest relationships. Generally speaking, there are at least three ways of handling anger.

The first way is not to handle it all! That may seem rather a non-point, yet it is a choice that we may well have made, even though it looks as though we have not! For we have decided that since such a reaction has been found to be effective in achieving our ends, and that others have come to expect it from us and have adjusted their attitude to us, we will "blow our top" whenever we want to! Consequently, we do not believe we can react in any other way because that is the disposition of our personality. Yet, as we shall see, in the process of becoming fully human, this is not a line of reasoning (and, consequently, behaviour) that is open to us. We may have an explosive temper. Such a temper is generally described as "having a short fuse" or "blowing your top", or we might be said to be "choleric" in disposition, but if we agree it is a weakness then help is at hand, for knowing our weaknesses and making them targets of God's grace is the essence of becoming what we were meant to be.

Another way of handling anger is to suppress it. In this case we speak of "deep-seated anger", "hidden anger", etc. This is possibly the most damaging of all reactions to anger. The cause of anger may well be legitimate, occasioned by some injustice, abuse or hurt suffered in the past. Our reaction of anger is still with us, and because we have not been able to confront the person who caused it, nor to express our deep sense of hurt we suffered, or receive satisfaction, or deal with the memory, we have chosen to bury it. Then we carry fire in our bellies, which requires great energy to control, and we risk falling into depression and self-pity. On the simple principle that it is "better out than in", we should find a trusted, wise, prayerful Christian friend, counsellor or minister to help us handle both the anger and its effect on us. It is all too easy to make a friend of it, feeding it, like a pet, titbits to maintain its energy; or simply lock it up in some basement or attic room of our being, like an unwanted guest.

Exploding with anger and suppressing all (righteous, justifiable) anger may be two extremes to avoid, but there is a third way: Ephesians 4:26 recognises the reality of anger, but warns you to let go of anger before it takes hold of you. Nowhere is this more important than in family relationships —between husband and wife, parent and child. In the context of the home there should be very few reasons for anger lasting overnight. As we saw with God's anger, be slow to be angry and be quick to relent.

But it would be simplistic and shallow not to recognise that there will be times in which—however justified we may be or feel ourselves to be in holding on to our anger—there will come a time when we must move from anger to forgiveness, and abandon anger, if we are to become truly human. Just as we were forgiven, when we received all that Jesus won for us on the cross, so we must release forgiveness, for our Lord has commanded us to do so.

ABANDONING ANGER

The choice we are considering in this chapter is "anger or forgiveness", and as I have indicated, it is often not a straight choice between the two. We may find that we are angry and then forgive, or we might forgive straightaway and not be angry, and be just sad or disappointed. Or we may feel that it is right to be angry and, as yet, feel it very hard to forgive, or again that anger is all that is required and forgiveness does not enter into it. If all this seems unnecessarily convoluted, it is simply a reflection on the complexities of our human interactions. But this final section of the chapter is a plea that we move when we can from anger to forgiveness. I say, "when we can" because this may be one of the most difficult movements to make. At times we may see it simply, to use a metaphor, as a short journey around the corner, whereas at other times it is one of the greatest pilgrimages of our life. For those of us for whom it has only ever been a "short journey around the corner", then we have no right to insist that another, for whom such a movement from anger to forgiveness is the greatest pilgrimage of their life, should do it at our command, or in a way prescribed by us. We can simply hold up three things to encourage this movement, namely, that there are some who have made the pilgrimage and are the greater for it; that there is help available to do it; and that if we journey this way we are following the steps and teaching of Christ.

Forgiveness means many things, but essentially it means letting go —letting go of the hurt, and of the consequent anger and recrimination, on the part of the one who is forgiving. And for the one being forgiven, ideally, it means at least acknowledging our own fault and need of forgiveness, and, at best, offering some reconciling action to generate healing of the breach that has occurred.[8] (Forgiveness is often conducive to healing, or an ingredient in it.) For the person doing the forgiving, forgiveness cannot be conditional upon its being received. Our release of forgiveness, to be real, has to be unconditional.

Where the hurt is deep, it will almost certainly be a process, a pilgrimage, in which many important milestones will be marked off. For the one who is forgiving, it will begin with the intention to let go, continue with the action of letting go, and in this there may well be a process of healing of memories and emotions.

For the one who is forgiven it should include a corresponding recognition, and then acknowledgement, of any wrongdoing, followed by words and actions that seek to re-build trust and reconciliation. In reality, it may not be possible to restore the relationship to the way it was before, but at the very least the anger, hostility and alienation will have been removed.

It is by considering those who have forgiven much that we can find the courage to abandon anger in any of its forms, and offer forgiveness —so letting go of our own hurts, grudges and self-pity, and perhaps enabling another to let go of guilt, shame and failure. There are always some heroic examples to cite to help us towards this abandonment.

One such story, much broadcast recently, comes out of the Vietnam War. It began with an incident in 1972, when a young girl aged nine, called Kim, was caught up in a napalm attack on her village. A photograph, which became known across the world, recorded her flight from the incinerating village. The picture is of Kim, severely burnt, running down her village road, naked, crying and with arms outstretched. Behind her are plumes of black smoke billowing from her destroyed village. It was a picture that shocked the world and I, with millions of others, remember it well. It is, in all probability, one of the most powerful pictures of human suffering to come out of that war.

What I did not know until a year ago was that a man called John Plummer organised that raid on the Vietnamese village. For twenty four years he had lived with that picture in his mind. He is now a Methodist minister in Virginia. In 1996, on Veterans Day, he was attending the annual service in Washington. Who should be the speaker but Kim. She said, "Behind that picture of me, thousands and thousands of people died. They lost parts of their bodies and their whole lives were destroyed and nobody took their picture." At this point, John was beside himself with emotion; he pushed through the crowd and identified himself to Kim as the one who had organised the raid on her village and had taken part himself. "Kim saw my grief and pain, my sorrow; she held out her arms to me and embraced me. All I could say was 'I'm sorry, I'm sorry,' over and over again. At the same time she was saying, 'It's alright, it's alright.'" Abandoned anger! Another survivor of war, this time of the Nazi concentration camp, Corrie Ten Boom, met one of her prison guards at a meeting after the war and forgave him.

In his seminal work *Exclusion and Embrace*, Miroslav Volf, a Croatian theologian teaching at Fuller Seminary, California, records a moment of challenge in the preface to this work. He had just finished a lecture on this subject of exclusion and embrace when Professor Jürgen Moltmann rose to ask one of his searching questions: "But can you (a Croatian) embrace a Cetnik (a Serbian fighter)?" Volf wrote of that moment as follows: "It was the winter of 1993. For months, the notorious Serbian fighters called "cetnik" had been sowing desolation in my native country, herding people into concentration camps, raping women, burning churches, and destroying cities. Can I embrace a cetnik, the ultimate other, so to speak, the evil other? What would justify the embrace? Where would I draw the strength for it? What would it do to my identity as a human being and as a Croat? It took me a while to answer, though I immediately knew what I wanted to say. No, I cannot —but as a follower of Christ I think I should be able to."[9] Many would stand with Volf with regard to their own "other", whoever that might be: declared enemy, estranged husband, absent parent, abusive neighbour. They need to know that there is a source of power, and example, to help them inch towards this goal of abandoning anger and moving towards forgiveness.

Of course, the origin of this movement from anger to forgiveness lies in the teaching and example of Jesus, who told a timeless parable of grace called the prodigal son, and who made it absolutely clear that if we desire forgiveness of our own sins we must forgive "seventy times seven", that is, in a free, unrestricted way. So, however justified we may feel in our anger, there comes a moment where, for our own sake, for the sake of the perpetrator and in compliance with Christ's teaching, we must abandon it. God's anger against sin is always perfectly righteous. Our own wrongdoing and waywardness was dealt with on the cross when Jesus, who had no sin, was made "to be sin for us", so that we might be completely forgiven and, "become the righteousness of God."[10] We must forgive as he forgave us, so that he can turn a face of welcome and gladness to us when we meet him face to face.

Notes

[1]   Exodus 4:14.

[2]   Isaiah 5:7.

[3]   Isaiah 5:24–25.

[4]   Hosea 11:8–9.

[5]   Psalm 145:8–9.

[6]   See Ephesians 4:26 (and Psalm 4:4).

[7]   See Jack Dominian, *Passionate and Compassionate Love* (Darton, Longman & Todd, 1991)

[8]   See Russ Parker, *Forgiveness is Healing* (Darton, Longman & Todd, 1993) p. 14.

[9]   Miroslav Volf *Exclusion and Embrace (*Abingdon Press, Nashville).

[10]   See 2 Corinthians 5:21.

9

Envy or Gratitude

"Green with envy" we say, but why green? After all, green is the most restful colour to the eye and the predominant colour of our countryside, unless we live in either the desert or high altitude or where the sun has parched the ground. Yet envy is far from restful to its harbourer; it is like a like a shoot of ivy (green, too!) that clings and grows and suffocates, and in the end, kills! Envy is green, presumably, because it is the colour of our eye when we desire something another has and which we passionately want for ourselves.

In fact, envy is one of the most personal, insidious and poisoning of thoughts which, if it takes root, can soon destroy our wellbeing. The problem with it is that it is especially personal. At first thought, envy might seem to be similar to greed when, in fact, they are distinctly different. Whereas greed is invariably directed to the acquisition of more objects (sometimes thereby reducing humans to the status of objects, as in the case of lust or the desire for power), envy is always personal. It is directed at another person of whom we are envious for any number of reasons. So we become envious of their wealth, their figure, their holidays, their children, their looks, their prospects, their popularity, their favour, their gifts, their opportunities, their man, their woman, and on and on it may go! In fact, we can be envious of just about everything and anything that we do not have and perceive that another has in annoying and galling abundance! Given the awful inequality of life, there is huge scope for envy. Since this inequality does not seem to be deserved, then the harder the inequality is to bear; for we say to ourselves, "I don't deserve to be without such and such", and, "What has she done to deserve it, or him, or that?"

According to the biblical narrative, envy was present soon after the beginning of human life and its effects could not be more important. It lay at the root of the first murder recorded in Scripture. It brought about the betrayal of Joseph, which led to the Israelites going down to Egypt, where they were eventually enslaved. It was the cause of a civil war between Saul and David and, finally, it was one of the principal earthly reasons why the high priests sought to crucify Christ. Therefore, it could not be a more powerful and dangerous human sin!

The first bloodshed depicted in the Bible was occasioned by envy. Cain could not bear the favour that God showed towards his brother Abel's offering. The reason why Abel's offering was preferred was because it was offered with faith whereas Cain's was not. Cain could have enjoyed equal favour if his offering was also presented with faith, love and thanks to God; but instead it was presumably offered without any of those transforming characteristics. The account of Cain's envy is all the more perverse and seemingly unlikely if you look beneath the surface of the story. Cain was the first-born; of whom his mother Eve said at his birth, "With the help of the LORD I have brought forth a man."[1] In her own delight and exuberance at giving birth to him, she named him Cain, meaning "to produce, or bring forth". So his being and existence was a continual reminder of his mother's pride in his life and production! Abel's arrival, however, was greeted with far less celebration. His name meant "breath" or "vapour", with connotations of transience and passing. Both had good occupations: Cain, the tiller of the soil, possibly a rich landowner and farmer; Abel, as Professor Gese of Tubingen suggests, a poor keeper of sheep.[2] Yet Abel, out of his comparative poverty and insignificance, produced an offering or sacrifice which was more acceptable. The reason for this acceptability was that it was offered in gratitude and faith. Cain produced an offering from his abundance, whereas Abel, from his poverty, produced the "fat portions" of the animal, which were considered the best.

So begins a thread that runs right through the Scriptures, in which a little offered humbly is always more acceptable than something grand and ostentatious being offered in a spirit of sullen compliance or showy extravagance. Our minds may race on to the New Testament and the story of Mary's offering of her body, in obedience to God's call to bear the Christ-child, or the widow who gave her mite in the temple. Each of them was praised for the faith that transfigured their offering. But even though Cain's sacrifice did not meet with God's immediate approval, he still had a way back to God's favour.

Indeed, Cain had a choice as he was told, "Why are you angry? Why is your face downcast? If you do what is right, will you not be accepted? But if you do not do what is right, sin is crouching at the door; it desires to have you, but you must master it."[3] However, envy turned to anger and anger turned to violence. Cain murdered Abel.

Too often, the same spiral of envy, anger and violence has occurred, not least where one group or race sees another as more favoured, more prosperous, or more successful than themselves. Envy and resentment become engines for violence and repression. The seemingly successful then become the target for retribution. There are plenty of examples of how whole communities have become the kicking boy for other communities, which perceive themselves to be either impoverished or humiliated by another's success. The list is familiar and depressing. It could be the Jew in Europe, the Indian in East Africa, the Chinese in Indonesia, the Tutsi in Rwanda or the Armenians in Turkey. Once one group perceives another group's enrichment as the reason for their own impoverishment then we are only steps away from a descent into violence. A whispering campaign can soon be orchestrated into a systematic call for blood. That was true in Nazi Germany in the late 1930s, in Rwanda before the genocide, and in Serbia before the Kosovan war of 1999. Now, on a global scale, it is clear that a combination of envy of the material success of the West, especially the USA, combined with resentment against the culture of the West and its seemingly dominant position in the world, is fuelling, in part, acts of terrorism against its symbols and people, whether it is the Twin Towers in New York, representing capitalism, or the hedonistic lifestyle of young surfers, as paraded in Bali. Envy and resentment are powerful engines for violence now, as they have always been. The growing disparity of wealth is fertile soil for the growth of envy and violence.

Cain chose to eradicate Abel. He chose not to deal with his envy and rage in some other way. He excluded his brother from life, but his brother's death inevitably affected him, not least through God's judgement upon him. So it is a deception to think that we can free ourselves from the object of envy through violence, because the act of violence goes on to haunt its perpetrators. And the blood of the innocent cries up from the ground, whether it is the Garden of Eden, "Ground Zero" or Kuta Beach. If envy is carried through to violence then it produces a bitter fruit. Cain's punishment was to go from the presence of God, to be restless, and no longer to be in harmony with creation. In the deepest sense he was a dislocated person.[4]

However, on a more hopeful note, one of the most extraordinary stories in the Bible of envy being transformed by God's grace is that of Joseph. It is rare to find anyone today who has not seen Andrew Lloyd Webber's and Tim Rice's *Joseph and the Amazing Technicolour Dreamcoat* with its brilliant matching of styles of music with the mood of the songs. This story of envy, honour and providence has become widely known. It is essentially a story of God's redemption of Joseph's envious brothers for the benefit of the Israelite nation. Joseph—the favoured son of the favoured wife, with the provocative dreams that his older brothers and parents would all bow down to him, strutting around in his exhibitionist coat, given as a sign of his father's favour—was a soft target for envy! "When his brothers saw that their father loved him more than any of them, they hated him and could not speak a kind word to him."[5] They were speechless with envy, or at least their speech was no longer seasoned with any kindness towards him. Once again, envy progressed to hatred, and hatred to violence, which stopped short of murder.

If envy caused Joseph's brothers to sell him into slavery and pretend to their father that he was dead, envy was also one of the chief motivations for the high priests seeking the execution and removal of Jesus. Even Pilate recognised this. Matthew records that, "It was out of envy that they had handed Jesus over to him."[6] Indeed, most of the seven deadly sins were on parade in the betrayal, trial and execution of Jesus. There was the greed and covetousness of Judas; the envy of the high priests; the spiritual sloth of the disciples, who rested when they might have kept watch with Jesus in Gethsemane; the anger of Pharisees who jeered at him as he suffered. It was not surprising that it was through the conspiracy of these sins that Jesus ended up hanging upon the cross. Having seen some of the all too clear traces of envy smeared over the narrative of the Bible, it is time to examine its cause, effect and antidote more deeply.

THE HABITAT OF ENVY

We have already noted that envy is distinct from greed because it is personally directed. We are envious of another because we perceive that they have something which either we want ourselves or we simply do not want them to have! But it grows in a particular habitat. Just as the keen naturalist or horticulturalist will know the kind of habitat in which to find either a particular animal or plant, so even the average student of human nature will know where to find the occurrence of envy. Recently, I was watching an exuberant Australian television presenter and "reptile handler" track down various types of rattlesnake, locating them by observing the right habitat and then searching successfully for them there; likewise, envy occurs in a particular but well recognised habitat. It is also as deadly as a rattlesnake!

We are not normally sickeningly envious of people who have what we might like to have but whom we do not know personally. I may want the wealth of a Bill Gates or the intellectual ability of a man who speaks six languages, or the musical skill of a woman who plays four instruments superbly, but if I do not know them my desire is probably a passing fancy, a weak sigh of, "Wouldn't it be nice if...!" But transpose that wealth, skill, ability or preferment to someone I know well, a colleague or member of my family, then there is the habitat for envy.

So envy occurs most frequently in tight circles, and perhaps above all in the family and amongst siblings. It is not surprising that some of the greatest and most well known accounts of envy in the Bible are to be found in families. We have already noticed Cain's envy and that of Joseph's brothers, but it does not end there. Most of the patriarchal narratives are laced with envy. There is Jacob's desire for Esau's position as oldest in the family; Sarah's envy of Hagar who bore Abraham Ishmael when she was barren; Rachel's jealousy of Leah, her sister, because she was not able to bear Jacob any son.[7] Since families are prone to envy, parents do well not to elevate one or other of their children so that they become the obvious target for their other children's jealousy. Jacob's obvious doting on Joseph did nothing to help family unity! On the other hand, "choice" and "favour" are incontrovertibly part of God's way of implementing his plans.

Nowhere is this clearer in the Old Testament than with Saul and David. The story of these two lives, at one level, is a tragedy of Shakespearean proportions. Saul, at the outset, was the darling of the people. Naturally, he was not born to lead; initially he was self-effacing, hiding as he did from the attention of Samuel, among the baggage.[8] But, soon after assuming power, he became proud, taking powers to himself which were not his, and failing to obey God's command. So David was chosen in his place. And as Saul's star continued to fall and David's rose ever higher in the estimation of the people, after his destruction of Goliath, Saul's envy became a veritable sickness. We are told:

> When the men were returning home after David had killed the Philistine, the women came out from all the towns of Israel to meet King Saul with singing and dancing, with joyful songs and with tambourines and lutes. As they danced, they sang:
>
>> "Saul has slain his thousands,
>> and David his tens of thousands."
>
> Saul was very angry; this refrain galled him. "They have credited David with tens of thousands," he thought, "but me with only thousands. What more can he get than the kingdom?" And from that time on Saul kept a jealous eye on David."[9]

Indeed, the next day, Saul attempted to take David's life, while David was playing the harp. But the fact was that David had now been **chosen** to succeed Saul, who had been cast aside, even if he had several more years to live. Saul's unwillingness to accept this plunged Israel into a damaging civil war, until both Saul and Jonathan died fighting the Philistines on Mount Gilboa.

So however much we may seek to treat people equally, there are two things we cannot change: the inequality of people's gifts, and the fact that in God's hands we have different roles, callings or destinies. It is often the inability to accept that which creates the seedbed for growing envy.

Envy, then, occurs in circles in which we are close to others: in families and also amongst professional colleagues, whether they be footballers, sportsmen, lawyers, doctors, academics, teachers and, yes, even clergy! Indeed, wherever people work closely together, and wherever there is a perceived pecking order, career and reward structure, there exists the potential for envy or jealousy.

THE EFFECTS OF ENVY

The effects of envy have already been shown in passing. They are hatred, anger, bitterness, resentment and sometimes violence, even murder or attempted murder. Whole populations can be caught up in the policies that emerge from a ruler's envy of another's power, position or success. Sometimes the policies may be masked by religion, ideology or nationalist rhetoric, but the source is still the envy and consequent hatred of a more powerful or influential ruler. History is littered with such animosities and their effects.

Amongst politicians in many societies, and in political situations, we often see the mutation of envy to depression, of hatred to revenge, albeit of a petty and peculiarly political kind. Of course, we cannot know all the twists and turns of political relationships, but they are symptomatic of our all too frequent disputes over power or "face". Once policy making in international or corporate life becomes so personalised, it becomes dangerous to whole populations or corporate structures.

But we should not be too surprised that these spats occur amongst the power wielding classes when even the disciples, who had by then spent three years with Jesus, were disputing over which of them was the greatest, during the Last Supper. You might think that it was a time for solidarity and mutual support, not to mention encouragement, but that was very far from the case. It always strikes me as both depressing and all too "natural" that right after the sharing of the Passover meal, or the institution of the Lord's supper, and when Jesus was about to go to the cross, that his closest friends and disciples should be disputing about which of them was the greatest! No wonder it was necessary for Jesus to explain once again the way that power works in the kingdom of God.

> Jesus said to them, "The kings of the Gentiles lord it over them; and those who exercise authority over them call themselves Benefactors. But you are not to be like that. Instead, the greatest among you should be like the youngest, and the one who rules like the one who serves. For who is greater, the one who is at the table or the one who serves? Is it not the one who is at the table? But I am among you as one who serves."[10]

So what might be the antidote to envy? A cardinal virtue for a cardinal sin!

THE ANTIDOTE TO ENVY

In the third section of this book we will look at the way in which a Christian may fight each of these classically defined "seven deadly sins" from the standpoint of "being in Christ". We shall unravel what that means in the process of becoming fully human later. For now, I will simply outline a way of coping with envy, knowing that this must be set in the context of grasping personally what is set out in the final part of the book. There appear to be five ways to deal with envy, each of which may need to be employed in combating this failing.

Firstly, as with all issues that we need to confront, we have to acknowledge its presence. It is not possible to begin to fight back without this initial step. Just as with alcoholism, drug addiction or pornography, the act of acknowledgement or confession is a vital first step. Nor should it only be done privately, but perhaps to someone who is not a party to the problem. It might be a Christian friend or minister. However, at the onset of envious thinking, we may simply need to deal with it by not allowing this incipient thought to take root but, as Paul says, "...take captive every thought to make it obedient to Christ."[11]

Secondly, we need to have the goodness and love of God towards us re-affirmed to us, or we need to re-affirm it to ourselves. It is too easy to fall into the trap of thinking God's love to be conditional upon the blessings we expect, or hope for or want. We may even get to the point where we believe that only if we have **that** house, child, married partner, career, promotion, opportunity, and so on, does God truly love and care for us. What we have then done is to measure his love on a scale which we have chosen or invented, rather than by the only yardstick by which we are to measure his love for us, which is the cross. This is a spiritual exercise, which will need both discipline and the encouragement of others if it is to truly sink into our thinking and hearts.

Or again, to avoid envy may mean not so much a renewed affirmation of God's love as a renewed affirmation of his justice. If we should feel envious or resentful of another because we have been unfairly or unjustly treated, then there are two courses open to us. Either we could pray, work towards and, in some circumstances, campaign for, the establishment of justice and fairness which may bring some restoration of our circumstances or reputation; or, as the apostle Peter tells us, we should learn to follow the example of Christ —who himself suffered unjustly and entrusted his cause to the Father.[12]

A re-affirmation of God's love or justice in our lives can act as a counterpoint to the invasion of envy, bitterness or resentment.

Thirdly, we should try not to compare ourselves with others. It is only natural to do so, and especially with those closest to us. There is a powerful culture of comparison in our society at present with the many kinds of league tables. Comparing ourselves with others can lead all too easily to being either envious of others or proud of ourselves. Instead, the Bible teaches us that we have all been called to run our race, which is bound to be different in distance, in contours, and in obstacles, to that of the person with whom we are comparing ourselves. Our task is to complete our race successfully —which means faithfully and fairly. It has rightly been said that we are not promised an easy race, but we are promised a safe arrival.[13]

Fourthly, as Christians we are encouraged to be thankful. Indeed the title of this chapter is envy or *gratitude*. The two cannot co-exist; the one can dispel the other, and gratitude is the best antidote to envy. Learning to cultivate an attitude of gratitude is homework well done. "Giving thanks" is, time and again, the major key of Paul's prayers; it appears to be the tenor of his living. Anyone who has travelled to Africa, where most of the world's poorest live, will always come away with the impression that, despite their poverty and deprivation there, most of the people have not given in to green-eyed envy, but are more thankful, more welcoming, and more generous than we are in the West, with all our goods and prospects. I remember returning from Nigeria after a ten-day visit, and recalling that although we had seen many families and children and what we might call poverty compared with our lifestyle, I had never heard a child cry! Those we met in Nigeria were a living rebuke to us who long for more possessions or who are envious of people with more of what we want but cannot afford. We have or want the possessions, but invariably look more miserable in having them!

Finally, like the great apostle Paul, we should learn to be content. It is something which is learnt, for he said:

> I know what it is to be in need, and I know what it is to have plenty. I have learned the secret of being content in any and every situation, whether well fed or hungry, whether living in plenty or in want. I can do everything through him who gives me strength.[15]

His contentment came from running his race, acknowledging his faults —the more to boast Christ's grace, realising Christ's love and goodness, and looking beyond his material circumstances, which went up and down, to the promise of salvation.

At root, he knew the truth of what the father said to the

envious older brother in the parable of the prodigal son: "Everything I have is yours."[15] The way to dispel envy is by concentrating our thoughts, prayers and speech on being thankful.

Notes

[1]   See Genesis 4:1.
[2]   Miroslav Volf *Exclusion and Embrace* (Abingdon Press, Nashville. 1996).
[3]   Genesis 4:6–7.
[4]   See Genesis 4:10 –16.
[5]   Genesis 37:4.
[6]   See Matthew 27:18.
[7]   See Genesis 30:1.
[8]   See 1 Samuel 10:22.
[9]   See 1 Samuel 18:6–9.
[10]   Luke 22:25–27.
[11]   See 2 Corinthians 10:5.
[12]   See 1 Peter 2:23.
[13]   See Hebrews 12:1 and 2 Timothy 4:7–8.
[14]   Philippians 4:11–12.
[15]   See Luke 15:31.

10

Pride or Potential

So we come to the final of what are commonly described as the "seven deadly sins"; and, to alter the phrase of a well-known Middle Eastern dictator, the "mother of all sins". Yet unlike the battle that he vainly promised, pride does not turn out to be a damp squib, but the source, origin and genesis of all other sins. Precisely because it is at the root of most, if not all, wrong attitudes or damaging actions, we normally overlook its lurking presence, concentrating instead on the visible branches, leaves and "fruit" that it produces, rather than upon the root itself.

Yet from the taproot of human pride come the other failings we have looked at. Greed for things, rather than simply food, is generally a desire to inflate our standing in the eyes of others, despite the fact—of which the writer of Ecclesiastes reminds us—that we must leave whatever we acquire behind! A relative, enquiring how much a rich man left behind at his death, was told, sardonically, "Everything!" Lust may simply be the pride of conquest; having **who** you desire rather than **what**, so that in obtaining him or her we may congratulate ourselves on the power of our image, or our "attractiveness", without regard to loyalty or love. Anger may often be the defence of injured pride which, when challenged, prefers to rise in contempt, cold disdain or rage rather than acknowledge that a criticism may be fair and just. Envy is another form of pride, because rather than freely acknowledging another's gifts, blessings or opportunities, we either openly or secretly feel that we deserve or require them. And if sloth and gluttony do not seem so easily to fit into this "family tree" of pride, they may prove to be not the immediate children, but the grandchildren! However bleak all this appears to be, the bad news of the Christian gospel is that all of us are infected with, and need de-scaling from, pride's callous effects. But the good news, as we shall see, is that we can be re-centred away from pride and egotism by an internal operation on the heart.

But this fault of pride is hard to admit or acknowledge. C.S. Lewis, amongst others, noted that whilst people might admit to rage, gluttony or even lust, they will scarcely ever admit to the sin of pride. It is as though there is an inbuilt mechanism in pride that camouflages it from its holder whilst simultaneously making it apparent to others. Pride has about it that "emperor's new clothes" characteristic, so that we cannot see what is transparently evident to others; and so it is linked to self-deception.

THE ORIGIN OF PRIDE

As we saw at the start of this book, in the opening section, pride was intertwined with—and indeed inspired—that original act of rebellion in the Garden of Eden. The thought was put in the heads of Adam and Eve that they were being denied something which, if they gained it, would make them become like gods, "knowing good and evil". This thought was insinuated into their minds by one who had already rebelled against the majesty of God, and was described in the prophecy of Ezekiel as follows:

> "Your heart became proud
> on account of your beauty,

and you corrupted your wisdom
because of your splendour.
So I threw you to the earth;
I made a spectacle of you before kings."[1]

So Adam and Eve, representing all humankind, grasped at becoming like God and fell from the fullness of their humanity. But in an exact reversal of this, as we shall see, Paul writes of Jesus:

Who, being in very nature God,
did not consider equality with God something to be
grasped,
but made himself nothing,
taking the very nature of a servant,
being made in human likeness.[2]
                                                    [my emphasis].

So we have this reverse parallel exchange! On the one hand humankind, in its representatives Adam and Eve, grasping at godhead, and in their pride trying to become what was always beyond their grasp —and, in so doing, marring the very humanity that was the image of God in them—and, on the other, Christ conversely giving up voluntarily the privileges of heaven to become a man and restore to humankind what had been lost. As Milton put it concisely: "Paradise Lost and Paradise Regained." In our case, the fault that lured us into such a grasp was pride, and as the common proverb has it: "pride comes before a fall!"

So pride was originally an unwillingness to accept a dependent status as creatures who are both accountable and subordinate. Pride led us to make a bid for a kind of power and authority which was never meant to be ours. And it is still pride which prevents human beings from acknowledging that we **are** creatures, and **are** dependent and accountable to God. So, to put it plainly, pride took us away from what we were created to be, and pride can keep us away from becoming what we were meant to be: fully human; for our humanity is only fully and properly expressed when we are dependent on God. For most of us that is a blow to our pride!

The evidence of pride was quickly displayed in the narrative of Genesis. We have already seen its immediate harvest in the judgement that fell on humankind in Adam and Eve, in the violence that proceeded from Cain's envy of Abel, and again in that curious but revealing story of the tower of Babel, which lies in the Genesis narrative immediately before the call of Abraham. The city, and the tower that was being built, were symbols of both human prowess and ambition. Ambition cuts both ways. On the one hand it is the engine that drives us to fulfil our potential and gifts which we have been given; and, on the other hand, it can lead to the vaunting and inflation of the self. Whereas the former is beneficial, as we shall see, the latter leads to arrogance and self-aggrandisement.

As pride lay in the very concept or foundation of the tower of Babel, so ever since then it has been the engine behind innumerable human empires, cities, buildings and corporate projects. Sometimes these ventures have been for the benefit of others, but more often for the individual or group who stood to benefit most from their success. As I write, the largest corporate scandal in history has come to light with the collapse of Worldcom, the second largest telecommunications business in the USA, dwarfing the previous collapse of Enron. The project was fuelled by at least three forces: the ambition and fraud of one individual; the failures of some accountants to inform employees and investors of the true state of the books, and the availability of money to pursue the old dream, "that gold may be found and fortunes made." Many human ventures seem to be created for the aggrandisement of some directors rather than for the investors or employees.

Again and again we have been through the same cycle of exploding bubbles: first bloating and then bursting. Notable examples have been the railways, the motorcar, the PC boom and, most recently and more spectacularly, much of the telecoms and dotcom industry. In only two years there was an unprecedented cycle of boom and bust, euphoria and misery in this market. Unlike the tower of Babel, it was not necessary to confuse the language of the dotcom speculators, as the seeds of this business collapse lay in the ambitions of its leaders, egged on by governments, to promote an unsustainable development. Although the market leaders mostly spoke a single language, English, another common language—that of ambition and speculation—had sufficient fissures in it to precipitate a freefall in financial markets. Those markets had been talked up in such a way as to promote greed and excessive optimism amongst investors. As a result there is a new business "club" called the 90% club, comprising businesses which have lost 90% of their value in two years —and for some that is a understated loss!

The origin of human pride is a thought insinuated into the minds of our forbears, that we should try and become more than what we were created to be. We were created *dependent* but we wanted to become *independent*; we were created to be *subordinate* but we wanted to become *superior*; we were created to be at the service of God and others, but we wanted to *be* god, and for him to be at our service. And the extraordinary thing is that, in the person of Jesus, he took "the very nature of a servant", so that our humanity could be reinstated.

The first steps, therefore, in dealing with pride are to establish its origin and reverse its ambition; to become dependent on God again, to subordinate ourselves to him and the interests of others, and to become the servants of God and our neighbours. Or, to put it another way, as the New Testament does, as we shall see, we must crucify human pride with Christ on the cross. Everything in us naturally recoils from such a humiliation of the self, but the surrender of ourselves in this way is the first step to restoration.

It is also the fundamental step to freedom. Here again is a paradox. In the original temptation in the Garden, which is both an event and a template for all our temptations, the tempter promised a greater degree of freedom to Adam and

Eve if they fell in with his plan: "You will be like God," he said, "knowing good and evil." But their act of disobedience led not to freedom but to slavery and to suffering. They knew "good and evil", not objectively but in their own experience. Conversely, a step of obedience of faith in Christ, of subordinating our will to his, of becoming dependent again upon his power, and of truly acknowledging both our creatureliness and accountability to him, leads us back into freedom in which we may develop and deploy all our gifts.

REALISING OUR POTENTIAL

In the award winning film *Chariots of Fire*, there comes a point in the film when the hero decides that he will "run for God". It was an important moment in the story, as from then on Eric Liddell made running his vocation. Other athletes have done the same. At the end of the World Cup 2002, one of the Brazilian winning side had a T-shirt on for probably a billion viewers to see. It simply stated that he belonged to Jesus. He had made football his career, his vocation and a platform for his witness to the world. In that single moment, a footballer made a statement which was read, and possibly thought about, by more people than a thousand ministers would speak to in a lifetime! Such is the power of sport, the *lingua franca* of our present age; such is the power of the media, and such can be the effect of a single man's desire to use his skill to proclaim his faith in Christ. These two individuals, competing in the highest competitions of their sport, used their potential to its utmost and fulfilled the talents they had been given.

The point is that we can be free from pride if, having submitted ourselves to God, we determine to use whatever gifts we have in the service of God and others. There has been a misapprehension down the years that the only way we can truly serve God is by becoming a clergyman or a missionary, and that such people enjoy a higher calling! However, this is just not true. It is certainly a privilege and responsibility to teach, pastor and care for God's people in that way, but another person may have an equally effective life by fulfilling the potential, under God, that he or she has been given. So vocations will be formed by the identification, use and development of each person's gifts.

In the parable of the talents there is an individual who is given only one gift. He is both fearful in his outlook and negative in his attitude. As you will remember, he hid his gift, frightened that he would lose it and so have nothing to show to his lord at the time of accounting. In the parable he is severely criticised by his master. The principle is simple: we are to develop through use the gifts we have been given. The musician will play; the businessman will run a profitable business on the Wesleyan principle of "earn all you can, save all you can and give all you can"; the athlete will run; the doctor will cure; the road sweeper will clean, and the student will study diligently, and so on. Each will develop the gifts and opportunities that he or she has been given, and that deployment will bring satisfaction to the user, help to the community and glory to God. In the right way, each will take pride in his work, by which is meant the satisfaction of doing something or achieving something to the best of their ability. Providing that this satisfaction does not lead to a person feeling that they are a superior human being to another, or that they need no longer be dependent on God, then their satisfaction—linked to thankfulness for the gifts they have been given, and for the help and opportunities they have been given for using them—is a healthy and health giving experience.

What is true of natural talents and abilities is true of spiritual gifts as well. These gifts, given for the most part for the upbuilding of the church and her equipping for worship and mission, are to be used in love within the fellowship of the church. They only become a source of pride when someone uses them to gain status, or hold sway over others, or as a means of either controlling church life or enhancing their own position in the church community. Again and again, both in Paul's and Peter's letters to the young churches of the first century, humility is enjoined on those who exercise leadership.[3]

Gifts can be a snare if they lead to pride, yet the very word "gift" has the clue to continuing humility and dependence on God. Gifts, by definition, are things which we did not gain or merit or come by ourselves, they are innate abilities which come both from natural endowment or supernatural gifting, for which we cannot justifiably take credit but which we can use creatively in a spirit of service.

So, if the source of pride is a desire to be independent of God, the continuing antidote to pride is a ready acknowledgement that all our gifts are from him, and that their best context for healthy development is within an ongoing relationship with him, marked by prayerful dependence. Each person has great potential, and part of the function of the church is, by its love, care and teaching, to enable people to discover and reach the potential which they have been given.

THE SOURCE OF HUMILITY

As has already been hinted, the antidote to pride is humility; but pride is so insidious that it can even turn humility into a reason for pride, as registered in that old quip— "Have you read my latest book: *Humility, and How I Attained it!* ?" On the other hand, false humility can equally become an occasion of pride, as someone refuses to acknowledge their gifts or to allow them to find proper expression.

One of the ways to humility involves remembering. Since remembering means recollection, it presupposes that we have previously understood and acknowledged as true what we are now remembering. There are plenty of things we can remember that will keep us humble. The psalms are full of such remembering. Amongst many other things, Psalm 103 reminds us to remember before God that we are but dust. This may well seem rather morbid but, as a clergyman with a churchyard in which ashes are still interred, I am frequently made aware that our bodily life on earth (with the Christian being promised a new bodily life in heaven) is, in the end, reduced to what seems like the equivalent in weight to a small pack of sugar! It cannot but help impress you that our material existence with all its demands, needs and attention, comes down to that! Unlike most people, I am obliged to contemplate this on a regular basis, and it certainly puts life into a different perspective. We are reminded that that we are dust, and the psalmist pulls no punches when he says:

> As for man, his days are like grass,
> he flourishes like a flower of the field;
> the wind blows over it and it is gone,
> and its place remembers it no more.[4]

Before they were settled in the Promised Land, the Israelites were told to remember or, rather, not to forget, the blessings they had received in the provision of this homeland.

When you have eaten and are satisfied, praise the LORD your God for the good land he has given you. Be careful that you do not **forget** the LORD your God, failing to observe his commands, his laws and his decrees that I am giving you this day. Otherwise, when you eat and are satisfied, when you build fine houses and settle down, and when your herds and flocks grow large and your silver and gold increase and all you have is multiplied, then your heart will become proud and you will forget the LORD your God, who brought you out of Egypt, out of the land of slavery.... You may say to yourself, "My power and the strength of my hands have produced this wealth for me." But **remember** the LORD your God, for it is he who gives you the ability to produce wealth, and so confirms his covenant, which he swore to your forefathers, as it is today.[5]

[my emphasis]

But of course they forgot, and went on forgetting, despite the innumerable reminders through the prophets. Many of the kings forgot, grew proud and then faced either rapid decline or punishment. Solomon, having started out so well, exercising the wisdom which he was given and enjoying immense wealth, forgot the source of his blessing, and then we are told his vast harem, not surprisingly, turned his heart from God: "As Solomon grew old, his wives turned his heart after other gods, and his heart was not fully devoted to the LORD his God, as the heart of David his father had been."[6]

Or again there was Uzziah, who reigned effectively and well for some forty years from the age of sixteen but, "After he became powerful, his pride led to his downfall. He was unfaithful to the Lord his God, and entered the temple of the Lord to burn incense on the altar" —so taking to himself a function that was not rightfully his. When confronted by Azariah and eighty other priests, who told him that he was doing what he had no right to do, Uzziah became angry, contracted leprosy, and died in virtual isolation.

In the very year of Uzziah's death, the great prophet Isaiah was sent to prophesy to the nation that they must return to their Lord, whom they had rejected. But the same cycle was repeated under succeeding kings like Ahaz, Hezekiah, Manasseh and Jehoiachin —with the exception of Josiah, who found and implemented the Book of the law—until Jerusalem and the kingdom faced destruction and exile at the hand of the Babylonians. The cycle of forgetting—or not remembering—led to pride and unfaithfulness, until the tragedy of the exile and the destruction of their national life overtook Judah, as Isaiah and Jeremiah had predicted. The people were then forced to remember in exile, on the banks of the rivers of Babylon, where "they sat and wept", and could not sing the Lord's songs in a foreign land, as their captors wanted.[7]

So it is not surprising to find in the New Testament the same injunction to remember. "Remember Jesus Christ, raised from the dead, descended from David. This is my gospel for which I am suffering in chains," says Paul to Timothy. In particular, we should remember, in this context, Jesus' constant teaching on humility. This took two forms.

Firstly, there was his outright criticism of the hypocrisy of the Pharisees who loved to get the deference of the people for their vaunted spirituality; and, secondly, his direct teaching on how to conduct ourselves in our discipleship so that pride will not overtake us. Much is found in the Sermon on the Mount on both points. There, he castigates the Pharisees for their ostentatious fasting and their exhibitionist giving and praying, and he enjoins on his own disciples secrecy, modesty and a determined unwillingness to cultivate the praise of others. Indeed, Jesus said the Pharisees' spirituality would always be at fault, as long as its motive force was seeking the praise of their contemporaries rather than the approval of God, as he made clear in this saying: "How can you believe if you accept praise from one another, yet make no effort to obtain the praise that comes from the only God?"[8] Repeatedly, Jesus calls his followers to humility, which is the subordination of ourselves both to him and, where appropriate, others, and reminds us that, "...everyone who exalts himself will be humbled, and he who humbles himself will be exalted."[9] In expecting such behaviour from his followers he was requiring no more of them, indeed less, than he had already required of himself in his incarnation, ministry and sacrificial death. The driving force of Jesus' ministry was that he came as a servant, not to be served but to serve, and to give his life as a ransom for many; washing his disciples' feet, and predicting that even at his return, his servant ministry would remain central to his existence. At a moment of squabbling amongst his disciples at the time of the Last Supper when, as we have already seen, such a squabble was as insensitive to Jesus' impending death as it was a failure to grasp the true nature of discipleship, Jesus gave them a further masterclass in humility in his words recorded in Luke 22:25–27, as we noted in the last chapter.

Throughout the New Testament, we are encouraged to "consider" Jesus. As the writer to the Hebrews says, "Consider him who endured such opposition from sinful men, so that you will not grow weary and lose heart."[10] Again, we are called repeatedly to "remember". As St Paul said to the

Ephesian Christians, "...remember that at that time you were separate from Christ, excluded from citizenship in Israel and foreigners to the covenant of promise, without hope and without God in the world."[11]

This kind of remembering has the double effect of both strengthening the disciple to persevere when the going gets tough and keeping him humble by virtue of this recalling of Christ's life and ministry, which rescued him from a hopeless existence. And finally Jesus himself gave us a meal whereby we could remember him, and in particular his death on the cross. So, if we compare ourselves to others, we may think of ourselves more highly—or as more lowly—than we should; but if we compare ourselves to Christ and remember him, then it is surely both death to any incipient pride and encouragement to follow humbly, knowing his love for us.

In conclusion, remembering our lives in the perspective of creation—that we are, in one sense, but dust—recalling the failure of leaders and nation in Old Testament times and comparing ourselves to Christ, should surely curb pride and promote humility. But, more likely, it will alert us to the fact that we have a struggle on our hands if we are to realise our potential whilst at the same time walking humbly with God.[12]

****

On my four thousand mile journey from Bath to Jordan in 2002, it was relatively easy travelling not by foot, horse or bicycle as many others have done, but by car. My journey took about a month, going at a leisurely pace. Others, mostly in previous ages, who have walked to Jerusalem have taken years to get there. From the tenth century, for around the next three hundred years, it was a well-travelled pilgrim route. However, during that period, the journey changed from being a peaceful pilgrimage to visit the Holy Land to being a military campaign to re-possess the holy sites during the period of the crusades, with all the controversial issues that they raise. The pilgrim's route to Jerusalem was the longest, hardest and most dangerous that could be undertaken; many did not return. Some travelled in twos or threes, others in large groups with some kind of military escort to help them get there. But they were fulfilling a deeply held desire to visit the places and country where Jesus had lived on earth. As Sir Steven Runciman says, in his classic account of the crusades:

> The desire to be a pilgrim is deeply rooted in human nature. To stand where those we have reverenced once stood, to see the very sites where they were born and toiled and died, gives us a feeling of mystical contact with them and is a practical expression of our homage. And if the great men of the world have their shrines to which their admirers come from afar, still more do men flock eagerly to those places where, they believe, the divine has sanctified the earth.[13]

But what we have been doing in the last seven chapters is to go, at least in thought and heart, along another path, or consider another pilgrimage, which maps out a journey of even greater magnitude but which everyone must face. Nor is this pilgrimage, if I can call it that, of our own choosing. It is quite simply there, and I have called it "Becoming Fully Human". Many may not even have identified the journey as one, thinking instead that it is just a stretch of disconnected episodes in life, which do not have much purpose other than surviving or, some would say, enjoying —and doing so to your own best advantage. Others will instinctively realise that there appears to be some journey in living but are hard pushed to describe what it is. Others will know that there is a journey, but find it overwhelming, baffling or lonesome.

In preparing to go on our journey overland to Jordan, we spent some time planning the route, which eventually took us through ten countries, six capitals and areas of Europe and the Middle East which are more deluged with history than any other route I can think of. Similarly, the route to becoming what we were meant to be takes most of us through territory along which we all have to travel. The journey was most ably and memorably described in *Pilgrims Progress*. The journey takes us to countries and capitals, so to speak, which most have visited and can describe, even if we would prefer not to. Part Two of this book has taken us to some of these capitals: from gluttony to avarice, from sloth to anger, from lust to envy, and finally to the chief capital of them all — pride. Now this route map, which we have used, is commonly called "the seven deadly sins". It is presented here in no particular order, although each seems to favour a particular stage of life. Many of us can find that we are disposed to visit frequently one or two particular capitals; the old divines would have called these our "besetting sins". There are other capitals, too, not put down on this map — theft and falsehood, to name but two. There are those which were once described but are now, in name, forgotten, one such being called acedia, which means little to us today. [John Cassian, a spiritual writer in former years, added this sin to the normal seven. He describes it as, "a wearied or anxious heart. It is akin to sadness, and is the peculiar lot of solitaries, and a particularly dangerous and frequent foe of those dwelling in the desert. It disturbs the monk especially around the sixth hour!" We may not be monks or desert ascetics but in our increasingly solitary Western society, we can surely identify a state of heart, which is "weary or anxious".]

However, there is another route map; indeed, I should say daily marching orders, which is briefer and more comprehensive than all the others, and which is given to us by Christ himself. This route map is: to love God with all your heart, mind, soul and strength, and your neighbour as yourself. A further map defines neighbourly relations in another way: "Do to others as you would have them do to you."[14]

But whatever map we choose to use, or are asked to use, we find that somewhere along the route mapped out the engine fails, or our legs give way, or the horse goes lame or public transport grinds to a halt, or we are involved in some terrible crash. And so we make little or no progress towards our destination of "becoming fully human". And the more we attempt it, the more obvious to us it becomes that we are simply not making it. Maybe others seem not to be bothering to pursue the route, or many settle down to enjoy to the full whatever capital they find themselves in. But some of those find in one capital or another that they are, like the prodigal son, "in a far country" for which they have no map, in which they feel desperately alone and begin to "be in want". Like him, they long to get back home.

One person who had more maps for the journey than most of us would wish to take was the apostle Paul. He had laws of all kinds, or, we might say, maps of all kinds: large scale and small scale; some with infinite detail, showing not just towns and cities but houses, fields and every feature and contour on the route, showing him how to avoid trouble and get to the destination. But despite all this he still lost his way and ended up in a mess; he said, in a cry of great frustration, "I know that nothing good lives in me, that is, in my sinful nature. For I have the desire to do what is good, but I cannot carry it out. For what I do is not the good I want to do; no, the evil I do not want to do —this I keep on doing. Now if I do what I do not want to do, it is no longer I who do it, but it is sin living in me that does it." He goes on to say, "What a wretched man I am! Who will rescue me from this body of death?"[15]

Sooner or later, most humans cry this cry in words of their own making. The words may not be as articulate, the logic not so well reasoned, the moral analysis not so sharp, but the heart cry is the same, proceeding as it does from great frustration and from being aware of the futility of death. The final question is the one we must answer if we are to become fully human: who will deliver me from this body of death? We have seen that we humans were created in the image of God but that the image has been marred. We would agree that we all face a struggle with those seven or more sins. Most of us would claim an occasional victory, but agree that, on the whole, we were losing the campaign. So what is the way to our humanity being restored, the image of God in us being re-created or renewed, of becoming what we were created to be, or, to use Paul's language, simply: "Who will rescue me?" The solution does not lie in a better education, a new ideology, more civilizing influences or a greater body of restraining law, all of which have been copiously used throughout history. The answer to Paul's question, "**who** will rescue me?" is Jesus Christ; but how does that **really**, that is in reality, happen? How does he help us be human?

If our tour of these seven capitals has served to show anything, it is that each capital in its own way can enthral but can never be satisfying. Each may lead to a further disintegration of that "image of God" in man, which was damaged but not destroyed in the Fall. Each presents us with a choice either to settle there or go on to a better and more fulfilling place. Each, too, involves us in a struggle, which we cannot win alone because our own resources are too depleted. So they serve to demonstrate to us that we need a guide who can show us the way through, and equip us to live a new kind of life. It is to this guide and to this equipment that we must now turn: to the only one who can lead us to become fully human. For this guide to help us, he must be the very embodiment of true humanity, who also has the power to rework the fractured image of God in us, so that it gives, once more, glimpses of glory.

Notes

[1]   Ezekiel 28:17.
[2]   Philippians 2:6–7.
[3]   See 1 Peter 5:1–7 or Philippians 2:1–13.
[4]   Psalm 103:15–16.
[5]   Deuteronomy 8:10–14 and vv. 17–18.
[6]   1 Kings 11:4.
[7]   See Psalm 137:1.
[8]   John 5:44.
[9]   Luke 14:11.
[10]   Hebrews 12:3.

[11] Ephesians 2:12.
[12] See Micah 6:8.
[13] Steven Runciman, *A History of the Crusades*, Volume 1, *The First Crusade and the Foundation of the Kingdom of Jerusalem*, Cambridge University Press 1951, p. 38. Used by permission.
[14] See Luke 6:31.
[15] Romans 7:18–20, 24.

Part Three

LIVING SOULS

11

Behold the Man!

It was another of those true and prophetic words spoken in semi-ignorance, which surrounded the crucifixion of Jesus. St John tells us that when Jesus came out onto the balcony of the governor's residence wearing the crown of thorns and the purple robe, Pilate said to the crowd, "Here is the man!" or in Latin, Pilate's native language, *Ecce Homo!* [1]

In speaking those now well-known words that day to the baying crowd, you wonder where Pilate, the Roman governor of Jerusalem, put the stress. If you were reading the English translation, as a disciple, you would probably want to put the stress as follows: "Here is **the** man!" You wonder what Pilate meant by these words of profound and lasting significance about Jesus. One imagines he was saying, in effect, here was **the** man who was centre stage in Jerusalem at that moment; the man around whom had gathered a storm of controversy; a man whom he found innocent but who, out of jealousy, the Jewish leaders wanted to be rid of.

But since their first utterance, Christians have found deeper meaning in Pilate's words. For Christians, Pilate was presenting to the crowd outside his residence **the** man who was both the model of humanity, the one who was truly human but who also was the Father's son, the Son of God, and the Messiah. The essence of this book's theme is that Jesus Christ is the model human being, the paradigm man, so that to be like him is to be fully human.

Later on, in a subsequent speech to the crowd, Pilate was to complement his former statement that Jesus was "the man" with another insight, when he said, "Here is your king."[2] It is likely that Pilate did not know who Jesus really was, although he did recognise Jesus as being without fault, not deserving execution, as well as being a profound teacher of whom the Jewish leaders were inordinately jealous and wanted to be rid of at all costs. Pilate also seems to have recognised, from his profound conversations with Jesus, that he had an authority which was undeniable, and so he called him a king, because Jesus often spoke of a kingdom to his followers. However, knowing that he was being caught up in their shabby plot, and not having the courage to resist it and free Jesus, Pilate famously tried to wash his hands of the decision that he was about to take, to hand Jesus over to the fate engineered for him by the Jewish leaders. So at the very least Pilate recognised Jesus to be both an extraordinary man and a man of undoubted authority.

In the next chapter we will consider the significance of Christ's death and the part it plays in our pursuit of becoming fully human, but for the moment we will explore further the meaning of Pilate's saying that Jesus is **the** man, in the light of the things we have already considered in this book. The principal concern in this chapter is to show that Jesus is quite simply the model for our humanity, so that, as we become more like him, the likeness of God is gradually restored in us. There are many names or titles under which Jesus is described in the Bible, and we shall look at three. Firstly, there is Jesus' own favourite description of himself, the Son of Man. Secondly, we have Paul's description of Jesus as the new or second Adam, and thirdly we will consider a description used by several New Testament authors: that Jesus is the exact image or representation of God.

THE SON OF MAN

"The Son of Man", Jesus' favoured self-description, was more than a circumlocution or device whereby he could speak in the third person about himself, so leaving others to decide whom the Son of Man was and whether Jesus was speaking of himself or another. By using this term, Jesus was able to make what is called an indirect claim, such as when he said to the sceptical Pharisees that his healing of a paralysed man was a sign that, "...the Son of Man has authority on earth to forgive sins."[3]

More often than not, the Son of Man sayings (of Jesus) tell us what he had come to do and what he would do in the future. So in Mark's Gospel we are told, "...even the Son of Man did not come to be served, but to serve, and to give his life as a ransom for many."[4] Or, in reply to Peter's plaintive question about what reward he and the other disciples would get in return for leaving everything to follow him, Jesus says, looking into the future, "I tell you the truth, at the renewal of all things, when the Son of Man sits on his glorious throne, you who have followed me will also sit on twelve thrones, judging the twelve tribes of Israel"[5] You hope Peter was satisfied! Once again, Jesus is speaking indirectly about himself and telling those who understood what he would do, both in his ministry then and in the future.

However, what was confusing to his contemporaries was that although they knew the figure of the Son of Man in the Scriptures to be a glorious and majestic one, as in Daniel's vision of the Son of Man in Daniel chapter seven, they found that Jesus linked this figure of glory and majesty with another mysterious figure in the Old Testament, namely the suffering servant who was to be found in the "servant songs" of Isaiah. Here is the Daniel picture:

> "In my vision at night I looked, and there before me was one like a son of man, coming with the clouds of heaven. He approached the Ancient of Days and was

led into his presence. He was given authority, glory and sovereign power; all peoples, nations and men of every language worshipped him. His dominion is an everlasting dominion that will not pass away, and his kingdom is one that will never be destroyed."[6]

In fact, Jesus took these two Old Testament themes, of suffering and glory, connected to these two figures, and applied both to himself, so that the Son of Man sayings depicted a person who would establish an everlasting kingdom and inaugurate that kingdom through suffering for his people. So the title Son of Man denotes both human suffering and divine glory.

These twin aspects of the title Son of Man are highlighted in other ways in the New Testament, in the sense that Jesus is both like us and unlike us. He is **like us** because he is the Word made *flesh*, so sharing in our humanity. Paul daringly develops this idea when he says, "For what the law was powerless to do in that it was weakened by the sinful nature, God did by sending his own Son **in the likeness of sinful man** to be a sin offering."[7] But equally, Jesus is **unlike us** in that no fault was found in him or, to use the Latin word, he was impeccable.

The writer to the Hebrews puts this clearly when he tells us, "He (Jesus) was tempted in every way just as we are—yet was without sin," and consequently he is a sympathetic high priest towards us and able to help us as he himself is without any sin. So in this title that Jesus loved to use to describe both who he was and what he had come to do, there is a double resonance. On the one hand this title shows his humanity, sharing in our likeness, (a likeness originally created by God—Father, Son and Holy Spirit—and which he had come to restore in us) and, on the other hand, this title, earthed in the picture of the Son of Man figure in Daniel, looks forward to the glorious kingdom of God which he had come to inaugurate and of which he is Lord.

The Son of Man sayings on the lips of Jesus are replete with this double emphasis. Jesus attaches this title, Son of

Man, both to his predictions of his betrayal, sufferings and death and to his return in power, in glory and for judgement. It is an awesome combination.

In visiting Istanbul this year, or Constantinople as it was called for most of its history from 315 –1439, I saw again the famous mosaics of Christ in Hagia Sophia, the great Byzantine basilica built by the Emperor Justinian and completed in 537AD. It was the third great cathedral church on that site, the first having been burnt down by followers of the golden tongued expository preacher John Chysostom, when he was deposed as Patriarch by the Empress Eudoxia on June 9, 404AD. The Mosaic of Christ Pantocrator, which is on a wall in the upper level of that building, catches in its expression this double likeness: on the one hand, the compassionate, knowing man and the other the solemn, all-knowing Lord. It demonstrates well both the humanity and divinity implicit in this title which Jesus used so frequently of himself.

In becoming human or taking on flesh, Jesus bestowed dignity on humankind. He identified with us. Jesus entered our existence as both our original Creator and then Redeemer, and used of himself this title that meant he was one of us: the Son of Man. He became like us in every way, yet without sin. In literal human terms, he became a neonate or an embryo (sanctifying the unborn); he was a vulnerable defenceless child (dignifying the innocence of children); he grew up and worked (dignifying education, upbringing and work); and he was a member of a family (hallowing family life), and he died, as we must die, too. In fact, no stage of life did he avoid, however messy, painful or ordinary it was. He was human, and by becoming human he gave honour to our human existence from conception to the grave and, as we shall see, his incarnation began the process by which our humanity may be restored.

So the title Son of Man quite simply combines the human and divine in the person of Jesus. On the one hand, it proclaims his solidarity with humankind, and that, like Adam, he too was taken from the earth. On the other hand, he was the glorious and majestic Son of God; he was the man from heaven. His divine nature was in human flesh. As Wesley put it, "Veiled in flesh the godhead see." And, as St Paul tells us in his famous Philippian hymn, Jesus emptied himself of the divine splendour of heaven to become a man, taking the form of a servant, finally dying on the cross to restore us to heaven and, eventually, to bring heaven to earth. He was perfectly humble, and obedient to the will of the Father.

THE SECOND ADAM

The teaching of Paul, which is centred on the idea of Jesus being the second or new Adam, can be simply stated as follows: Adam brought death into the world and Jesus brought life. Through the first Adam death reigned, but, through the second Adam, life came to all who received the grace of Jesus.

Nowhere is this contrast more crisply stated than in Paul's great chapter on the resurrection, 1 Corinthians 15, where he says:

> But Christ has indeed been raised from the dead, the firstfruits of those who have fallen asleep. For since death came through a man, the resurrection of the dead comes also through a man. For as in Adam all die, so in Christ all will be made alive.[8]

Anyone who is familiar with Handel's *Messiah* will know the remarkable moment when the choir sings, to triumphant music, "For as in Adam all die, so in Christ all will be made alive." It is one of the great moments of the entire work. To continue the musical illustration, Paul's contrast with Adam is like counterpoint, a passage of music in which two melodies contrasting in mood or style are placed next to each other. The stories of Adam and Christ are opposites, and by placing them together as Paul does in Romans 5:12–21, he shows the tragedy of Adam and the triumph of Christ. There are many points of contrast, or thesis and antithesis, or counterpoint, in their lives, which Paul proceeds to highlight by way of analogy and comparison.

Firstly, there is the contrast between Adam's disobedience and Jesus' obedience. Adam trespassed, or fell from his state of communion with God, as we have already seen, whereas Jesus learnt obedience as God's Son.[9] We are told frequently in the Gospels what this obedience meant for Jesus: his resistance of the temptations in the wilderness; his conformity to his Father's pattern of words and works; and, above all, his willingness to suffer on the cross. Through this obedience, Jesus was able to bring the gift of life.

It was through obedience that Christ's holiness and perfection was revealed. The holiness of Jesus was present in the details of his everyday living, and evident in his responses and interactions with the people around him, whether they were disciples or opponents. So his was no ivory tower holiness, but one in which he transparently lived out his teaching over his lifetime.

He told us to pursue humility, or meekness. He said of himself, "Take my yoke upon you and learn from me, for I am gentle and humble in heart."[10] He then fulfilled his own teaching by taking up a towel, doing the work of a servant and washing the disciples' feet. He told us to forgive our enemies, saying, "But I tell you: Love your enemies and pray for those who persecute you...."[11] Then, on the cross, he prayed for the soldiers who crucified him, "Father, forgive them, for they do not know what they are doing."[12] As Raneiro Cantalamessa wrote, "An examination of the Gospels immediately shows us that Jesus' holiness is no mere abstract principle or metaphysical deduction but real holiness lived out minute by minute in the most concrete situations of life."[13] The open secret of Jesus' holiness was faithful obedience displaying itself in love for the Father and for others. In this obedience he had freedom. The dynamic for this freedom and holiness was love for the Father. As Jesus said, "...I always do what pleases him."[14] So Jesus held together what we moderns have almost completely separated, which is love and obedience. He loved, and so obeyed and, in his obedience, succeeded where Adam failed. He was the new true man or, as Paul says, the complete, whole and perfect man.

The second contrast, which Paul draws between Adam and Christ, is the consequence of their respective actions. Adam's action in choosing to disobey brought condemnation on successive generations of humans, as we have already seen in the early chapters of this book. That condemnation followed the first hand experience of guilt and shame resulting from the act of disobedience. It resulted in being separated from the presence of God and experiencing dislocation in our human relationships.

By contrast, Jesus brought justification, a technical or forensic Pauline word, which means being made acceptable and righteous before God, by faith in Jesus and his redeeming sacrifice. What Paul was at pains to explain in the early chapters of Romans is that we are justified through faith in Christ and in no other way. So the first Adam brought condemnation on his successors, as we all share in his failure, and the second Adam, Jesus, brings acquittal, to those who believe, of any moral charge laid against us. So Christ's forgiveness covers our failures and makes us completely acceptable to our Creator.

The third contrast that Paul draws between Adam and Jesus is that Adam's disobedience led to condemnation resulting in death, whereas Jesus' obedience leads to justification and life. So we can rightly say, in summary, that death comes through Adam, and life through Christ. But we need to explore what these sweeping terms mean. When Paul speaks of death issuing from Adam's disobedience, and infecting all mankind, he means both a spiritual and physical death. Spiritual death, which Paul has earlier described as being the wages of sin, means not being able to have a friendship with God, and being separate and alienated from him. Physical death needs no elucidation. By contrast, Jesus came to bring life. The life he offers is firstly relational, or to put it another way, a relationship with him is life. As John, the most relational of the apostles, makes known through the words of Jesus,

"Now this is eternal life: that they may **know** you, the
only true God, and Jesus Christ, whom you have sent."[15]

Knowing Christ is eternal or spiritual life. But the life
Christ offers through a relationship with him has a physical
as well as spiritual effect, so reversing the sentence of
physical death passed on Adam and bringing, as Paul says,
immortality to light through the gospel. So in Adam there is
death, but in Christ there is life.

If this seems a rather dense piece of theology, which is
hard to get hold of because some of the terms are not exactly
everyday language and the concepts are not familiar, then
the picture on the cover of this book comes visually to our
aid. It is a fresco found in the church of St Saviour Chora, in
Istanbul, which I visited during a two-day stay in the city on
my journey to Jordan. The church is close to the city walls
built by Theodosius. "Chora" means in the countryside or
fields, as originally the church was "outside the city wall"
until they were rebuilt under Theodosius in the fifth
century. Although the church was then inside the city, it
retained its name. Inside, the church is full of the most
wonderfully preserved mosaics and frescoes, probably some
of the finest Christian mosaics in the world, of which the
fresco on the front of this book is the most striking. It is not
a scene I have seen depicted anywhere else, and it is a faithful
visual representation of Paul's teaching in Romans 5:12–21. It
is simply known as Resurrection, or Anastasis. It depicts
Jesus rising from the dead and, in dynamic fashion, hauling
Adam with his right hand and Eve with his left from their
tombs. Behind them stand characters from the Old and New
Testaments. It is a breathtaking and vibrant presentation of
the resurrection of Christ reversing the death brought upon
humanity by Adam and Eve. It also well illustrates the words
of Paul, who speaks of the abundant grace which Christ offers
to all:

For if the many died by the trespass of the one man,
how much more did God's grace and the gift that came

by the grace of the one man, Jesus Christ, overflow to the many![16]

The language is as super-abundant as the fresco is vibrant! A final point of contrast between Adam and Jesus is that the lavish grace of God in Christ will more certainly lead to life for those who receive it than the effect of Adam's sin will lead to death. So we should let Paul speak for himself as it could not be more eloquently put than in these words of his:

For if, by the trespass of the one man, death reigned through that one man, how much more will those who receive God's abundant provision of grace and of the gift of righteousness reign in life through the one man, Jesus Christ.[17]

Receiving this abundant provision of grace and righteousness from the risen Lord is the first, essential step to having the image of God restored in us and becoming fully human!

THE IMAGE OF GOD

We saw in the earlier chapters of this book how Adam and Eve together were made in the image of God and, as far as the Bible is concerned, this is the defining characteristic of being human. We also saw what were the constituent parts of being made in the image of God: our moral, spiritual, relational, rational and creative characteristics. We saw too that, as a result of the Fall, that image became marred so that we are now left with a dichotomy in human nature, on the one hand still exhibiting the characteristics of this image of God in our human lives, but on the other hand displaying a fatal flaw which corrupts those characteristics and alienates us from our Creator.

This fatal flaw is variously described in the Bible as the principle of sin, or the old nature or the flesh or an evil heart, and with these things we must contend and struggle in those areas of life which we looked at in the central section of the book. These "seven deadly sins" are just the outward symptoms of the deeper problem, which I have described as this fatal flaw. The issue we must now think about is whether and how the image, once marred, can be restored.

Like Humpty Dumpty, we fell! But can the pieces be put back together and, if so, how? The short answer is that the image can be perfectly restored over time, but the process begins in this life and is fulfilled in the next. The restoration is the work of the Father, Son and Holy Spirit. Just as God, the Holy Trinity, paused before the creation of man in the Genesis account and said, "Let **us** make man in our own image," so also it is he, three persons and one God, who has taken the initiative, made the sacrifice and provided the power for the remaking of the divine image in us, so that once again we may become what we were intended to be, namely fully human beings.

The Father sent his Son, having prepared a people to receive him. Previously, prophets or messengers had been sent, but in one of the most poignant of Jesus' parables, which he told shortly before his own sufferings, the parable of the tenants, Jesus told how the owner of the vineyard (the Father) resolved to send his only son to his recalcitrant and rebellious tenants, who were abusing his vineyard, not sending either the rent or any of the fruit to the owner, and beating or killing the messengers. The owner of the vineyard said, "What shall I do? I will send my son, whom I love; perhaps they will respect him."[18] As we know, they did not; and in the parable, seeing their chance to dispossess the owner by killing the heir, they hoped that the vineyard would pass to them. The irony was that the Father sent the Son so that what had been lost could be restored, and the inheritance, which had been squandered, could be put in place again. Or, to change the metaphor, the Son came, sent by the Father to restore the relationship of love and trust which had been broken down, and to restore the image of God in humankind that had been marred. And the one could not occur without the other.

So Jesus came not only as the Son of Man or as the true man, the new Adam, but also as the exact representation of God the Father himself. The word "image" has changed its meaning in our society, drifting from its former meaning of being a likeness or representation to being now merely a presentational stance. The media are the great image-makers. Politicians, who have to manifest themselves through the media, are sometimes accused of being all image and no substance, all "spin" and no solidity. Image has thus come to mean what is on the surface, which may well be quite different from what is below the surface, and we have come to live with this perception.

It is a tendency in all human affairs for hypocrisy, deceit and falsehood to take root easily, and in so doing to create a split between what is either thought or held inwardly and what is expressed outwardly, or between what we profess with our words and what we do in our actions. This is dishonesty or a lack of truth. The opposite of this is integrity: where what you see on the outside is what is there on the inside or, to put it simply, what is seen is what you are. Or again, what is promised or heralded with words is done in deeds. Whereas all other humans suffer from this intrinsic division to a greater or lesser degree, Jesus did not. Philip once made this request of Jesus: "Lord, show us the Father and that will be enough for us", to which Jesus said, "Anyone who has seen me has seen the Father."[19] Jesus was teaching the disciples that what you see in him is an exact likeness of the Father. With Jesus, what is expressed on the outside through word and action is a window into the reality of God. So Paul, on various occasions, calls Jesus "the image of God", or, "the image of the invisible God",[20] and the writer to the Hebrews wrote, "The Son is the radiance of God's glory and the exact representation of his being...."[21] Finally, John, in his prologue to his Gospel, wrote, "The Word became flesh and made his dwelling among us. We have seen his glory, the glory of the One and Only, who came from the Father, full of grace and truth."[22]

So, because Jesus shares not only "the likeness of sinful

man",[23] but is also "the image of the invisible God", he alone is equipped to restore to humankind that inheritance which was once given originally but which became marred and flawed. And at the same time he can restore the relationship of love and trust which had been broken. Just as in the fresco, Anastasis, in the church of the Saviour, the risen Jesus is seen hauling Adam and Eve from their graves, so in reality Christ can take our flawed and marred life and fill it with the life of heaven; his divine power remaking our own shattered image. But for Jesus to restore the image of God in us he must be both fully man and fully God, so that in his "fullness" we may become what we were meant to be.

However, there have always been well-aimed assaults upon that essential nature of Jesus, either denying that he is the unique Son of God or denying that he ever came "in the flesh". Often, the prevailing intellectual attitudes in the culture of the day colour the way we understand who Jesus is. Let me explain with an illustration from history.

****

To return, for a moment, to my travels that summer. About eighty miles south of Istanbul, on a large inland lake surrounded by acres and acres of olive groves, is the Turkish lakeside resort of Iznik. It is, in fact, the old Byzantine city of Nicaea. The Byzantine walls around the city partially remain. There are the remains of several churches long since destroyed in days of the Seljuk Turks and the Ottoman Empire. More significantly, there are the remains of the council chamber in which the Council of Nicaea took place in May 325AD. The Ecumenical Council, summoned by the Emperor Constantine, was the most emphatic attempt to resolve the issues surrounding the person of Christ in the fourth century. In the preceding years, the influential presbyter Arius, from Alexandria in North Africa, had systematically set out to undermine belief in the divine nature of Christ, publishing his conclusions in 318AD.

His position was the almost inevitable outcome of the long years of dispute in the early years of the Christian faith about the nature of Jesus as being both human and divine. As early as 90AD, when John was writing his Gospel, and even earlier in his Epistles, John was arguing that Jesus had really come in the flesh. In the prologue to his Gospel, John is at pains to establish that the Word became flesh —real flesh. In his Epistles, John again defended the fact that Christ came in real flesh.

This is how you can recognise the Spirit of God. Every spirit that acknowledges that Jesus Christ has come **in the flesh** is from God, but every spirit that does not acknowledge Jesus is not from God. This is the spirit of the antichrist, which you have heard is coming and even now is already in the world.[24]

The battle was joined, to defend and maintain the truth that Jesus came in human flesh (though without sin) — against the world of gnostic Greek thought, in which the flesh was denigrated and despised. J.N.D. Kelly, in his classic work on the early church, drew attention to the way in which, underlying the varied gnostic groups, there lay a body of concepts which could mutate, and change these groups which were looking for answers to fundamental questions about spiritual reality.[25]

Fundamental amongst these ideas was their form of dualism which separated the spiritual and the physical— denigrating the latter. It was because they regarded matter, and hence the body or flesh, as intrinsically evil that they could not abide the idea that God had become flesh. From the second half of the first century onwards, the church had to do battle with their erroneous teaching. It was against their teachings that Irenaeus fought in the second century: "Vain indeed are those who allege that Jesus appeared in mere seeming [i.e. not properly in the flesh]. For these things were not done in appearance only, but in actual reality."[26] That is, Jesus really did become flesh. Much of Irenaeus's defence was against the prevalent notion derived from Greek philosophy that the flesh was intrinsically evil, and because of this intellectual stance the very idea of the humanity of Christ was called into question or denied outright.

If one result of that prevailing intellectual culture was to deny what the Gospel proclaimed and Irenaeus contended—that Jesus actually and really came in the flesh—then the other way out of this intellectual difficulty was to say that Jesus was simply not God. Yes, he was an inspired individual with "knowledge" from the heavenly sphere, as the Gnostics taught, but he was not God in flesh. It was this teaching which found its climax in Arianism, which asserted as its premise "One God, who alone is ingenerate, alone eternal, alone without beginning, alone true, alone possessing immortality, alone wise, alone good, alone sovereign, alone judge of all."[27] The result of this doctrine of God, combined with the general view of the flesh still being inherently evil, meant that the divinity of Christ was denied by Arius and his many followers. They did this chiefly on the grounds that God had an indivisible nature and therefore could not appear on earth without spoiling the greatness of the godhead. It was left to Athanasius after the Council of Nicaea to defend the teaching that Jesus was fully God and man.

The Council of Nicaea was convened by Constantine to lay to rest the false teaching, and in its own historic language to state that the Son was of the same substance as the Father. They coined a new Greek word, which was to be a benchmark of orthodoxy in explaining the dual nature of Christ as both human and divine. The word was *homoousios*, meaning that Jesus was of the same substance as, or one in being with, the Father. It took a further hundred years until the Council at Chalcedon, before the two natures of Jesus were adequately explained and defended in a creed.

The purpose of revisiting some of these ancient but critical disputes in the early church is to show that our view of Jesus is deeply influenced by the prevailing intellectual culture. In a culture in which the body was despised and material things were considered evil it was only a matter of time before the humanity of Jesus was brought into question. Having not succeeded in jettisoning the idea that God came in flesh, the attack changed from being an assault on the idea of God taking flesh in Jesus to one of Jesus not really being divine or of the same substance with the Father. To substantiate this attack, the starting place changed too, from being a denigration of the material things as evil, to an exaltation of the godhead such that no idea of God becoming flesh could be entertained without it being construed as an affront to the dignity or sovereignty of God. And, of course, in this there is more than a slight echo in Islam, which can neither countenance Jesus being God, nor God suffering in Christ for the failures of humankind. Islam appeared in the Middle East in the seventh century, and that is not altogether surprising, given the background of Arianism which had a similar doctrine of God. So in the early centuries, amongst many other false teachings, the church had to defend itself against both Gnosticism and Arianism.

But just as the intellectual climate of those early centuries of the church's existence provided fertile ground for distorting the truth about Jesus, so in more recent times our own Western intellectual climate has also provided fertile soil for disbelieving these same truths, though for different, modern reasons. There are some obvious strands of thought, which have contributed to this fresh assault on the doctrine of Jesus as the man who was God. The first was the rise of scientific materialism, which originated in the Enlightenment and grew in confidence through the nineteenth and twentieth centuries. Until the outbreak of the two World Wars, enormous optimism was attached to the progress of science. As scientism swept all before it, theologians felt under pressure to drop the miraculous from the life of Christ, so the incarnation, resurrection and ascension were all explained away. They believed it was no longer plausible to a scientific world to proclaim a Christ who was supra scientific, so they trimmed Jesus to fit in with the intellectual climate of the day. Words like "myth" became fashionable to describe what could not be explained by science; the miracles were no longer regarded as historical events. And people spoke of a Christ of faith and not of history, as they were embarrassed by the history but still found Jesus an "inspiring figure". In this exceedingly sceptical presentation of Jesus, the divinity of Jesus, the doctrine that he was truly God, soon came into question. Some theologians believed that Jesus would be more credible if they explained away the supernatural bits. But what sort of Jesus would they be believing in? What we can say is that the intellectual culture of the day affects our Christology, that is our view of Christ, unless the beginning and ending point is the biblical record.

In the last few years, though, there appears to have been in our culture an imperceptible shift away from such a secular, scientific, materialist mood, which is partly due to the rise of the New Age movement, growing interest in man-centred spiritualities, and the popularising of the supernatural.

Another intellectual mood that has come to dominate Western culture, and which also has affected profoundly our contemporaries' view of Christ, is the philosophical denial that anything called truth can exist. After all, Jesus did say, "I am the truth", but if you have already taken up the position that no such thing as truth exists, then what is Jesus saying? In so called postmodern Western society, many have bought into the idea that whatever we experience is the only reliable definition of truth. So if every experience is a legitimate expression of truth, then each experience is valid and true —and no discrimination between any of those truths should be allowed, for that would be intolerant. As Os Guinness wrote, "The Christian faith is not true because it works; it works because it is true. It is not true because we experience it; we experience it, deeply and gloriously, because it is true. It is not simply "true for us"; it is true for any who seek in order to find, because truth is true even if nobody believes it, and falsehood is false even if everybody believes it. That is why truth does not yield to opinion, fashion, numbers, office, or sincerity; it is simply true and that is the end of it."[28]

But our general intellectual climate, in which truth is

relativised and public truth has given way to private experience, has a profound effect on our view of Jesus. It begins to be thought that he cannot be "the truth" for that must deny the truth as someone else has perceived or experienced it. This powerful current intellectual trend means that everything is comparative, and the only arbiter between these different perceptions of truth is whether it is beneficial in your private life. If it is, then it is valid for you, which is all that can be asked in our pragmatic world. But Jesus said "I am **the** truth", and that statement is based on the truth that he is God in human flesh, as St John says at the beginning of his Gospel.

This powerful intellectual current in our modern world of denying the existence of public truth, a trend that was especially highlighted by Bishop Newbigin, runs quite counter to the notion of there being a defining and final truth. It is not surprising, therefore, that the belief that "Jesus is Lord" is seriously counter culture.

The final point about the intellectual or cultural mood, which prevails in our modern world, concerns living **for** the body rather than simply living **in** the body and for something greater than bodily life. This mood and cultural climate in the West is an exact reversal of the gnostic Greek view of the body, which, as we have observed, was believed to be intrinsically evil.

In our modern society, the body is the place in which we gain our greatest experiences. These could be culinary, sexual, or mind–altering. Naturally and obviously, all experiences have to be had in the body, otherwise they could not happen, but our aim today is not to answer the deeper question as to the purpose of living, but rather to find out how we can more exquisitely satisfy the aspirations of the body!

Once again, we have made everything into means but have lost any view of what the end is —as Jacques Ellul said we would, in his seminal post-World War II book, *The Presence of the Kingdom*. He wrote, "The first great fact that emerges from our civilisation is that today everything has become "means". Man becomes an obedient consumer, and with his eyes shut he swallows everything that economics puts into his mouth."[29] In fact, we have turned the means into the end, and no more so than with the body. Whereas the Gnostics sought to deny the reality and sanctity of the bodily life, seeking only a greater meaning from outside it, our current Western society has gone to the opposite extreme: it deifies the body, seeking no redemption of it. If the body is the theatre where all desires can be satisfied, and it is severed from the harness of purpose and the engine of faith, it becomes literally all-consuming. But Jesus came in the flesh not to condemn the body but to transform it, so that we may find our true identities, realise that faith in him enables us to fully live in the body, and be given a purpose and a goal without which bodily experience becomes a shackle that restrains our true humanity.

In conclusion, Jesus was both the perfect image of God and the perfect image of man. This was what the Church Fathers fought to maintain at Nicaea and Chalcedon, in the face of the onslaught against the humanity and deity of Christ. That onslaught arose out of the prevailing intellectual and cultural winds of the day, which were undermining the biblical truth about Jesus —as then, so now. But it is only because Jesus was fully human that he can restore our own fallen humanity, and it is only because he is God that he has the power and authority to do so. Amid all the disputes that raged over the definition of Jesus as both man and God, it is easy to lose sight of him as a person who wept, suffered, loved, challenged, transformed and taught those around him, and who is presented to us in the Gospels in countless encounters with people for whom he had come. Attracted by the sheer magnetism of his person, people then had to answer the question, "Who is this? Even the wind and the waves obey him!"[30] And, as they entered into relationship with him, they realised that they were changing and that they were becoming more like him: more generous, merciful, loving and just. But that restoration could only take place through the agony and triumph of the cross, which could set us on the path of becoming human again. It is to the cross that we must now turn, as the necessary sacrifice by which our humanity may be restored.

Before we turn to look at the cross and resurrection, and how they usher in our new humanity, the final word of hope should stay with Paul, the greatest expositor of the new humanity Christ gives us:

> And just as we have borne the likeness of the earthly man, so shall we bear the likeness of the man from heaven.[31]

How such a thing became possible is firstly revealed in the incarnation, but made possible through the cross. It is to the cross and resurrection of Christ that we must now turn. The new humanity was lived out in Jesus, and it is through his death and resurrection that this humanity is put within our grasp, and we too can become women and men of heaven!

Notes

1. See John 19:5.
2. See John 19:14.
3. See Mark 2:10.
4. See Mark 10:45.
5. See Matthew 19:28.
6. Daniel 7:13–14.
7. Romans 8:3, my emphasis.
8. 1 Corinthians 15:20–22.
9. See Hebrews 5:8.
10. Matthew 11:29.
11. Matthew 5:44.
12. Luke 23:34.
13. Raniero Cantalamassa, *The Holy One of God.* (The Liturgical Press, Collegeville, MN56321, 1990), p.12. Used by permission.

[14]   See John 8:29.

[15]   John 17:3, my emphasis.

[16]   Romans 5:15b.

[17]   Romans 5:17.

[18]   Luke 20:13.

[19]   See John 14:8–9.

[20]   2 Corinthians 4:4, Colossians 1:15.

[21]   Hebrews 1:3.

[22]   John 1:14.

[23]   See Romans 8:3.

[24]   1 John 4:2–3, my emphasis.

[25]   See J.N.D. Kelly, *Early Christian Doctrine*, 2nd edition, (A & C Black, 1960), p. 29.

[26]   See *Ante–Nicene Fathers* (1975), Book 5:2.

[27]   See J.N.D. Kelly, op. cit. p. 227.

[28]   Os Guinness, *Time for Truth* (IVP, 2000, p. 84, & Baker Book House, USA).

[29]   Jacques Ellul, *The Presence of the Kingdom* (Colorado Springs, CO: Helmers & Howard), 1989 p. 51.

[30]   See Mark 4:41b.

[31]   1 Corinthians 15:49.

12

The Cross

About a hundred miles south east of present day Iznik, or Byzantine Nicaea, was the Roman province of Galatia. Going north from his home town of Tarsus, or from the operational headquarters of the early church at Antioch, Galatia would have been the first province Paul entered, having crossed the Taurus mountains.

On the first missionary journey, the Holy Spirit moved Paul and his companions to take a route, first westwards to Cyprus and Pamphylia, and then north east to Galatia, with which he would probably have had some previous knowledge. The church at Antioch—which comprised a diverse group of gifted leaders that included "Barnabas, Simeon called Niger, Lucius of Cyrene, Manaen (who had been brought up with Herod the tetrarch) and Saul" — had laid hands on Paul and Barnabas and, after fasting and prayer, had sent them off on their first missionary journey.[1]

The round trip took them eventually to the towns of southern Galatia. At Pisidian Antioch, Iconium, Lystra and Derbe, Paul preached the gospel. In these Galatian towns churches were founded, sometimes in the face of fierce opposition, as in Pisidian Antioch and Iconium.[2]

213

Later, in his second missionary journey, Paul was to re-visit these Galatian towns before his summons in a night time vision to cross over into Europe and make known the gospel in Philippi. But at some point subsequently, probably in the face of severe opposition from the Jews, these new converts to the faith in Galatia were in great danger of making shipwreck of their faith, as they gave credence to the false teachers who were harassing them.

In effect, they were at the point of making a U-turn in their faith, deserting the message of the gospel and the theology of the cross which they had understood from Paul, and going back to the idea that only through works of the law rather than through faith in the promises of God can anyone make themselves acceptable to him. So, in utter amazement, Paul wrote to these Galatian Christians, "I am astonished that you are so quickly deserting the one who called you by the grace of Christ and are turning to a different gospel —which is really no gospel at all."[3] They were deserting the message of the cross, and what had been accomplished for them there, and were going back to a man-made message with no power to save.

It was Martin Luther who was reported to have said that if you want to understand Christianity you must begin with the wounds of Christ. The cross is the apex of God's revelation to man. Why did Jesus hang on a cross for six hours, like a common convict, suffering the worst punishment Roman justice and repression could devise? And if he was the very image of the invisible God, why did his Father allow it —and the Son embrace it in obedient love for his Father and for the world? And what was achieved for humankind? These are some of the central questions that surround the death of Jesus on the cross. The theology of the cross is in itself the subject of a large number of books, which seek to explain both its many sides and profound effects.[4] Suffice it to say here that, at its heart, the cross demonstrates supremely in history the truth of what Paul tells the Galatians in an impassioned way, namely that the Son of God, "...loved **me** and gave himself for **me**."[5] As Karl Barth, probably the

best known theologian of the twentieth century, is reported
to have said when asked to summarise the Christian faith,
using the words of a children's song: "Jesus loves me, this I
know, for the Bible tells me so"! Equally, the words of a song
I sang with others thirty years ago expresses most, but not
all, we need to know about the cross:

> At the cross of Jesus, pardon is complete,
> Love and justice mingle, truth and mercy meet.
> Though my sins condemn me, Jesus died instead;
> There is full forgiveness in the blood he shed.

The tune may not be all that popular today, but the truths
are eternal and well expressed. The essence of this summary
of the cross is that Christ loved us by doing for us what we
could not do ourselves, which is to make atonement or
payment for the guilt of our wrongdoing. That atonement
(literally, making one with) required his death, his blood
being shed. Our wrongdoing is an offence to God and needs
to be removed before we can be at peace with him. So he
offers, through his grace, this promise of forgiveness through
the cross. If we accept and believe this promise then we will
be reconciled to him eternally. Then we will know his
presence with us by the Spirit in our hearts, and become a
member of his family, from which we cannot be disunited by
death. But the Galatians were in danger of turning away from
believing and trusting that Christ had done for them
everything necessary for their salvation and that they had
only to believe, receive and live out this truth. The false
teachers who had sprung up amongst them told them instead
that they had to go back to fulfilling the obligations of the
law in order to obtain forgiveness and merit with God. No
wonder Paul said, "You foolish Galatians! Who has bewitched
you? Before your very eyes Jesus Christ was clearly
portrayed as crucified."[6]

If the central truth of the cross is, "that Christ died for our
sins according to the Scriptures",[7] the question that we are
considering in the context of this book is: what effect does

215

that have on my humanity? If previously, before believing we are walking paradoxes, that we have a bias towards pleasing ourselves at others' expense—that we are *incurvatus se* (turned in upon ourselves), as the Reformers taught—the question we are now considering here is: "what changes in us when we believe the message of the cross?" What changes inside us, to help us become more fully human, as a result of believing in the death of Jesus for us?

It is primarily Paul who grapples with these issues, both in the Epistle to the Romans chapters 5–8, and also, in relation to the cross, specifically in his letter to the Galatians. Because this is one of the more difficult parts of Paul's teaching to get hold of and understand, there does not appear to be much said or taught about it these days, yet understanding it is essential to our progress towards becoming fully human, or becoming like "the man from heaven" as we were intended to be. These questions will be the subject of most of the next three chapters. But for now we shall look at the way the cross empowers us to become more truly human.

There are three aspects of the cross which we shall look at in relationship to these issues. They are: the embrace of the cross, the power of the cross to change us, and the example of the cross.

THE EMBRACE OF THE CROSS

Without this embrace we cannot become truly human. That is a stark statement, but from the standpoint of Christianity it is entirely true, and it does not arise as a figment of human imagination but from the words of Jesus, in probably his best known and most loved parable, that of the prodigal son. In recent years, the writings of Henri Nouwen, Miroslav Volf and Philip Yancey have greatly helped us to plumb the depths of this pre-eminent parable of grace. The metaphor which we are thinking about here, of embrace, comes at the centre of the parable. Everything leads up to it in the parable, and then leads away from it. It is the hinge of the parable taken as a whole and precipitates the reactions of the older brother, just as the cross is the hinge of history. For everything leads up to the cross and subsequently leads away from it. We know the words well, but nevertheless we should hear them again:

> ...But while he was still a long way off, his father saw him and was filled with compassion for him; he ran to his son, threw his arms around him and kissed him.[8]

Of course, the embrace as described in the parable, which is a story of the operation of God's grace, is only made possible by the historical event of the cross. To put it in current theological parlance, the narrative of the parable of the prodigal son is made possible by the overarching meta-narrative of the sending of his son by the Father for the salvation of the world.

As we know, there are two sensational and arresting moments in the parable. Firstly, the prodigal son said that he wanted his share of the inheritance, presumably one third of his father's assets, because the older son in Jewish inheritance law had a double portion of inheritance. In asking for his inheritance he was saying in effect, "I wish that you were dead" —which is a reaction of many to the notion that God the Father wants his rightful place in our lives! The second sensational moment in the parable was the notion of the Father running to embrace his returning son for whom he had been patiently waiting. Fathers **then** simply did not run, especially to meet an errant son who had previously said, in effect, "I wish that you were dead." But the father who had given away wealth which had then been squandered, ran, out of compassion, to embrace his son, and not a word of reproach was said to him. The son received only the best: his father's embrace, new clothes, new standing and a huge party. All of this serves only to underline the later irony in the story of the older brother who could neither embrace his father, with whom he was angry, nor his brother, of whom he was both jealous and contemptuous. But returning to the embrace, I often ask the question: how was it possible that the father could act so freely, spontaneously and non-judgementally toward his wayward, prodigal son? And the answer is that the embrace was made possible by the other overarching, cosmic embrace, which surrounds the whole Bible story —the embrace of the cross!

It was Irenaeus who once again pictured, symbolically, the two arms of the dying Christ on the cross as those of the Father and then Spirit, reaching out to a lost world. And of course, theologically, that is true, for each member of the Trinity was intimately involved in the sacrifice God made for us there. The Father sent and initiated this sacrifice, the Son uniquely offered himself once for all, and the Spirit eternally applies the effect of the cross to humankind. The cross is that embrace which prefigures all other embraces, and it lies behind the embrace of the father for the son in the parable of the prodigal son. As Miroslav Volf so beautifully puts it in his book *Exclusion and Embrace*:

> The cross is the giving up of God's self in order not to give up on humanity; it is the consequence of God's desire to break the power of human enmity without violence and receive human beings into divine communion. The goal of the cross is the dwelling of human beings "in the Spirit", "in Christ" and "in God". Forgiveness is therefore not the culmination of Christ's relation to the offending other: it is a passage leading to embrace. The arms of the crucified are open—a sign of space in God's self and an invitation for the enemy to come in.[9]

Or, as Paul put it,

> For if, when we were God's enemies, we were reconciled to him through the death of his Son, how much more, having been reconciled, shall we be saved through his life![10]

The rite of "passage" of which Volf speaks necessarily

involves repentance, as in the prodigal's coming to his senses and saying to himself, "I will set out and go back to my father and say to him: "Father, I have sinned against heaven and against you. I am no longer worthy to be called your son; make me one of your hired men."[11] Repentance, in his case, does lead to the seeking of forgiveness and reconciliation; and this forgiveness culminates in an embrace, in which the penitent prodigal finds space in the heart of God. However, the embrace also typically involves not only throwing arms around another but then **opening** the arms so that the "other", having been forgiven, reconciled and accepted, may get on with living. The question that concerns us in the context of becoming fully human is: what changes occur to the person who is embraced by the Father, through the cross?

Before moving on to answer this vital question, I must re-iterate that these changes to an individual can only truly follow the beginning—or the renewal—of a relationship with the Father, through the Son, and, as we shall see, in the Spirit. It is only in this context of having, and knowing you have, this relationship with the Father through the Son that changes may take place, are taking place and will take place to enable us to become fully human.

For the moment, and from this parable, we can notice that the son was re-clothed. His shoes, which were either worn out or lost, were replaced by new ones. His clothes smelt of a mixture of pigs, sweat, travel and the detritus of months of penury following riotous living. They needed more than a few cycles in a washing machine; they needed to be thrown away! In place of them he was given a new robe. This picture in Jesus' story of being re-clothed matches the greater doctrinal detail that Paul gives us, mostly in his epistles to the Romans, Galatians and Corinthians. So, having first understood that both our repentance and his forgiveness are implicit in the Father's embrace, the difficult question we must now face and try to answer is: how do we change as a result of that embrace?—And what difference do we experience, both in this struggle to become fully human and in the battles we encounter with those seven deadly sins?

THE POWER OF THE CROSS

The crisis that faced the Galatian church, in the towns that Paul and Barnabas had previously visited, was their denial of the benefits and effects of the cross. Instead, they preferred to believe, amazingly, that the Father wanted from them the hard labour of keeping the Jewish law, its rites and ceremonies—not just the moral commandments of the Decalogue—rather than simply receiving the ongoing grace of the gospel, and living in the power of the Spirit.

In a great cry from his heart, Paul teaches them that they were forsaking life for death, promise for servitude, potency for sterility, and that they should look no further than the cross, by which they were forgiven, by which they had been changed, and as a result of which they enjoyed the presence of the Spirit as a guarantee of heaven. No wonder he told them of his astonishment that they were so quickly deserting the one who had called them by the grace of Christ, and were turning to a different gospel which was really no gospel at all. Paul's argument with them was that not only were they making void the promise of forgiveness, the gift of righteousness and being justified, all of which comes through believing in the cross, and receiving the Father's embrace, but also that they were leaving behind the way that God had provided for them to become what God wanted them to be. For the cross has in it not only the means whereby we are forgiven and made at peace with God, but alongside, inside and intertwined with this objective change to our relationship with God, there is also a dynamic power to help us to become fully human. Often this is overlooked, but both here in this Epistle to the Galatians, as well as in Romans chapters 5–8, Paul makes it clear.

Paul writes, by way of teaching from his own apostolic experience and understanding:

> For through the law I died to the law so that I might live
> for God. I have been crucified with Christ and I no longer

live, but Christ lives in me. The life I live in the body, I live by faith in the Son of God, who loved me and gave himself for me.[12]

The principle motive force for Paul's life was no longer trying to observe the law in his own strength or resolution. Rather, knowing Christ's love for him, which was pre-eminently shown at the cross, he would now make obedient faith in him the cornerstone and main priority of his life.

So it is probable that whilst the Galatian Christians may not have seen the law as a means of gaining favour with God in the first place, they evidently still felt that it was vital for Christians to observe the law and so avoid any suspicion of antinomianism —that heresy which Paul was wrongly accused of preaching, namely that our sinning provides greater scope for God's forgiveness and a wider field for his grace to abound. (Paul's detractors had said, "Why not sin that grace may abound!") But Paul is saying here that he has died to the law, by which he means he has been released from its demands; it no longer has any claim on him, he need not set out to fulfil it, and it can no longer condemn him. Why? —and here comes the "crucial" point of his argument — because he has "...been crucified with Christ and I no longer live, but Christ lives in me." It is at this point in Paul's argument that people's eyes glaze over, and they wonder what is meant.

What we must now explore further is: in what sense has the Christian been crucified with Christ? And what real effect does this crucifixion have both upon me and the way I see my struggle with those classic seven deadly sins, indeed with all sin? Although there will be an evolving answer to these questions over the next two chapters, the specific area we are considering here is: what does being crucified with Christ mean, and what dynamic flows from that in our search and desire to become fully human? They are not easy questions to answer, but we must attempt both to explain and to understand, if we are to fully grasp the effect of the cross for the believer.

The benefits of Christ's death on the cross are both objective and subjective. The objective benefit is that believing and trusting in Christ's death on the cross, and the atonement he made there, leads to a change in our status. It means that through his death we are no longer enemies of God but **become his friends**. There is an objective change to our status. We are now friends and members of his family. We are reconciled. We are forgiven. The obstacles and barriers, which previously existed, have come down. We are no longer without hope in the world. All this is the result of Christ's death for us when we believe. We cannot improve on this state of affairs by our own efforts, although many Christians persistently think they can improve their standing with God by praying harder, doing more, attending more meetings, going to more conferences, worshipping for longer. But that is quite untrue! No, our objective relations with God have been perfectly restored by what another has done on my behalf. This is what Paul means when he says, "Therefore, since we have been justified through faith, we have peace with God through our Lord Jesus Christ...."[13] This peace–with–God perfectly describes the state of our relations with God once we have believed in his promise of forgiveness.

But we live in an age where we have a problem in accepting something which is objective, and that is because we now gauge most things today by how we feel. It is always interesting to me that any reporter interviewing a sportsman after their performance will almost inevitably ask the question: how did you feel when you rounded the last bend with sight of victory, or got your double century at the crease? —To which the breathless athlete has to mouth the usual phrase: "great", "good" or "beaten". I rather hope they would say to the reporter to tease this line of enquiry: "Well, I felt deeply depressed!" A slightly more interesting line of enquiry might be: "What were you thinking and feeling?" But in fact, when it comes to our faith, we need to hold in balance both the objective benefits of the cross and the subjective effects of Christ's death, because if on the one hand there is an objective change to our standing before God through faith in Christ's death, there is also an actual experiential change in us as well. Yes, there really is!

The experiential change is as significant as the objective change of status (from enemy to friend, through embrace) and it is to short sell the effects of the cross to describe one as being more important than the other. Paul teaches that both occur. When a person believes, then their standing before God is objectively changed. This results entirely from Christ's sacrifice on our behalf, so that our efforts play no part in making us friends or keeping us friends, only his work for us on the cross can do that. As Archbishop Temple famously said, "There is nothing I can contribute to my own salvation except the sin from which I need to be redeemed!" But equally, as well as our status being changed, we ourselves **are** changed in a number of highly significant ways. In the next chapter we will see that the gift of the Holy Spirit to indwell our lives gives the believer an ongoing experience of God, which we simply cannot do without in the struggle to become fully human. But for the moment, in relation to the cross, we shall consider how we ourselves are changed not only outwardly in our relations with God but also inwardly in terms of our own human nature.

Derek Tidball boldly and truly observes that the ego as well as the law was put to death by the cross of Jesus Christ.[14] This is entirely consonant with Paul's statement to the Galatians that, "I have been crucified with Christ and I no longer live, but Christ lives in me." Tidball's point summarises what it means to live the Christian life. Paul shows the Galatians that the demand of the law is both superseded and set aside by the cross. It is superseded in that we now primarily aim to please Christ, rather than setting out to observe the law. The curse or condemnation, which comes from comparing our lives with the moral law, is set aside because all claims upon us arising from the law have been met on our behalf by Christ. I suppose this is rather like saying that if we have negligently crashed our car into another's, and a claim against us has justifiably arisen, the insurance company has stepped in and settled the claim. In the case of our insurance we have paid an annual premium; in the case of Jesus settling the claim, he has done entirely so out of his grace!

So if we understand that the cross has set the claim of the law aside, in what sense did the cross also break our ego? For this is a statement yearning for greater explanation in terms of our quest of becoming fully human. For surely in this inward experience of our egos being in some sense put to death lies the secret of dealing with those deadly sins, which we have previously traced and which diminish our true humanity. What does it mean to have our egos crucified, and how could this come about? It does not mean that, in either some physical or metaphorical sense our bodies actually have been pinned with Christ to the cross; obviously we live two thousand years distant from the event of Christ's death, and in no way can we say that we have been physically crucified with him. Nor is Paul simply using a metaphor, to help us regard ourselves in a new light by putting a new gloss on our Christian lives; that would mean encouraging us to think something about ourselves which, if we believed it strongly enough, might be expected to change our self perceptions, so modifying our behaviour. That, too, would simply be a form of brainwashing or just a clever use of words: believing something to be true, so that it becomes "true for us". No, on the contrary, what Paul says is that when we believed in the death of Christ for us, not only did our standing change, but a real, actual, change has occurred **in us** as well.

The particular change we are looking at here is that the power of the ego, or the control of the self-life is really broken. Surely this is what Paul means when he says:

> For we know that our old self was crucified with him so that the body of sin might be done away with, that we should no longer be slaves to sin —because anyone who has died has been freed from sin.[15]

Few verses in the New Testament could be more important

than this one if we are to rightly regard ourselves as Christians and are to move towards the goal of becoming fully human. It is worth pausing on it for longer.

I heard a story a number of years ago of two people travelling together in a railway compartment; one was a kindly, scholarly and fairly ancient bishop, the other a young Salvationist: one in purple the other with bonnet! The Salvationist was fairly suspicious of the bishop, uncertain that he could be part of the true fold! After debating with herself for the most of the journey, she came out with her question in a rush: "Are you saved?" she said, baldly and boldly to him.

He put down his book in a kindly way and, peering over his half-moon glasses, said, "Well, it depends what you mean." Then, using the three tenses of the Greek word "to save", said: "I have been saved from the penalty of sin; I am being saved from the power of sin; and I will be saved from the presence of sin. Does that help?" One imagines that the Salvationist got more than she was looking for, and I am pleased to say that the bishop knew his Greek New Testament well, not so that he could wow her or anyone else with his ease with Greek, but so that he could properly teach the faith as he should, so that the flock is not in error either in believing too much which is not warranted, or on the other hand too little, so diminishing their expectations.

For our purposes, the second tense of salvation is what we are thinking about here. For the Christian is being saved from the power of sin by a triple alliance; that alliance is between what Jesus accomplished for us on the cross, the indwelling Spirit, and the intent and conformity of our will to the way of life which God intends for us.

The first part of this alliance is what interests us here, namely that our old self or ego or nature was crucified with Christ so that we are no longer a slave to it. Now we have already considered some of those ways that are, and have been classically described as, sinful, or to put it another way as diminishing to our true humanity. They are being greedy, envious, lazy, embittered, proud and so on; put in anything you care to which diminishes what we should truly be. Left to ourselves, we might say that we cannot but be or do these things because that is our nature; and indeed we may go on to say that we have good cause to be like that because we were badly treated in childhood or by someone else, or that we encountered bad things and endured adverse circumstances, all of which give us no alternative than to behaving in this particular way. So it seems that we are locked into a circle of behaviour from which we **believe** we can never cut loose; so in a real sense our pattern of behaviour is self-fulfilling. Whether we justify it to ourselves because we reckon ourselves to have been badly treated, or, more commonly, simply believe that we can do no other, we do it and reap the consequences, often reinforcing a pattern which we may expect to live with for the rest of our lives! Naturally, for some that sounds like a recipe for despair, so we insulate ourselves from such bleak thinking by alleviating our pain with the usual panaceas, but deep down we are hurting. And we do not give ourselves too much time to think, as we see no way out.

Some will say to me, "Do you have to be so bleak?" Others may admit that this is a fair description of our predicament. But is there a way out from this cycle? Emphatically, yes there is! And it would be more than a pity to miss it because Paul's language and categories of thought seem either inaccessible or arcane. What is needed is either a proper understanding of what he teaches (which we too often gloss over) or a change in what we believe! For deep down, many people simply do not believe that life could change or, more to the point, that **they** could change. Yet we are told that if we believe that Christ died for us then **our old self was crucified with him** with the result that we need no longer be dominated, enslaved or controlled by the power of sin. What Paul teaches every Christian is that when I come to believe that Christ died for me there is an inward change in me which amounts to a death and a resurrection in myself. Our old, selfish tendency is put to death as surely as Jesus was put to death on the cross, and the effect of this is not that we are sinless from now on, but that the power of that old life, which once held us in its grip, has been broken so that we can live differently, and have a desire now to please our Creator and follow in the steps of his Son. But of course we must go on choosing to do that with the help of the Holy Spirit. Not only has there been this death in us but there has also been a resurrection, too —the resurrection of a new life in us, which continually helps us to become what we want to be, which is to be like **the man** whom we have started to follow.

To the Christian, we have to ask the question, "Do you really believe that?" To the person who is considering the Christian faith, we have to say, "Do you see what is promised?" —namely, that we need no longer be enslaved by those things which in our better moments we do not like anyway. That is all! Now that, surely, is a message of hope, for it breaks us free from a dead weight which holds down our humanity from rising up and becoming, as far as possible in this life, what God intended for us.

This does not mean that our fundamental personality is altered so that we become unrecognisable but, on the contrary, our personality is enhanced —so that we become the best that we could be! Nor does it mean that thereby we have a by-pass around suffering and struggle, but it does mean we have a companion in suffering and sometimes we may even find purpose within it. The cross does something inwardly for us: it mysteriously changes us by actually putting to death an old self which had previously dominated us. As the good bishop said, "We are being saved from the power of sin", because that has been made possible intrinsically by the cross. We recall what Paul said to his Galatian churches: "I have been crucified with Christ and I no longer live, but Christ lives in me"; and what he said about himself, he expected all Christian believers to say and believe about themselves, too.

At this point we will leave our discussion of this part of the effect of the cross, having made the point that it brings about an inward change in the Christian by putting to death our old self with Christ on the cross. What this means in practice, and how this part of the jigsaw is a help to us becoming fully human, we will explore further in the chapter entitled "The Way we Live Now". But before moving on to explore this, we must look at one more way in which the cross helps us to become what God intended us to be. This is best described as *following the way of the cross*.

THE WAY OF THE CROSS

One of Archbishop Cranmer's most lovely collects has these words as part of his prayer: "Almighty God, whose most dear Son went not up to joy but first he suffered pain, and entered not into glory before he was crucified: mercifully grant that we, walking in the way of the cross, may find it none other than the way of life and peace." The paradox is, of course, that walking in the way of the cross *should be* a way to life and peace, but it surely *is*! For undoubtedly there are so many occasions in life when the example of the cross, and the inspiration of how Christ himself embraced the cross, is a transforming dynamic in the process of becoming human. So much of what Jesus taught consists not only in what we might call didactic, propositional teaching—that is, truths about his Father, himself and the Holy Spirit—but, also, actual power and authority in operation, in the *living out* of that teaching before a watching world. This distinguished him from the average teacher of his day. This living out of teaching, combined with his acts of mercy and power whether in healing, deliverance and provision, made the crowds repeatedly cry out, "What is this? A new teaching—and with authority!"[16]

So what is the way of the cross? In essence, it is the laying down of the self in obedience to and faith in the Father, and the resulting pattern of life and attitudes that follow. This way of the cross was illustrated in countless actions of Jesus around the time of his passion. Some of these actions were as follows: the forgiveness of his enemies ("Forgive them, Father, for they do not know what they are doing"); his care for his mother; his silence in the face of unjust accusation; his sadness and forbearance toward the disciples in the face of their desertion; his physical commitment to the cross, refusing drugs to alleviate the pain; his steadfastness and courage, setting his face to go to Jerusalem and not shirking this divine plan for salvation. The illustrations could go on. But it is Jesus' nobility, dignity and courage in the face of suffering which is part of the way of the cross. And it is often following this way which makes others become more fully human than before.

Interestingly, it is in the forgoing of our own comfort and convenience for another that we come closest to following in this way of the cross. Taking up our cross and following Christ can mean many things, including the subordination of our own self–interest to God's will as we discover it in Christ, but what may be a surprise is that it turns out to be a "way of life and peace". Without the cross we cannot become fully human, nor can we possibly follow along this "way" without the Holy Spirit.

The Galatian church was in danger of deserting the cross, and the gospel of the cross which Paul had preached to them and which they had believed. It was through the cross that they had been forgiven, incorporated into the family of God, released from the claims of the law. It was through the cross that God had made a real inward change in them, which was the breaking of the power of an old way of life. It was through the cross that the world, with its allurements and seductions, had been overcome. But Paul posed the Galatians one other vital question, the pivotal question of his cross–examination of their position:

> I would like to learn just one thing from you: did you receive the Spirit by observing the law, or by believing what you heard? Are you so foolish? After beginning with the Spirit, are you now trying to attain your goal by human effort? [17]

Becoming fully human depends on the cross, and it is not

achieved by human effort but by co-operation with the Holy Spirit. It is to him that we must now turn, who helps us to follow this way, makes real the internal changes in us as a result of our being crucified with Christ, and informs us inwardly of our change of status, from enemy to friend, so that we actually, experientially, know it inside.

Notes

[1]   See Acts 13:1–2.
[2]   See Acts chapters 13–14.
[3]   Galatians 1:6–7a.
[4]   Amongst which I would particularly recommend *The Cross of Christ* by Stott, and *The Message of the Cross*, by Tidball.
[5]   See Galatians 2:20, my emphasis.
[6]   Galatians 3:1.
[7]   See 1 Corinthians 15:3.
[8]   See Luke 15:20.
[9]   Miroslav Volf *Exclusion and Embrace* (Abingdon Press, Nashville 1996), p. 126
[10]   Romans 5:10.
[11]   Luke 15:18 –19.
[12]   Galatians 2:19–20.
[13]   Romans 5:1.
[14]   See Tidball, *The Message of the Cross,* p. 236.
[15]   Romans 6:6.
[16]   See Mark 1:27 (and Matthew 7:28–29).
[17]   Galatians 3:2–3.

13

The Spirit

So how are we to become fully human? Or to put it another way, how may we have the image of God restored in us so that the qualities of our true and original humanity become more obvious? The fundamental answer to this question is that left to ourselves we cannot do it. No amount of observing good examples as to what we should be like, nor commands as to what we should think, do or feel, will of themselves succeed in making us what, in our better moments, we would wish to become. Although God the Father told us what to do in the Ten Commandments, and God the Son showed us how to live, because of a power vacuum in us we can no more fulfil those commands or follow that example on our own as touch the stars unaided! We simply find ourselves incapable of such compliance with his will. It is precisely in this context of our natural deficiency of inclination and absence of spiritual power that the Holy Spirit comes to our rescue. He lifts us into a new realm.

Jesus was unmistakably clear in his teaching to the Jewish leader Nicodemus, that if we are to enter this new realm then it would only be through the operation or working of the Spirit. Jesus said, "Flesh gives birth to flesh, but the Spirit gives birth to Spirit."[1] Without the Spirit we could not be born into this new existence or realm which Jesus called belonging to his kingdom. At last, Jesus would inaugurate a new age, which the prophets had been looking forward to and predicting, and in which the work of the Holy Spirit would be central. The new covenant would be inaugurated. Paul was fully aware of the glory implicit in this new covenant, and conscious of the excitement about its amazing consequences, when he wrote to the Corinthian church:

> Now if the ministry that brought death, which was engraved in letters on stone, came with glory, so that the Israelites could not look steadily at the face of Moses because of its glory, fading though it was, will not the ministry of the Spirit be even more glorious?[2]

So when a person believes in the Son of God, who was lifted up on the cross for us, then he or she enters this new realm in which the Spirit comes to live inside them. It is then that the individual confesses that "Jesus is Lord", by the power of the Spirit of God.

Christianity without the Holy Spirit is like having a car without an engine. The chassis may look fine, the seats may be comfortable, it may look like a car but if you look under the bonnet or try to drive it then you know that it is not really one at all. There is not much pleasure in sitting still, no adventure, as there is no risk of movement, and it cannot serve any function except look deceptively decorative. Yet down the years too many have reduced Christianity either to an *ethical* observance society (in which we all are trying to behave) or a *religious* observance society, in which we enact various rituals without hope of real change. This is Spirit–less Christianity, and as such is not Christianity at all. The Spirit is above all else dynamic, as Jesus told the apostles before he left them at his ascension: "I am going to send you what my Father has promised; but stay in the city until you have been clothed with power from on high."[3] In fact the work of the Spirit is variously described in terms of wind, breath, fire and water, all of which are dynamic pictures of power. So it is he who provides the power for the Christian life; indeed, he is the one who brings us into the realm of Christ's kingdom.

Now in this process of becoming fully human we are reliant on the help and power of the Spirit. Pre-eminently, the Spirit brings us to Christ, makes the presence of Christ real to us, transforms us to become like Christ and equips us to serve Christ and others in the world. In fact this is a rounded description of a so-called charismatic Christian, and to be honest, in these senses, every Christian must be a charismatic Christian! The aspect of the Spirit's work that we are especially focussing on here is his helping us to become like Christ who is **the** man; so that in becoming more like him who is **the** man we are becoming more fully and truly human. So how does the Spirit restore the image of God in us? Once again we will use Paul's teaching to the Galatian Christians as our chief guide in exploring what exactly the Spirit does in helping us become what God intended us to be.

MAKING THE CONNECTION

The Galatians, as we saw in the previous chapter, were in danger of slipping away from the gospel. And Paul had to ask them pointedly, "Did you receive the Spirit by observing the law, or by believing what you heard?" Of course they received the Spirit by hearing the promise of the gospel and by believing what they heard, and not by any human efforts of their own. When they believed, they received the promise of the Spirit themselves and discovered his work in their lives. One of the principal and most wonderful aspects of his work is re-creating a relationship between an individual and the heavenly Father. He has been aptly termed the "go–between God" —going between the Father and us, and making known the reality of the Father's love in our very hearts.

There is a world of difference between having an intellectual conviction that there is a God who exists, and knowing him intimately as Father. We cannot manufacture this knowledge as it is experiential, and no amount of encouragement to believe this will enable another to experience it unless the Spirit bears witness with our spirit that we are his children. One of the principal works of the Spirit in our lives is to give us this knowledge experientially —that is so we know it, as someone wisely said in our "knower" and, in a measure, feel it. Few people have put this better than Jim Packer, who in his classic *Knowing God*, suggested that the teaching of the New Testament can be summed up by reference to its revelation of the Creator's Fatherhood. He rightly stresses the centrality for Christians of that Fatherhood.[4]

As Paul wrote to the Galatians,

Because you are sons, God sent the Spirit of his Son into our hearts, the Spirit who calls out *Abba*, Father. So you are no longer a slave, but a son; and since you are a son, God has made you also an heir.[5]

So we are not simply invited to believe in the Fatherhood of God as a propositional, doctrinal statement *about* God, but to enjoy, as sons or daughters, the living experience of him as our Father. But some people may have greater difficulty in appreciating or believing that they could possibly have a Heavenly Father who cares for them, as their experience of fatherhood makes it hard for them to grasp this. Anyone who has been a minister for a number of years realises that people have myriad views of what fatherhood means. For some, their father was either a distant or absent figure, for others he was a deserter who left their mother to do all that was necessary in bringing them up, to yet others he was a betrayer —betraying their mother for someone else whom he came to prefer. To another he is a distant memory, albeit happy, or simply a photograph, as he died in their infancy; to another he was a father re-discovered who had been thought dead when he suddenly appeared to be alive; to another he was a father who refused to acknowledge your existence because it was "socially difficult" (i.e. you were born out of wedlock at a time when such things were still socially unacceptable) and, worst of all, your father might have abused you physically or sexually or in some other particular way. I have known people who have suffered several of these failures in human fatherhood.

Equally, there are as many, hopefully more, who look back with affection and a warm glow on the care, interest, love, wisdom, security and strength that their fathers (and indeed both their parents) provided for them. Their ability to comprehend and experience the Fatherhood of God is more straightforward, because they already have a healthy view of fatherhood or parenthood. Others, with the Spirit's help, must overcome feelings of rejection, desertion, betrayal, abuse or varying degrees of neglect. Another group of all too common fathers in our achievement-orientated society are those who only bestow their favour when it is earned, and when their own high expectations and standards of achievement are reached. Such fathers are conspicuously operating an economy of good works in exchange for gaining appreciation, in contrast to our heavenly Father's economy of grace, in which he favours any who turn to him with faith.

Jesus taught his disciples to pray, "Our Father...." In other words, he told us to come to him as Father, and in that expression he revealed something of what God is like. But he did not just tell us, but provided a way for us to experience and know that he really is a Father to us, by adopting us into his family and giving us the Spirit to bear witness with our human spirit that we are his children.[6]

And this is his indication to us of his great love for us, as the "apostle of love", St John, tells us:

How great is the love the Father has lavished on us, that we should be called children of God! And that is what we are![7]

So the Spirit brings home to our hearts the reality of the Father's love for us, and that we are both his children and his heirs. Or, to put it another way, he is the one who makes the living, vibrant connection between our life and his. He does this with various degrees of intensity and feeling, which is his design for each of us. Indeed, one of the hallmarks of the Spirit's work in us is his variety. Again Paul makes this very clear when dealing with the Corinthian church, who fell into various errors with regard to the Spirit, concerning which they needed to be sorted out by the apostle. So Paul tells them,

> There are different kinds of gifts, but the same Spirit. There are different kinds of service, but the same Lord. There are different kinds of working, but the same God works all of them in all men.[8]

There is variety in what the Spirit gives, how he works and how he wishes us to serve. It is curiously ironic that the very church, which purported to be most "pentecostal" amongst the New Testament churches, namely the church at Corinth, was in danger of becoming more restrictive in terms of their expectations of the Spirit. They had made the gifts of the Spirit into trophies rather than tools, paying attention to two or three gifts but probably neglecting others. They came to prize the gift more than the giver, and to value the exercise of other gifts more highly than the gift of love. So in his corrective teaching to them, Paul on the one hand encouraged them to know the Spirit's life more and more, but on the other hand warned them not to replace the diversity of gifts with their more uniform view of his work, and not to prize the possession of gifts more highly than the exercise of love. And the greatest love, which we could know, is the love of the Father poured out into our hearts by the Holy Spirit.

It is the experience of this love in its various levels of intensity which is the primary work of the Spirit in the believer's life. So many people in various ways have borne witness to the work of the Holy Spirit in this respect. And they come from all corners of the church: the Catholic, the

Orthodox, the new churches and my own Anglican church. The test of the validity of these experiences of the Spirit is whether they lead to a greater knowledge of Christ, a greater service of Christ and a greater Christ-likeness in character and a fruitfulness of life, for, as Jesus said, "...by their fruits you shall know them."

D. L Moody and Blaise Pascal were separated by many years, language and church experience. They could not have been more different in calling and circumstance. The former was one of the great evangelists to have come out from America, on a par with Billy Graham in the twentieth century. He recalled an experience of God in New York which he recorded as follows:

One day in the city of New York, oh what a day, I cannot describe it, it is almost too sacred an experience to name. I can only say that God revealed himself to me and I had such an experience of his love that I had to ask him to stay his hand.[9]

Equally, Blaise Pascal an inventor, mathematician and philosopher, wrote of an experience he had of God's presence on November 23, 1654, the oft-quoted record of which began thus:

From about half-past ten in the evening till about half-past twelve, FIRE. God of Abraham, God of Isaac, God of Jacob, not of the philosophers and scholars (savants). Certainty. Certainty (certitude). Feeling (sentiment). Joy. Peace.[10]

These two are representative of many, many people who have found that the Spirit's witness may become suddenly strong, and indeed overwhelming.

Packer has expressed the view that the certitude and rapture which Augustine, Bernard, Luther, Calvin, Owen, Whitfield, Spurgeon and many others experienced is the direct fruit of the ministry of the Holy Spirit.

I for one am glad that we have moved on from the terminological arguments of the 1960s and '70s over whether we have been or need to be baptised, filled, drenched or released in the Holy Spirit, but have rather moved to a simple insistence that we need to receive as much of the Spirit as the Father will give us, which in turn means yielding as much of ourselves to the Spirit as he has pointed out needs his touch, presence and transformation. And lest any think they have arrived, it is the experience of Christians down the ages that the Spirit continues to point out areas of our lives which are not yet operating in perfect obedience to him! So the initial work of the Holy Spirit in the believer, having brought him/her to new birth in the kingdom, is to give us this inner awareness that "Father" is the reality of God for us, and that we are his children (by adoption), and indeed heirs; and then, having done this, he changes us so that we show greater and greater evidence of belonging to this heavenly and human family.

"Becoming fully human" means allowing that relationship to have its proper, supreme place in our lives. Knowing God as Father allows our humanity to blossom. Jesus taught in the Sermon on the Mount that such knowledge should remove anxiety over life itself, remove the cause of hypocrisy, since we need only aspire to please him alone (rather than perpetually comparing ourselves with others) and encourages trust in him who has even the hairs of our head counted! Knowing whose child you are is a prerequisite spiritually to becoming like the Father who gave us birth into his kingdom through the Spirit. It is the most wonderful connection to have made or relationship to be restored. But the Spirit's work by no means stops there.

FILLING THE BASKET WITH FRUIT

One of the most satisfying gardening experiences I have is to go into our patch at different times of year and fill whatever basket I have with the ripe fruits, whether strawberries, raspberries and redcurrants in the summer or apples, pears and plums in the early autumn. You are hard pressed to find people who do not like fruit, though I do have to admit that our young son, and he is twelve, has yet to taste any fruit, as he says he does not like any of them! That said, most people do find fruit irresistible. Paul, in this same letter to the Galatian Christians, teaches that our lives are like trees on which the Holy Spirit is actively producing fruit. They are the fruit of the Spirit, which sit alongside those other effects of the Spirit in the New Testament —the gifts of the Spirit.

Just as fruit grows slowly over spring and summer, heralded by blossom and then advertised to passers-by by its colour and seeming succulence, so the Spirit is active in the life of the believer to produce the fruits of true humanity, which likewise are attractive. For which right–minded person would not want themselves, a family member or a close friend to have these qualities of "love, joy peace, patience, kindness, goodness, faithfulness, gentleness and self-control"? It is possible that someone seeking to find fault might say that such a recipe for human nature sounds insipid; but that is because they have probably constructed their own stereotype around these qualities for a reason which itself is in need of redemption!

The trouble is that human failings are often far easier to depict than goodness. Stories to do with ambition, pride, greed and sex have always been fascinating to us, whether in the pages of Macbeth or between the covers of modern magazines! —although, in fairness to Shakespeare, he surely had more artistry than today's popular journals or soaps, even if the subject matter is at times, in essence, the same.

There are, for all of us, age–old choices to be made, which we have already traced in the seven choices already described in Part 2 of this book and which we meet, in one form or another, every day. These choices provide continual opportunities in daily living to exhibit "love, joy, peace, patience, kindness, goodness, faithfulness, gentleness and self-control". Paul shows us that the Holy Spirit helps us to make the right choices —by giving us new desires, indeed a new heart; by reminding us of what is God's will for our conduct; and by actively growing this fruit in our lives as we follow him.

Paul teaches there are two dynamics at work in us.

> So I say, live by the Spirit, and you will not gratify the desires of the sinful nature. For the sinful nature desires what is contrary to the Spirit, and the Spirit what is contrary to the sinful nature. They are in conflict with each other, so that you do not do what you want. But if you are led by the Spirit, you are not under the law.[11]

We may choose to follow the Spirit, keeping in step with him, and so allowing him to produce this fruit on the tree of our life, or we can ignore his urgings and choose to follow what Paul calls the sinful nature, which still exists in our lives, although its power to control us has been broken with Christ on the cross, as we saw in our previous chapter. In order to make this choice we must be convinced that the ways of the old sinful nature are both harmful to us and injurious to our relationship with the Father. Often, the strength of temptation is such that we may well find that it appeals to our old self life which is still present with us though its controlling power has been broken. At those moments of real temptation to fall into rage or sexual wrongdoing, ambition, jealousy, or any of those powerful sins—which Paul lists in Galatians and which we discussed earlier in this book, which all tend to diminish our humanity—we must remind ourselves that the power of this sin–inclined nature has been broken; that its seeming strength is in part bravado, and that the Spirit is the one to call upon to help us overcome the temptation. As we shall see, that is a struggle for all of us but it is the way we live now. In short, the cross and the Spirit are the exit provided, and, as when faced with a fire, we should look for and take the essential means of escape.

A friend once told me this: that whenever he stayed at an hotel for a night he always ascertained before turning in where the nearest way of escape was, in case there was a fire in the night! Paul concludes this section by referring himself to these twin means of escape, the cross and the Spirit, when he writes:

> Those who belong to Christ Jesus have crucified the sinful nature with its passions and desires. Since we live by the Spirit, let us keep in step with the Spirit.[12]

The way of escape is both crucifixion and companionship, dying with Christ and walking in the Spirit.

So the Spirit, having regenerated us, having brought us into the kingdom, made known to us our relationship with the father (adoption), now sets about what used to be called our sanctification or transformation, part of which is growing this crop of fruit in our lives, with our co-operation. It is a process, which does not let up for the whole of our lives!

TRANSFORMATION

To watch transformation going on is a fascinating thing. On a road at the edge of my parish, I noticed that builders have moved into an old house, which they are transforming into a family home of some splendour. On a piece of land behind another local house, a formal garden is being made. I was reminded that most of us, if we are honest, would love to look around and see what the new owners have done. This is analogous to the Christian life. When we truly start to follow Christ, we have a new owner and he sets to work transforming either the wilderness of our life or the jaded rooms of our existence into, to use another's phrase, "something beautiful for God".

To put it another way, many of us have been fascinated and shocked by the sudden loss of value in some telecommunications stocks, which has precipitated something called a "debt for equity swap", meaning that the banks, which have huge amounts owing to them by the crashed companies, remove or cancel the debt, amounting to billions of pounds sterling, in exchange for equity in the new business. Here is another picture of our Christian life. Jesus Christ takes the "crashed stock" of our personal lives, cancels the debt through his death on the cross, and takes up the position as **the** equity holder from then on. This is what the apostle teaches in these words: "You are not your own; you were bought at a price."[13]

But the process goes even further than a straight debt for equity swap. What also occurs is that a new manager comes in, to take forward the ongoing transformation process. The Holy Spirit—known as the Comforter, or Paraclete—is the one who draws alongside us. There is no adequate English translation of the latter, Greek, word. Packer reminds us that it means, by turns, "counsellor, helper, supporter, adviser, advocate, ally, senior friend."[14] He is the one who is sent to indwell us, and gradually to transform our life.

The principle of transformation is one that we can readily understand today. Attempts are being made to transform institutions and public services. The British government is attempting to follow a transformational model to change what they would term failing schools or hospitals. In one hospital in the region where I live, a new administrator was appointed to ensure a move from failure to success. It is not enough to pay off any debt, without at the same time sending in an expert, to help turn the school or hospital around. The amazing thing in God's plan is that he himself comes, a person of the godhead, to indwell everyone who has taken up his offer of forgiveness ("debt for equity"), and to oversee and help each individual in the process of transformation, which is underway.

It is not surprising to read Paul writing once more to the Corinthian church:

> And we, who with unveiled faces all reflect the Lord's glory, are being transformed into his likeness with ever-increasing glory, which comes from the Lord, who is the Spirit.[15]

Nothing could be clearer, nor more beautifully expressed, than this description of the process of becoming fully human!

The Spirit is restoring in us the likeness or image of God. This process of transformation is under way when we believe; it is not complete until heaven. In the meantime, each of us is a place of God's workmanship.

Many years ago I enjoyed a few holidays with a group of friends in Tuscany. We would visit Florence, to see the treasures of Renaissance art there. In those days it was easy to see them without pre-booking times in the most famous galleries and museums. One of the most memorable galleries was the Academy, which displayed some of Michelangelo's masterpieces. Alongside the huge and dynamic statue of David were a series of sculptures, by which Michelangelo showed the process of sculpture. The first of this series of sculptures was a piece of marble with barely a semblance of form and only the faintest definition of a figure emerging from the stone block. The second piece showed the emergence of two heads and shoulders; the third, legs and arms; and from the fourth there was emerging, as if by some act of powerful metamorphosis, the complete figures of prisoners emerging from the marble. It is astonishing to see the emergence of such life-like figures, expressing feelings of grief and tenderness, literally emerging from the hard, cold Italian marble, through the genius of Michelangelo. They are the work of an unsurpassed genius, who as a matter of interest, joined a group of devout Christians called the Nicodemes. This series of sculptures provides another picture of the work of the Spirit transforming our broken, hard or bankrupt lives into the likeness of Jesus, the Son of God. As Paul says, in his great eighth chapter of the Epistle to the Romans, it is by the Spirit we are being "conformed to the **likeness** of his Son" —and we are given this destiny by the Father. It is the Spirit who brings home the experience of being in the family of God; who begins the process of fruit production in our lives; and who continues the process of transformation in the interests of the new owner, bringing out the contours of Christ in the lives of his followers, who so become more fully human.

So it is through the life and incarnation of Christ as **the**

man, through the liberating death of Christ on the cross, and through the presence of the indwelling Spirit of Christ, that we may be transformed into the **likeness** of Jesus Christ, having our true humanity restored through the Spirit's gifts and graces. The context in which this happens is the focus of our final two chapters.

Notes

[1]   John 3:6.

[2]   2 Corinthians 3:7.

[3]   Luke 24:49.

[4]   See J. Packer, *Knowing God*, Hodder & Stoughton.

[5]   Galatians 4:6–7.

[6]   See Romans 8:16.

[7]   See 1 John 3:1.

[8]   1 Corinthians 12:4–6.

[9]   See David Watson, *I Believe in Evangelism* (Hodder and Stoughton, 1976), p. 182. Reproduced by permission of Hodder and Stoughton Ltd.

[10]   Quoted in: J. Packer, *Keep in Step with the Spirit*, IVP p. 78.

[11]   Galatians 5:16–18.

[12]   Galatians 5:24–25.

[13]   1 Corinthians 6:20.

[14]   Op. cit., see p. 61.

[15]   2 Corinthians 3:18.

14

The Way We Live Now

Few, if any, would deny that it is a struggle to become fully human. In Part 2 of this book we looked at some of the choices and conflicts that most of us face in life. In the last three chapters we have looked at the steps towards restoring our humanity. These steps involve us in thinking about both ends and means. What is the end or goal of our humanity? This is a crucial question. It is not a question that our postmodern society sets itself to answer, for, on the whole, it is much more preoccupied with means than with an end. Destiny questions seem to be unfashionable. Yet the Christian faith is all about destiny and seeks to answer the question: what is our destiny as human beings? —Or, to put it another way: for what were we created? What we have seen in the past few chapters is that Jesus Christ is **the** man who is the paradigm for the rest of us. And becoming fully human is to become like him. The more Christ–like we are, the more truly human we are. Nor is it possible to begin to become like him without help. The help that Christ himself gives is to show us the pattern of a truly human life, his life; to die for us so that we might be released from all those forces which harm and destroy our true humanity; and, lastly, to give us the Spirit, to inhabit our mortal bodies and undertake the process of transformation with our co-operation. But the context for this is our weakness, and because of that it is a struggle.

The way we live now is in the context of a struggle. The Christian experiences a struggle in the process of becoming fully human. At the outset the Christian is reminded of this at his or her baptism. We are told to fight against "the world, the flesh and the devil", and that we will have to continue Christ's faithful soldiers and servants for the rest of our lives. The Christian life is referred to as a fight, so that Paul at the end of his life says, "I have fought the good fight, I have finished the race, I have kept the faith."[1] And no-one wrote with greater feeling about the nature of this struggle than he did in Romans 7:18–20, as we have already seen.

The vexed question, which has taxed commentators, Christian authors and teachers alike for centuries, is who is the "I" in that passage, or to whom is Paul referring? ("I know that nothing good lives in me....") Of course we know it is Paul writing, but is he referring to his experience as a Jew and not as a Christian? Or, to put it differently, is Paul writing in this section of Romans about his life before he was a Christian —or now that he is one? After all, the answer to that question will make a difference to what we can expect from our Christian living and how we may fare. The fact is that many teachers of the faith are divided on the interpretation of this passage. Some believe Paul is talking about his experience of moral failure as a Christian. They say that Paul is using his own experience to depict this universal struggle to become what we know we should be. Others say that such an interpretation is too gloomy. For if Christians who have known the Spirit of God, his love and grace, at work in their lives, have to say, " I have the desire to do good but I cannot carry it out", what does it say about the effect of receiving such blessings? John Stott takes the view that the person depicted in Romans chapter seven, whilst regenerate, is not a mature believer, evidently being still "under" the law, and not yet filled with the Holy Spirit.[2]

Maybe the best way of interpreting this passage is in the light of other passages of Scripture, some of which we have already seen. We have already noted that Paul teaches elsewhere that when we believe not only is our standing before God changed from being an enemy to a friend, but that there is an inward change in us, so that we are told that we have died to sin, meaning that it need no longer control us. We have seen that there is a real change in the Christian. Equally, the prophets of the Old Testament defined the new covenant as giving the believer a new heart and having a new spirit within them; and Paul says, anyone who is in Christ is a "new creation". What sort of a new creation or new heart or new spirit is it that leaves the individual believer in the same position as before — seeing the good, but not being be able to do it? To say that Paul in these verses is describing his experience as a Christian would be to diminish the effect of belonging to the new covenant, of having the Spirit dwelling in the heart and life of the believer, and of having the power of the old life broken. All these three effects Paul teaches elsewhere in his letters. However, if Paul is indeed describing his pre–conversion life, it would be a mistake to then go on to say that the Christian does not still have the experience of struggle in the process of becoming fully human. In fact, it is precisely because there has been the sort of teaching in the church that says that we can reach some state of perfection or steady–state–holiness, in which there are few, if any, dips below a constant standard of near perfect godly behaviour, that more realistic people have said this passage of Paul's is the true description of the Christian's experience. I can understand that, but our first impression of this passage is surely both the natural one and the right one, given Paul's teaching elsewhere —that Paul is describing his pre-Christian experience in his struggle to fulfil the Law.

But even if we say that Paul is describing his experience before he fully knew the grace of God and the help of the Spirit and the effect of the cross on his inward life, that does not mean that there is not still a struggle. For Paul's description of himself before being a Christian is still applicable to a part of him after he became a Christian —and indeed to any Christian **after** having become a Christian. For as Paul makes perfectly plain to the Christians in Galatia, we still have the ongoing choice of either living by the Spirit or living according to that old sinful nature or flesh, which is still around us but need not control us.[3]

Paul says, "Live by the Spirit, and you will not gratify the desires of the sinful nature." So our will is involved in choosing either to be led by the Spirit (and so choosing not to be led by our own old sinful nature) or by the flesh (meaning what is in us that is still opposing or rebelling against God.) This does involve us in an ongoing struggle or conflict, as Paul says in his instruction to the Galatians. We must learn to live by the Spirit —that is "the way we live now" in the process of becoming fully human. But we engage in this conflict knowing a number of vital things: that the Father has embraced us, and has given us a new robe of righteousness; that we have the indwelling Spirit; and we know that the old nature need not control our life. So Paul says to the Romans: "You, however, are controlled not by the sinful nature but by the Spirit, if the Spirit of God lives in you...."[4]

To summarise, the path to becoming fully human involves us in a struggle. It is not a struggle which we must lose because there is an unassailable impotency in our lives. We have been equipped with the Spirit, who can keep us clear of inevitably falling prey to our sinful nature, which is present but no longer dominant, or to the flesh, by our following the Spirit's leading. And we may only follow his leading if we keep in the step with the Spirit. This keeping in step is an act of the will and an act of co-operation, in which we choose not to enter into the acts of the sinful nature, but rather choose to keep in step with what the Spirit desires. We looked at some of those choices in earlier chapters. In choosing well we are keeping in step with the Spirit. Choosing may involve a great struggle sometimes, and what we should be aiming at is a gradual transformation, in which we move from one degree of glory to another. If we take care of openness to the Holy Spirit, the results will take care of themselves! Or, to change the metaphor, the fruit of the Spirit will swell and ripen on the branches of our life.

IN WEAKNESS

We also, in a certain sense, live in weakness. It is hard to find a person who is on the path to fuller humanity who is not aware of their weakness —not that this makes us gloomy, far from it, for we shall see that it should only increase our hope, our honesty and our humour, all of which we shall look more at later in this chapter. But awareness of our human weakness should keep us from triumphalism, hypocrisy, smugness and arrogance, all of which is usually sniffed out by our candid critic at a thousand paces!

Weakness comes in all shapes and sizes. Some weakness comes from our upbringing and our childhood, some from what we inherit from our families, even going back three or four generations. Some weakness is due to patterns of behaviour, which have taken up residence in our sinful nature before we were Christians. Some of those established patterns may be stubborn and deeply ingrained, and may require considerable prayer, love, support and counsel if they are to be sifted. The struggle with those things may be protracted, and again we note that the model of Christ's life, the power of the cross and the dynamic of the Spirit co-operating with our own will are means of gradual change, "from one degree of glory to another". Occasionally, a glorious miracle may take place, by the power of the Holy Spirit, and the pattern of behaviour can be radically and quickly changed. Just as some people's conversion to Christ can occur over time, so change for most people will occur gradually, but for others there may be a sudden and dramatic change from a way of life which is incompatible with Christ's call to discipleship.

But there are other kinds of weakness, which are not essentially moral, but physical or psychological. To put it another way, some people's weaknesses are related to their state of mind or personality. Some may be prone to anxiety, over–confidence, impetuosity, diffidence, timidity, fear; they are, if you like, states of mind, which they must deal with in the development of becoming fully human, and everyone must be working on some trait or disposition, which is part of their make-up. For most of us, that is an ongoing struggle in which the word of God straightens out our thinking, the power of God helps us with our weakness, and the cross provides a continual source of forgiveness, new starts and grace. To some extent the church has neglected this pastoral teaching of late, and surely when the world is more and more fascinated with the inner life of people, which is exhibited in ever more television soaps and "reality TV" programmes like *Big Brother*, it behoves the church to teach more clearly on the path of becoming fully human which is especially its concern.

For all the invective heaped upon them, the group of writers and preachers who most effectively charted the course down which a human soul must travel to become fully human were the Puritans. The best known of the Puritan writers is John Bunyan who, in charting the pilgrim's progress shows how, with the help of the word, the cross and the Spirit, he dealt with the many temptations and trials he found *en route* to the celestial city. Likewise, our own particular foibles and weaknesses provide the context for some of the struggles with which we must contend on the path to becoming fully human.

But not all weakness is due either to received or established patterns of behaviour or our own particular frame of mind. There is also the weakness caused by the interplay of our body, mind and spirit. If this seems rather mysterious, then the most well known example is the weakness from which Paul suffered, and of which he speaks to the Corinthians, showing that God had left him with—or allowed Satan to trouble him with—a "thorn in the flesh". Some Christians have been at great pains to show that this could not possibly be a physical blemish or problem, although it is quite clear that elsewhere the great apostle did have bad eyesight, and complained that, as a consequence of it, his handwriting had deteriorated.[5] Whether it was a physical or psychological problem, and presumably it is more likely the former than the latter, it was nevertheless a real aspect of his life, and it was bad enough for Paul to have pleaded three times to God that it be removed! However, Paul got a highly significant reply from God in answer to this request, which was: "My grace is sufficient for you, for my power is made perfect in weakness."[6] So what is indisputable is that Paul did suffer weakness from whatever source; it was a considerable hindrance to him; and God said he should live with it, so that his power would be made perfect in Paul's weakness.

Why is all this so important? Because it reminds us that the path to full humanity does not lead us to physical, moral, and psychological perfection in this life. In fact we all must wrestle with physical, moral or psychological issues throughout our lives. What God promised Paul is that in this process our new humanity would be forged, and that his power would be made perfect in our weakness. Nor is this to say that God does not heal, or does not deliver. He can and does do both, whenever he chooses. But the working of his grace is not mechanical but personal; it is varied and not uniformly the same. It is the straitjacketing of God's grace—an insistence that he works according to our own programme—which so often leads into difficulties, and into placing pressure rather than love upon the individual.

You could imagine some of the more zealous Corinthian Christians visiting Paul when he was suffering a bad bout of "thorn in the flesh", and telling him that God could remove it. Of course he could, but for the reasons that Paul states, he chose not to. What we can say assuredly is that God's pre-eminent purpose in us is our holiness even more than our comfort. We are in danger of forgetting that in the Western church!

Down the ages there have been a myriad of Christians who have shown that their weakness is no obstacle to God's use of them, in fact the reverse. Martin Luther, not surprisingly, given the circumstances of his life, sometimes grew depressed. He faced what was called *anfechtung*, for which there is no equivalent English word. It "may be a trial sent by God to test man, or an assault by the Devil to destroy man. It is also the doubt, turmoil, pang, tremor, panic, despair desolation and desperation which invade the spirit of man."[7] Luther suffered from such attacks, and he the man who rediscovered the justifying grace of God for the church after it had been buried for generations under the relics, indulgences and penances of the medieval church! To counteract such moods he sometimes went out to dig in his garden, spread muck on the fields, or cry out in the night to his beloved Katie, "Forbid me to have such temptations and recall me from such vain vexations!"[8] —or enjoyed beer and music at his table with convivial companionship!

The great Christian poets Cowper, Rossetti, and Manley Hopkins all suffered from gloom and depression —and, in Rossetti's case, anxiety. Yet all wrote most wonderfully of the Christian faith. Rossetti wrote one of our best-loved carols, *In the Deep Mid–Winter*.[9] The very vulnerability created by their weakness made them hunger more deeply for a true knowledge of God. This is not to make a virtue of their weakness itself, but their weakness becomes a context in which God shows his grace and makes them more sensitive to—and consious of their dependence upon—his presence. But if such well-known Christians exhibited a measure of glory through the frailty of their weakness, this is, in fact, true for every Christian.

As Paul says, "But we have this treasure in jars of clay to show that this all–surpassing power is from God and not from us."[10] It is in the context of weakness that God works new humanity in us, conforming us to the image of his Son who, although more powerful than any, hid that power in the weakness of human life. So weakness, and the vulnerability that is consequent upon it, is not to be fled from, but is the very stuff in which our true humanity may be shown forth. It is also a cause for Christian hope.

HOPE IN THE FACE OF DEATH

So the Christian lives in a state of struggle, and is conscious of weakness, but also lives in hope. In the Pauline trilogy of faith, love and hope, **hope** is the forgotten factor of Christian discipleship. You could say that hope in Christian discipleship needs to be rehabilitated. We can think of movements within the church which have stressed both faith and love, but who can really think of a movement of hope in the church? Hope is the forgotten facet of Christian living; the Cinderella at the ball of Christian celebration! Again, this is a direct result of the culture in which we live, which expects to receive everything now. If this is true of our consumerism it is also sometimes true of our expression of the Christian faith. The fact is, as the bishop in the railway carriage well knew, the greater part of our salvation lies in the future, and what we receive now is a down payment. It seems that hope is not always invited to the feast, and why, we ask, is that?

One of the reasons may be that hope is not as fashionable today as faith and love. Paul has certainly given us a clear order for this premier league of Christian virtues. Love remains at the top because, as he taught, it will outlast the other two great Christian characteristics.[11] It will do so because faith and hope are only needed for this life and will have no part to play in heaven. But in this earthly life we need both faith and hope to keep us in balance.

The reason why hope has such a poor press today is partly because it is out of kilter with our present age, partly because our view of hope is so superficial and partly because it seems that we focus our faith so much on the present that we leave the future out of our perspective. If that all seems rather a conundrum, let me explain.

As we have already said in earlier chapters, we have sought in our Western culture to take the waiting out of wanting; that is a cultural given of our society. We all know that we live in a culture which wants fast and instant access to the web or to a consumer product or to locations around the world by virtue of faster and smoother travel. We get impatient if we do not have quickly what we want! Yet it is clear that God is not in a hurry! He never was. Indeed, he has set things up in such a way that we have to learn to wait.

After all, he has now kept the world waiting over two thousand years for the return of his Son. And we are told only he knows the timetable for that event, for not even Christ himself knew when he would return to planet earth. Because the fulfilment of the kingdom of God is dependent on that momentous event, we are all therefore consigned to live in hope for the duration of our own lives (unless he should return). The earth or environment also lives in hope for its planetary history to be fulfilled. This is Paul's teaching in his famous eighth chapter of Romans, where he says,

> The creation waits in eager expectation for the sons of God to be revealed. For the creation was subjected to frustration, not by its own choice, but by the will of the one who subjected it, in hope that the creation itself will be liberated from its bondage to decay and brought into the glorious freedom of the children of God.[12]

So the whole of creation is waiting, in hope, for its liberation from the bondage of decay. We are acutely aware of the failures of the international community to care for the planet, as demonstrated at the UN conference at Johannesburg in 2002, which ended in considerable disarray. Hope is now a hallmark of creation's existence, because one day, amazingly, it will be liberated from the bondage of decay imposed on it by human abuse.

Likewise, every Christian hopes. It is an essential aspect of our discipleship. Now we only have the first down payment of the Spirit; only the first fruits. The idea of first fruits would have been very familiar to the agrarian Jewish society, although perhaps not so familiar to the urban society of Rome, to whom Paul was writing about this. The idea of first fruits is a perfect illustration of Paul's point.

Generally speaking, fruits do not ripen all at once. In late August I can go to a plum tree in our garden and find just a few plums that are ripe, and eat them. They are the first fruits, which in Jewish law were customarily given to God as thanks for the whole crop. But most of the crop is still to come. This is the picture of the Spirit's presence in us. Now we have only a modicum of what will finally be made available. So we are hoping for the rest. And while we wait with creation itself, with which we are intrinsically linked, we groan; and this groaning is a sign of our frustration in waiting. But wait we must because "we are saved in hope" until either Christ returns or we die.

In our present instant society, we want to take the groaning and the waiting–in–hope out of our discipleship, so that in both our living and in our Christian teaching we often do people the grave disservice of making them think that we can have it all now. If that is the impression we give, it is a distortion of the Christian faith. What we have now is the first fruits, with the guarantee of more to come. But the greater part of our salvation for which we hope lies in the future and in heaven.

Another reason why hope can be overlooked is because we have such a weak idea of what hope really is. In the Walker Art Gallery in Liverpool there hangs a picture entitled *Hope*, by the Victorian painter G.F. Watts. It shows a female figure in what could be described as a diaphanous nightie, seated piteously on the world, blindfolded. She is playing a lyre with three strings, two of which have already broken. That is hoping against hope that things will turn out all right! It is, of course, not what is meant by Christian hope. The foundation of Christian hope is God's work in Christ who died and was raised to life. The lifestyle of this hope is to live in the power of the Spirit, sharing in whatever suffering comes to us, but which cannot be compared with the glory, which is to come. The goal of this hope is the fulfilment of the kingdom of God, which was inaugurated in Christ's earthly ministry and will be completed at his return. Our hope is based, therefore, on what has been done in the past and on what is promised for the future, and of which we have experiential knowledge now in the Spirit. It is this hope, which can both deal with and surmount the fear of death, that should be a hallmark of Christian living. Few things are more humbling than the quiet trust of a dying person in God's gift of eternal life; that is hopeful living, and healthy 'euthanasia', in its literal sense, good or happy death, not the meaning it has, sadly, come to bear (involving killing).

JOYFULLY

So the way we live now, as we become fully human people, is with a struggle, in weakness, hopefully and, finally, joyfully. Paul sets out the causes of this joy in the closing verses of his eighth chapter of Romans. The foundations of this joy are these facts: that nothing can separate us from the love of God; that no charge will stand against those whom God has chosen; and that, in all the circumstances of life, God is at work for the good of those who love him. The natural disposition of the Christian should therefore be joyful! It is a paradox that we can both feel the intensity of the struggle and at the same time be conscious of an unparalleled joy. Yet this is the apostolic witness. More than in any other of his writings, it is Paul's second letter to the Corinthians that bears this out. It is a letter which appears to run on the twin rails of glory and suffering. This dual theme is, in fact, demonstrated in the apostle himself, who writes:

> Rather, as servants of God we commend ourselves in every way: in great endurance; in troubles, hardships and distresses; in beatings, imprisonments and riots; in hard work, sleepless nights and hunger; in purity, understanding, patience and kindness; in the Holy Spirit and in sincere love; in truthful speech and in the power of God; with weapons of righteousness in the right hand and in the left; through glory and dishonour, bad report and good report; genuine, yet regarded as impostors;

known, yet regarded as unknown; dying, and yet we live on; beaten, and yet not killed; sorrowful, yet always rejoicing; poor, yet making many rich; having nothing, and yet possessing everything.[13]

Perhaps the phrase that summarises Paul's frame of mind is, "sorrowful, yet always rejoicing". It is a paradox, hard to understand, but nevertheless reflects the attitude of Christ who was both full of joy and a man of suffering and acquainted with grief.

So in the process of becoming fully human we will be more than aware of our weaknesses, but rejoicing in our hope. Once again we may learn from Luther. It has been observed that he loved nature, art, playing and composing, as well as poetry and gardening; he took delight in the created order, which helped him to perceive the wisdom of God; and he valued the simple, trusting faith of children.[14]

Despite the *anfechtung* there was joy. This joy was based on the foundational belief that "nothing can separate us from the love of God". This joy works itself out in glad and generous hearts and humour. This humour, which I have found close to the surface in the lives of all those who are becoming truly human, shows itself in various ways, one of which is having a wry opinion of ourselves. This means pursuing our calling with wholehearted devotion whilst at the same time acknowledging that we are not indispensable to God's purposes! Yes, amazingly, he can manage without us, although we find it hard to believe! This humour takes delight in the sheer variety, scale and richness of his creation.

So it is, in this four-sided frame of living, that we make our slow progress to becoming fully human, engaging in struggle, acknowledging our weakness, living in hope and continuing to rejoice. This is the way we live now, fixing our eyes on the model man, and living close to the cross and in the power of the Spirit. But we do this in a community called the church, and with mixed feelings we must now look at this place of transformation —which **hopefully** is what it is!

257

Notes

[1]   2 Timothy 4:7.
[2]   See John Stott, *Epistle to the Romans* (BST series), p. 199.
[3]   Galatians 5:16–18.
[4]   Romans 8:9.
[5]   See Galatians 6:11.
[6]   2 Corinthians 12:9b.
[7]   Roland Bainton, *Here I Stand*, Abingdon Press, Nashville, TN, USA, p. 31.
[8]   Ibid., p. 285.
[9]   See: Dr Gaius Davies, *Genius and Grace*, or *The Stricken Deer* by Cecil, on the life of the poet and hymn writer Cowper.
[10]   2 Corinthians 4:7.
[11]   1 Corinthians 13:13.
[12]   Romans 8:19–21.
[13]   2 Corinthians 6:4 –10.
[14]   A most helpful account of Luther's character will be found in: James Atkinson, *Martin Luther and the Birth of Protestantism* (Pelican, 1968).

15

The Place of Transformation

The church is the community where we should be becoming fully human, but I turn to thinking about it with mixed feelings, because the church seems rather like that girl with the curl of nursery rhyme fame, who, "...when she was good, was very, very good, but when she was bad she was horrid"! Straight away, we who are church members must admit that the church, both historically and presently, is both wonderful and embarrassingly awful! The reasons for this are not far to seek. As has often been pointed out, although called to honesty, we are prone to hypocrisy; although called to generosity, we can seem extraordinarily nit-picking; although called to love, we can be surprisingly full of rivalry and partisanship; although called to minister to the equivalent of the "tax collector and the sinner", we can seem both remarkably insular and exclusive; and, although called to peace, the church has often in times past seemed blindly belligerent —yes, and even, in the distant past, bloodthirsty; and for all of that, and more, we owe the watching world a deep apology. There is much to repent of, both in the present and in the past. But to balance the scales, there are many exceptions to these considerable blemishes on the record of the church. There are many remarkable saints, both known and unknown—and churches, missions and communities—which have served the kingdom of God in our world, displaying the just and gentle rule of Christ.

What seems indefensible is to be defensive about the bad bits, but admit sadly that the church, rather than being all too human, was and is, in fact, the reverse: all too inhuman. For we have been at pains to show that true humanity is to be like Christ. We must face square on that if becoming fully human is an essential by–product of truly belonging to the church (by which I simply mean a community of believers, wherever they may be found, and however organised) then we have often signally failed to display that humanity to those who are looking in—whether enquiringly, hopefully, or sometimes plain mystified—from the outside. What they may see is a group of people forever taken up with their meetings, groups or ceremonies, but curiously reticent to speak in plain language about what makes them tick and how they see the world. As the rest of the world looks in from the outside, it is looking for evidence that our Lord makes a difference. The world is listening to our words and trying to see whether our words match what they observe, for, as always, actions speak louder than words —for without actions they cannot see the kingdom, and without words they cannot understand. Too often, there is not much evidence that needs explaining, and the words are often incomprehensible! Of course this is not the whole story, because there are many who do not want either to see or listen because it would lead to a change in their lifestyle, or because the "god of this age" has blinded them.[1]

But the conclusion to which this book is nonetheless moving is that to be truly human is to be more like Christ, in whom we see the Father. To grow closer to God through Christ is to have his image in us restored, and so at the same time to become like him. This was God's plan to reverse the effects of our disobedience which is traced back to Adam. The community in which this transformation takes place is the church in its widest definition.

But as God's kingdom is wider than the church, this transformation goes on wherever the kingdom is found. And the kingdom is found wherever the just and gentle rule of Christ holds sway and he is named as Lord. Let us not be too hasty in saying where that is. This transformation is going on wherever men, women and children love and follow Christ, the King. Normally this will be within the church but sometimes it will be outside; after all, to which church or synagogue did the dying thief on the cross belong? Yet he was admitted to paradise on the recognition of Christ's kingship and confession of his need. If the church, in God's plan, is to be the place or community in which we find transformation "from one degree of glory to another", what are the ways in which this comes about? Already we have looked at "a framework for understanding" concerning the way in which this transformation can come about. As Graham Tomlin writes in his book *The Provocative Church,*

> Transformation involves a new framework for understanding the world and ourselves as the rightful property of God. It involves the establishment of new habits, new patterns of life, new approaches to people and circumstances. It means living as if all that Christian theology is true: that Jesus is Lord of heaven and earth, that he has risen from the dead, and therefore death is ultimately a broken, defeated enemy no longer to be feared. It means living as if Christ died for my sins, and therefore even though I continue to commit them, ultimately they are dealt with and I need not live covered with shame. It means treating each person I meet as someone created in the likeness of God, precious and with dignity, with the potential of sharing God's nature again. It means living as if this really is a world graced with God's goodness, a world to be celebrated, protected and preserved as God's possession and gift. It means living as if I am loved, unconditionally, warmly, constantly and totally.[2]

Within this "framework of understanding", God begins and continues this process of gradual change, which involves changes of behaviour, sloughing off old patterns of life which do not follow our confession of being one of Christ's followers, and planting new ones —challenging (and transforming) attitudes towards ourselves, others, and God. It is a lifetime's process without let up, but therefore ever challenging to us, and it literally keeps us young. It involves us in making those choices which we examined in Part 2 of this book.

The particular means that God employs to transform us in the context of the church, which we shall look at more closely, are: his word, the sacraments, fellowship and prayer. In order for this transformation into becoming more fully human to take place, we must be open to being addressed by God in his word; live out what is signified by the sacraments; speak to God, and listen to him, in prayer; and share in the fellowship of the church. We shall look at each in turn.

OPENNESS TO GOD'S WORD

St Peter tells us that "men moved by the Holy Spirit" wrote from God. Peter puts it well when he says that the authors of the Bible were "moved" by the Spirit. They were. They were moved to write and record the events they witnessed or were about to witness, giving their divine significance, as led by the Holy Spirit. The Spirit did not remove their personalities and circumstances, but used them, inspiring them in such a way that we see God's actions from the standpoint, heartbeat and perspective of different men; so what we have is both human and divine. In so doing, they gave to humankind an authoritative, God–breathed record of all that we need to know for our salvation. As with all combining of the supernatural with the natural, whether it is the person of Christ, the realities of the sacraments, an explanation of the atonement or the miracle of the resurrection, the categories which we have been given by the biblical authors themselves are normative. What is certain is that where God's power works through human or physical means, we can soon exhaust our categories of understanding or explanation. In the case of the Scriptures, which authenticated themselves in the life of the early church, the medium for understanding God's grace is words. These words, written by men over thousands of years in all kinds of styles, were inspired by the Spirit of God. So now, as we read them, they are taken by the same Spirit who inspired their writing and are wielded by him in the hearts of individual Christians and in the life of the community of the church. Indeed, as St Paul says, the word of God is "the sword of the spirit". If we are to truly benefit from this word, which always leads us to Christ, then several qualities are especially necessary: honesty, sincerity and openness.

I well remember a leader of another South London church telling me the tragic story of a church member's suicide. What was especially poignant was that this man had belonged to the church for several years. He had been a member of a small group, which amongst other things studied the Bible together on a regular basis, but the tragedy was that, for whatever reasons, he had not been able to say anything about his problems to any other member of the group. You ask yourself the question: what prevented him from doing that? Was it too 'unreal'? Was there some filter at work in the group which meant that real issues for its members could not be discussed? Or was it that he could not simply speak openly to the others about his doubts and fears, which grew to a point of overwhelming him? It is too easy for such groups to fall into the pitfall of simply being a place where accepted propositional statements about our faith are exchanged but few people say what are the real struggles they have, with work, money, the family and so on. If a group is the wrong place to share whatever concerns a person may have, then some other more confidential, trustworthy and unjudgmental relationship needs to exist, so that the truth may come out and healing be found.

Honesty is an especially important quality in church, because there are so many reasons why someone can feel the need to be dishonest. They do not want to lose face; they dare not admit to a problem because of fear of disapproval; they do not want to disappoint, and they want to be seen to be on the winning side when it comes to their own discipleship. The result can sometimes be that the very person who has wrestled with some problem for years gets to a point where they can no longer go on living a lie, and suddenly they do a complete *volte face*, with sometimes huge repercussions to their family or church —especially if that person is a leader. Honesty must be the key to dealing with the problem: honesty in the person himself or herself, so that they can admit that they have a problem, but also a culture of honesty in the church, so that if they were to talk of their innermost secret somewhere in the church they would not be "run out of town". But sadly, too often, churches are places of make-believe (make others believe that all is fine and dandy) rather than places where weaknesses can be shown in the process of becoming fully human. Honesty in response to God's word is probably a culture which is contagious —and it needs to begin with the leadership of the church.

The fact is that we also all read Scripture with cultural spectacles. Or, to put it another way, we all have a tradition in which we have been nurtured, which can act as a filter, so that we only see those bits of Scripture which conform to that tradition. Often, we will have very good reasons for leaving out parts of Scripture which we may believe are no longer operative in today's church. What is ironic is that people who hold the highest possible doctrine of the inspiration of Scripture can be the very ones who, for other reasons, are willing to leave bits out which do not fit into the tradition which acts as a control on how they interpret it. In this regard, humility must be the starting point to openness. Openness is essential to the reading of Scripture because through reading it we expect to hear from the Spirit who inspired it in the first place, and who addresses us in Scripture now. It is through humility leading to openness and honesty, leading to integrity, that we may find our lives gradually moulded by Scripture. The reading of Scripture, which in turn must lead to the moulding of our lives in obedience to the call of the Spirit through it, is vital in the process of making us fully human. The community of the church, which itself is gathered around Scripture, can help us to hear, understand and obey its message, day by day.

THE SACRAMENTS

There are two sacraments which were given to us by Jesus, and they both look in two directions: backward and forward. In the first instance, both of them look back to the cross, in different ways. We shall look at both of them in turn, beginning with baptism.

Normative baptism in the New Testament is adult baptism after a profession of faith in Jesus as Lord and Saviour. This was what was envisaged by Peter at the day of Pentecost when he urged the crowd which was listening to him to respond, saying to them, "...Repent and be baptised, every one of you, in the name of Jesus Christ for the forgiveness of your sins. And you will receive the gift of the Holy Spirit."[3] However, notwithstanding this normative practice, I would argue, along with Calvin in his *Institutes*, that God's promise of grace is made to the whole family, so that children of a believing parent or parents may receive the sign of being within the covenant, which is baptism in the new covenant as it was circumcision in the old. As the child grows up, he or she would need to make the Christian profession, thus owning or accepting what was said on his/her behalf by parents. But this is not the place to fully consider the merits or otherwise of infant baptism. The point we are more concerned with here is that baptism looks backward and forward.

Baptism looks back, in that through it (and this is especially evident in baptism by immersion) the new disciple understands that he has been "crucified with Christ". We saw, when considering Paul's teaching in Romans chapter 6, how he counters the suggestion that God's grace is simply a blank cheque to sin, that "grace may abound", writing: "...don't you know that all of us who were baptised into Christ Jesus were baptised into his death?"[4] He means that in some way, which we looked at earlier, a part of us died with Christ on the cross, which led to an internal change making us different. The thing which died was the dominance of our old nature, so that now, in the Spirit, we are capable of pleasing God. Baptism also marks a break with past allegiances. Those allegiances to race, class and gender, which previously dominated our lives, are replaced by belonging to a new family and kingdom —which encompasses every race as equal, makes no distinction between classes, and esteems equally the roles of male and female. Baptism looks back to this death and burial with Christ of the old way of life. This radical change is signified as the candidate plunges under the water in baptism. In our own church we have hired a birthing pool from the midwifery department of the local hospital, and with our bishop presiding in his robes (outside the pool!), several adult candidates have been baptised in that way in past years.

If the sacrament or sign of baptism looks backward to the death of the old way of life, with Christ on the cross, it also looks forward to a new life of active service of God in the power of the Spirit. As we saw earlier, this is best encapsulated in the liturgical words we use at the baptism, when the minister says to the candidate, "Fight valiantly as a disciple of Christ against sin, the world and the devil, and remain faithful to Christ to the end of your life", and in the prayer, "May almighty God deliver you from the powers of darkness, restore in you the image of his glory, and lead you in the light and obedience of Christ." Baptism looks forward to a lifetime's service, a lifelong fight against powers which work in opposition to the kingdom of God, and a lifelong process of the image of God being restored in the candidate, so that he or she may become more fully human. When the significance of those words in the prayer becomes clear, we see that it is a prayer we can continue to pray for any Christian who has embarked on the path of discipleship.

Equally, the Lords Supper, Holy Communion or Eucharist looks back as well as forward. It, too, looks back to the events of Christ's crucifixion and resurrection, in particular to the meal that Christ himself gave us to remember his death and its significance. When we take and eat the bread and wine in faith, they are signs to us of our forgiveness and acceptance on the grounds of Christ's death. But the meal, too, looks forward to the return of the King, the fulfilment of the kingdom when a heavenly feast with the King may be enjoyed. In the meantime, in the near future, as Volf says, "at the Lord's supper Christians remember the One who gave his body 'for them' so that they would be shaped in his image."[5]

The sharing in the bread and wine is, once again, part of the process of having God's image restored in those who believe. One of the eucharistic prayers of *Common Worship* says, "As we eat and drink these holy things in your presence, form us in the **likeness** of Christ, and build us into a living temple to your glory."[6]

The sacraments of baptism and the Lord's supper remind us that in Christ's death we are set free from the past and its old allegiances, and given new eternal allegiances. Volf writes, "At the very core of Christian identity lies an all-encompassing change of loyalty, from a given culture with its gods...."[7] That could not be more important, for it reminds us of the creation of new ties of loyalty to other Christians, supplanting ethnic, social or economic ties. Yet, in reality, how far short we fall of this ideal, whether we look to those parts of the church in Rwanda which were caught up in the perpetration of violence in that country's holocaust, or to our backyard, where we fail to cross bridges of culture in our own churches. Nevertheless, despite all the failings on the part of ecclesial institutions and ordinary Christians, both sacraments have their place in the process of God's image in us being gradually restored, and so of our becoming more fully human.

FELLOWSHIP

We are to become fully human within the context of community. Jean Vanier, the founder of the worldwide L'Arche community has helpfully pointed out that we need to be in a place of belonging in order to grow in maturity, and to be and act in a more human way. He underlines the social dimension, stressing that we learn to trust—and that we are loved—in community with others. Absence of community means that we miss some of what God has for us.[8]

Indeed, we were not meant to be alone. On the one hand there is the community of family, with all its varied and extended relationships working out from marriage. On the other hand there is also the community of the church, God's family into which we come through faith in Christ. This is a worldwide family, in which we are all brothers and sisters.

The most common analogy that Paul uses to explain the church is that of a body in which there is great variety of function and honour, but unity of purpose and existence. In this body we may each have our different gifts and experiences of God working, but we cannot remain untouched by the needs and joys of others. So Paul writes, "If one part suffers, every part suffers with it; if one part is honoured, every part rejoices with it."[9] So the mutual pastoral care, which individual members of the local church give to each other and to the secular community in which the church meets, should be a hallmark of its existence.

In our own church this is shown in many ways begun by the church members, such as: meals being provided by members of the church for those who have recently had babies; a lunch club for older members, called the SAS, or "Senior All Saints", with the motto "Who cares, wins!" —and copious jokes about them going into action with all sticks blazing! Work amongst parents and children, the holding of marriage and family courses and early morning breakfasts for men are common, not only to us but to many thousands of churches up and down the country. Often they form an outreach to the community in which God's love may be shown at a point of need, and they may also be a form of pastoral care and fellowship within the church itself but open to all. In both cases they are a sharing of fellowship.

However, the essence of Christian fellowship is a common experience of sharing in the grace of God. It is this common experience, brought home to our hearts by the Spirit, which forges the bond that is fellowship. As St Paul said to the Philippian church, "If you have any encouragement from being united with Christ, if any comfort from his love, if any fellowship with the Spirit, if any tenderness and compassion, then make my joy complete by being like-minded, having the same love, being one in spirit and purpose."[10] The point is that fellowship should lead to unity through humility. The sadness is that self–interest too often gets in the way, so preventing the fellowship working itself out in unity. So repeatedly, in the New Testament, leaders and members of churches are called back to humility and compassion, which in turn will promote fellowship.

Fellowship is the soil in which our new humanity in Christ grows. It is also a cause for further development of fruit of the Spirit, as we integrate with people in the church who are quite different from ourselves. It is together with all the saints that we are able to grasp, "...how wide and long and high and deep is the love of Christ, and to know this love that surpasses knowledge."[11] As we grasp more of the extent of this love, we are further transformed from one degree of glory to another.

Indeed, fellowship is both the goal of Christ's work here on earth and one of the means that enables us to become fully human. It is the goal of Christ's work, as Paul explains to the Ephesian Christians:

> His purpose was to create in himself one new man out of the two, thus making peace, and in this one body to reconcile both of them* to God through the cross, by which he put to death their hostility. He came and

preached peace to you who were far away and peace to those who were near. For through him we both have access to the Father by one Spirit.[12]

[*Jew and Gentile]

I quote this piece at length because it shows the "purpose" behind Christ's coming, which was to reconcile humankind both to him and to each other or, to put it another way, to create fellowship between us and God and fellowship between each other. This fellowship is founded on the reconciling ministry of Jesus, and is made real to us in the Spirit. A fellowship is brought about which is the means of maturing our own humanity, helping us to become what we should be. One of the chief expressions of this fellowship is prayer.

PRAYER

There are two kinds of prayer that I want us to think about. The first kind is for our own community, the second is for others. They are not exclusive. They overlap in many places, but they have two foci.

The first form of prayer is summarised best by the Lord's Prayer. It is a community prayer, in which we are encouraged to pray for "ourselves". Together we worship and praise, remembering "our Father who is heaven", who is deserving of all our ascription of praise. All worship and prayer should begin by setting the context that God is great, he is our Father, and his "name" —or character— is holy, and to be rightly feared for, "The fear of God is the beginning of wisdom." In worship and in times of prayer, it is always worth beginning in this place, as in doing so we set the context for everything which may follow. Then together we pray for the coming of God's kingdom, that is for the just and gentle rule of God to come to the passions and circumstances of sinful humans. Once again we align ourselves with this coming kingdom, which we are called both to announce and bring in. We pray that it may come perfectly on earth, as it is already perfectly present in heaven. Having set our sights both on God and his coming kingdom, we bring our needs—whatever they may be, symbolised in our most basic need, namely bread—to God, who already knows all about them before we ask. But our souls must be continually guarded against two things: unforgiveness, and the assault of evil, or the evil one. Indeed, the former is often an entrance for the latter. If we do not forgive others, we will not ourselves receive forgiveness. If we do not ask forgiveness for what we have done, or failed to do, then we may leave the gate open to evil, or the evil one. Forgiveness—in each of these ways—is often the best protection from evil, and we have already touched on this vital theme earlier in this book. So here is Jesus' timeless prescription for prayer. We will never go beyond it, nor will intercession ever leave its principles without becoming unbalanced or eccentric. It is also in the context of this kind of praying that we become more fully human, and that we learn to listen to God.

The other focus of prayer, which has already been included in our thoughts about the Lord's Prayer, is simply praying for others. It was when Job prayed for his friends that the Lord restored him. We are called not simply to restrict our praying to our own needs as a Christian community, nor only to our own personal needs—whether for daily necessities, protection from harm, forgiveness and deliverance in time of trial—but also for the community and people amongst whom we are set; for our world and environment; the nations and their governments; our own nation and its leadership, as well as the institutions and the homes of our neighbourhood. Such intercession is all about praying for the coming of God's kingdom in every area of our world. But as we identify in prayer with the needs, cries and suffering of the world, we too become more fully in touch and more truly human. In all of this we can pray both with our minds and in the Spirit.

These, then, are some of the means within the church for our transformation. Having grasped the framework of understanding which follows faith, and which we have looked at in the earlier chapters of this Part of the book, we can be assured that we may grow in our openness to the word, in the spiritual use of the sacraments and what they signify, in enjoying the fellowship of other disciples, and in praying. The church is primarily a community created and called together by God himself, and it is in this community and through these means that we can become increasingly human, and God's image or likeness can be gradually restored in us to what he intended it to be. Our hope would be that people seeing this evolving humanity would ask us to give an account of the hope that is in us. As Peter said, "Live such good lives among the pagans that... they may see your good deeds, and glorify God...."[13] Our hope and aim must be that our churches are places where we are becoming fully human.

Notes

1   See 2 Corinthians 4:4.
2   Graham Tomlin, *The Provocative Church* (SPCK, 2002).
3   Acts 2:38.
4   Romans 6:2.
5   Miroslav Volf, *Exclusion and Embrace* (Abingdon Press, Nashville, TN, USA) p. 25.
6   Eucharistic Prayer G. My emphasis. Extract from *Common Worship: Services and Prayers for the Church of England* is copyright © The Archbishops' Council, 2000 and is reproduced with permission.
7   Op. cit., p. 40.
8   See Jean Vanier, *Becoming Human* (Darton Longman & Todd, 1999) p. 59.
9   1 Corinthians 12:26.
10   Philippians 2:1–2.
11   See Ephesians 3:18–19.
12   Ephesians 2:15–18.
13   See 1 Peter 2:12.

16

Becoming Fully Human

Jesus said that he came to give life so that we may have life and "have it to the full", unlike the thief, who, "...comes only to steal and kill and destroy".[1] If we substitute the word "humanity" for "life", then we are not far off Jesus' original meaning. Jesus came to give us back our full humanity, but the evil one comes only to diminish and destroy it. Evidence of this destruction is all around us in Western society. Millions of foetuses are aborted every year, there is increasing pressure to end life when it is seemingly past its "sell by date", and we are in danger of turning the gift of life into another commodity, in which we can select from the choices provided by genetic knowledge. If it is true that technology may often become divorced from God–given, Christ–centred values, and modern procedures are, in so many spheres, no longer informed by the classical tradition of Christian ethics, then we are surely entering a new dark age where we have never been before.

It is in this arena of "life issues" that the question of what it means to be human is being increasingly focussed. The values of love, compassion, mercy and truth are locked in combat with those which are coming to dominate our society, namely: convenience, control, pursuit of pleasure, and self-protection in its profoundest sense. It is ironic that the more we seek to build a society in which we gain greater control of our lives, eliminate risk, seek greater convenience and pleasure and ensure more protection of our rights, the less human we become. The reason for this is simply that we have missed the mark of what true humanity really is. In the words of St Francis, "It is in giving that we receive, it is in pardoning that we are pardoned, and in dying that we are born to eternal life." Our humanity is not increased by ever-greater independence but greater dependence on each other in community. And we must remember that Jesus said, "Whoever finds his life will lose it, and whoever loses his life for my sake will find it."[2]

Whereas the Western world, generally speaking, seeks ever more ingenious ways of preserving its life, often to the detriment of so many others who must sustain it, the very thing it seeks to preserve slips through its fingers. For Jesus teaches the exact opposite of what our instincts would tell us. We look for self–protection; he talks of self-abandonment to his will. We seek convenience; he talks of obedience. We seek to preserve our rights, whereas Jesus gave up all rights to restore our humanity.

The hallmark of true humanity, as we saw at the outset, consists in our having been made in the image of God our Creator. Our humanity subsists in that collection of qualities infused into our being at the point of creation. Those qualities include our capacity for loving relationships with others, intelligent thought, artistic creativity and, above all, a capacity for a relationship of friendship with our Creator. The image which includes these characteristics was marred, but not obliterated, in the act of defiance and independence by our human ancestors, Adam and Eve, the consequences of which we all share. It was an historic fall from paradise. But God gave the possibility of a restored humanity through the coming of Christ, truly God, **the man,** who came to restore our fractured and tarnished image. This process of restoration can only begin when we receive the gift of new life through faith in Jesus, when we receive him as Redeemer, Friend and Lord. Resources then are made available to us. Forgiveness from the cross covers over our past and future failure, and the Spirit of God comes to indwell us, bringing about an internal revolution. This revolution gives us both new desires and a new power to become what we were originally intended to be. And, although the believer is given a righteousness by God at the point of belief, we are also given **then** the resources to become, degree–by–degree or bit–by–bit, what God has already made us in Christ. This developmental change has traditionally been called sanctification.

However, this process involves many struggles, which we have looked at in the central Part of this book, and from which we are never immune. But if we have the wisdom to see what is good for us, and use the power available to help us, and go on being filled with the Holy Spirit, then we are treading the path to full humanity, which we do in hope and often through suffering. Through many struggles, we gradually become more and more the people we were intended to be, and so progressively become more fully human.

The secret is that to become fully human is to become holy. If the title of this book had been "Becoming Fully Holy", would you have ever bought it? And if you had not, then what, in all honesty, would have been the underlying reason for that? The reason would probably have been that our image of such an idea—being fully holy, I mean—is in need of rehabilitation, because for many people (although not all I grant) it conveys negativity, withdrawal, disengagement, and a piety which is all words and little action. To be sure, holiness means to be *in* the world but not to be *of* it; or, as Paul taught, not being squeezed into the mould of the world around us. So there is always a rightly negative side to holiness, as there was in the Old Testament, when the Israelites were called to be distinct from the other nations around them. But too often the distinctiveness turns into pride and exclusivity, as it did eventually with the Pharisees. Too often, so–called holiness is reduced to a single issue, again like the Pharisees, who were big on tithing their herb gardens, with their mint and cumin, but neglected the weightier aspects of the Law, namely mercy and justice. Too often, our holiness has a ceremonial or liturgical façade, whether that is expressed in one style or another, and is church service centred, like that of the priests in the Old Testament, who often knew how to arrange a good celebration, with plenty of impressive sacrifices and songs, but who neglected justice and mercy. No one has put this with greater eloquence and vehemence than the prophet Amos, who wrote:

> "I hate, I despise your religious feasts;
> I cannot stand your assemblies.
> Even though you bring me burnt offerings and grain
> offerings,
> I will not accept them.
> Though you bring choice fellowship offerings,
> I will have no regard for them.
> Away with the noise of your songs!
> I will not listen to the music of your harps.
> But let justice roll on like a river,
> righteousness like a never–failing stream."[3]

Or again, too often the ostensibly holy person is quick to condemn others; thanking God at the same time that "they are not like" a certain sinner who has crossed their path. Like the Pharisee in Jesus' famous story, they are thankful that they pray, tithe their money, fast twice a week and are definitely a cut above people who do not do these things. But they have mistaken their own pride for holiness, and believe that somehow they are more acceptable to God than, say, a broken man who knows he has done wrong and sobs his prayer of confession in the back pew of a dimly lit city church, where there is no–one except an ancient cleaner tidying the books!

Holiness has got a bad name generally because, in the common mind, it is associated with pride, hypocrisy, exclusivity, negativity and sheer blindness. Alternatively, it is an idea which seems to some to be out of touch with reality, especially when Christians have claimed, quite erroneously, that they have reached some sort of moral perfection or plateau through some special spiritual experience. All Christians are people following Jesus, the one and only truly human person, with his guidance (wisdom) and help (the Holy Spirit), with a permanent safety net for their ongoing failures (the cross), and a hope that one day the struggle will give way to bliss (heaven).

True holiness is simply defined. It is to become like Jesus. To be holy is to be like Jesus, and to be human is to be like him. *Ergo,* to be holy is to be human, and to be truly human is to be truly holy. Both humanity and holiness find the truest and fullest expression in Jesus. So true holiness is "something beautiful for God"; it is immensely attractive, and is the fenestration through which others may glimpse the reality and presence of God.[4] All this stems from two simple credal statements, which are: that we are made in the image of God; and that Jesus is **the** perfect **human** [as well as divine] self–revelation of God. So to become like Jesus is to become what we were intended to be.

The evidence of our humanity is shown in our attitudes. Attitudes are what determine actions; and attitudes also determine our choices. Some of the principal attitudes, which we see in the life of Jesus, are love, faith, obedience, humility, generosity, compassion and self-sacrifice. These are the same attitudes that Paul tells the early churches to put on, as in his letter to the Colossians:

Therefore, as God's chosen people, holy and dearly loved, clothe yourselves with compassion, kindness, humility, gentleness and patience. Bear with each other and forgive whatever grievances you may have against one another. Forgive as the Lord forgave you. And over all these virtues put on love, which binds them all together in perfect unity.[5]

Again and again, Paul asks the churches to choose the right attitudes, and put them on like clothes. These are the clothes of true humanity; they are found only in a wardrobe marked "Jesus", and as with all clothes they must be put on daily. This bridal trousseau is given to us at the point of faith or, to carry through the wedding analogy, when we say to God, "I will." Thereafter we must continually put on the right clothes for the right occasion, but they are all there in the wardrobe.

Becoming Fully Human is a call to everyone. At the outset we looked at the question, "What does it mean to be truly human?" Only when we have considered the **goal** of our humanity can we really answer this question of how to become truly human. We do not live in a society which has much time for "goals", or "ends"; we have become almost exclusively concentrated on means. But the Christian faith gives a coherent set of answers both to the question of what we were intended to be and to questions about how to become what we were intended to be! In Western society, the old choices, connected to the seven deadly sins, are dressed up in new, more sophisticated forms, but these choices have never been more alive and kicking. So there are few more pressing issues than how can we become what we are intended to be.

****

We end, as we began, in conversation....

"So, if I wanted to start on this journey of becoming fully human, what would I have to do?"

Well, we all start in the same way, by making contact, making a prayer —that is, to the God who made us, and to whom we will give an account of our lives, telling him we are sorry for mucking up, that we need his wisdom and help, thanking him for taking care of our failures through the cross and asking him to make us the humans he wants us to be. That does not mean that we all become uniform or the same; rather, it simply means that we can fully become what we were intended to be: fully human. If you like, here is a prayer you could use. It is a way of starting:

Jesus, Son of God, you are the perfect man, and you are also "the way, the truth and the life". Forgive me for my sins. Thank you for dying for me on the cross, so that I may live. I now put my trust in you, and believe in you alone; I ask you to come in and take charge of my life, from this moment, as my Redeemer and Lord. Please now help me to become fully human; please give me your wisdom, and enter my experience; fill me with your Holy Spirit. Help me to be everything that you want me to be, with you in charge of my life. Come, Lord Jesus, and transform the poverty of my life through the riches of your grace. Amen.

By the way, if you prayed this prayer, do tell someone you can trust that you are set on the path of Becoming Fully Human.

Notes

1. See John 10:10.
2. Matthew 10:39.
3. Amos 5:21–24.
4. See Hebrews 12:14.
5. Colossians 3:12–14.

Edited by Patrick Whitworth:

MEETINGS WITH JESUS

Foreword by Nicky Gumbel

Men and Women from the Gospels
come face to face with the Son of God

ISBN 1901949117

£7.99